Rudolf Otto

Jesse Russell, Ronald Cohn

Publisher: LENNEX Corp
Pubmix is a trademark of LENNEX Corp,
Address: Mitchell house, 5 Mitchell Street, EDINBURGH, EH6 7BD, Scotland, United Kingdom
Email: info@pubmix.com
Website: www.pubmix.com

Published in 2012

Printed in: U.S.A., U.K., Germany, Spain, Russia, India, Brazil, China or Australia.

ISBN: 978-5-5113-6828-3

Contents

Articles

Rudolf Otto   5

Religion   7

Numinous   21

Peine   22

University of Marburg   25

Theology   29

Mysticism   35

Paul Tillich   42

Mircea Eliade   53

References

Article Sources and Contributors   87

Image Sources, Licenses and Contributors   90

Article Licenses

License   92

Rudolf Otto

Rudolf Otto (September 25, 1869–6 March 1937) was an eminent German Lutheran theologian and scholar of comparative religion.

Life

Born in Peine near Hanover, Otto attended the Gymnasium Andreanum in Hildesheim and studied at the universities of Erlangen and Göttingen, where he wrote his dissertation on Martin Luther's understanding of the Holy Spirit, and his habilitation on Kant. By 1906, he held a position as extraordinary professor, and in 1910 he received an honorary doctorate from the University of Giessen. In 1915, he became ordinary professor at the University of Breslau, and in 1917, at the University of Marburg's Divinity School, then one of the most famous Protestant seminaries in the world. Although he received several other calls, he remained in Marburg for the rest of his life. He retired in 1929 and died of pneumonia eight years later, after he had suffered serious injuries falling some 20 m from a tower. Persistent but unconfirmed rumors identified this as a suicide attempt.[1] He is buried in Marburg cemetery.

Rudolf Otto.

The Idea of the Holy

Otto's most famous work is *The Idea of the Holy*, published first in 1917 as *Das Heilige - Über das Irrationale in der Idee des Göttlichen und sein Verhältnis zum Rationalen* (*The Holy - On the Irrational in the Idea of the Divine and its Relation to the Rational*). It is one of the most successful German theological books of the 20th century, has never gone out of print, and is now available in about 20 languages. The book defines the concept of the holy as that which is numinous. Otto explained the numinous as a "non-rational, non-sensory experience or feeling whose primary and immediate object is outside the self". He coined this new term based on the Latin numen (deity). This expression is etymologically unrelated to Immanuel Kant's noumenon, a Greek term referring to an unknowable reality underlying all things. The numinous is a mystery (Latin: *mysterium*) that is both terrifying (*tremendum*) and fascinating (*fascinans*) at the same time. It also sets a paradigm for the study of religion that focuses on the need to realize the religious as a non-reducible, original category in its own right. This paradigm was under much attack between approximately 1950 and 1990 but has made a strong comeback since then, after its phenomenological aspects have become more apparent, and written about by Karl Rahner's presentation of man as a being of transcendence.

Influence

Otto left a broad influence on theology and philosophy of religion in the first half of the 20th century. German-American theologian Paul Tillich acknowledged Otto's influence on him, as did Romanian-American philosopher Mircea Eliade and Otto's most famous German pupil Gustav Mensching (1901–1978) from Bonn University. Eliade used the concepts from *The Idea of the Holy* as the starting point for his own 1957 book, *The Sacred and the Profane*. Otto was one of the very few modern theologians to whom C. S. Lewis indicates a debt, particularly the idea of the numinous in The Problem of Pain. Others to acknowledge Otto were, for instance, Martin Heidegger, Leo Strauss, John A. Sanford, Hans-Georg Gadamer (critical in his youth, respectful in his old age), Max Scheler, Ernst Jünger, Joseph Needham and Hans Jonas. Ideas of Otto have been discussed also by non-Christian theologians, like Eliezer Berkovits.[2]

Partial bibliography

- *Naturalism and Religion* (1907), London: Williams and Norgate, Full text online [3] at Google Books
- *The Life and Ministry of Jesus, According to the Critical Method* (1908), Chicago: Open Court, ISBN 0-8370-4648-3. Full text online [4] at Google Books
- *The Idea of the Holy* (1923), Oxford University Press, ISBN 0-19-500210-5 Full text online [5] at Google Books
- *Christianity and the Indian Religion of Grace*, Madras 1928
- *India's Religion of Grace and Christianity Compared and Contrasted*, New York 1930
- *The philosophy of religion based on Kant and Fries*, London 1931
- *Religious essays: A supplement to The Idea of the Holy*, London 1931
- *Mysticism east and west: A comparative analysis of the nature of mysticism*, New York 1932
- *The original Gita: The song of the Supreme Exalted One*, London 1939
- *The Kingdom of God and the Son of Man: A Study in the History of Religion*, Boston 1943
- *Autobiographical and Social Essays* (1996), Berlin: Walter de Gruyter, ISBN 3-11-014518-9

Notes

[1] Lindsay Jones (ed. in chief). *Encyclopedia Of Religion: Second Edition*. Thomson Gale, 2005, p. 6926. ISBN 0028657438.
[2] God, Man and History (http://www.amazon.com/God-Man-History-Eliezer-Berkovits/dp/9657052157), pp. 166, 170
[3] http://books.google.com/books?id=Zf1-3CCi6v0C
[4] http://books.google.com/books?id=U6YMAAAAIAAJ
[5] http://books.google.com/books?id=0-9YrD6H0xUC&printsec=frontcover&dq=Rudolf+Otto&hl=en&src=bmrr& ei=lZXMTYvjIeH40gHaq5z0BA&sa=X&oi=book_result&ct=result&resnum=1&ved=0CCoQ6AEwAA#v=onepage&q&f=false

References

- Gooch, Todd A. (2000). *The Numinous and Modernity: An Interpretation of Rudolf Otto's Philosophy of Religion*. Preface by Otto Kaiser and Wolfgang Drechsler. Berlin and New York: Walter de Gruyter. ISBN 3-11-016799-9.
- Almond, Philip C., 'Rudolf Otto: An Introduction to his Philosophical Theology' (Chapel Hill: University of North Carolina Press, 1984).

External links

- Brief page on Otto (http://www.friesian.com/otto.htm)
- Otto and the Numinous (http://academic.brooklyn.cuny.edu/english/melani/gothic/numinous.html)
- Applications of Otto's term 'numinous' (http://www.ncf.ca/~dy656/earthpages3/articles_numinosity.htm)
- Rudolf-Otto-Congress 2012 (http://www.uni-marburg.de/fb05/fachgebiete/hermeneutik/tagungen/ rudolfotto/otto?set_language=en/)

Religion

Religion is a collection of cultural systems, belief systems, and worldviews that establishes symbols that relate humanity to spirituality and, sometimes, to moral values.[1] Many religions have narratives, symbols, traditions and sacred histories that are intended to give meaning to life or to explain the origin of life or the universe. They tend to derive morality, ethics, religious laws or a preferred lifestyle from their ideas about the cosmos and human nature.

The word *religion* is sometimes used interchangeably with *faith* or *belief system*, but religion differs from private belief in that it has a public aspect. Most religions have organized behaviors, including clerical hierarchies, a definition of what constitutes adherence or membership, congregations of laity, regular meetings or services for the purposes of veneration of a deity or for prayer, holy places (either natural or architectural), and/or scriptures. The practice of a religion may also include sermons, commemoration of the activities of a god or gods, sacrifices, festivals, feasts, trance, initiations, funerary services, matrimonial services, meditation, music, art, dance, public service, or other aspects of human culture.

Symbols representing some world religions, from left to right:
row 1: Christianity, Judaism, Hinduism
row 2: Islam, Buddhism, Shinto
row 3: Sikhism, Bahá'í Faith, Jainism

The development of religion has taken different forms in different cultures. Some religions place an emphasis on belief, while others emphasize practice. Some religions focus on the subjective experience of the religious individual, while others consider the activities of the religious community to be most important. Some religions claim to be universal, believing their laws and cosmology to be binding for everyone, while others are intended to be practiced only by a closely defined or localized group. In many places religion has been associated with public institutions such as education, hospitals, the family, government, and political hierarchies.

Some academics studying the subject have divided religions into three broad categories: world religions, a term which refers to transcultural, international faiths; indigenous religions, which refers to smaller, culture-specific or nation-specific religious groups; and new religious movements, which refers to recently developed faiths.[2] One modern academic theory of religion, social constructionism, says that religion is a modern concept that suggests all spiritual practice and worship follows a model similar to the Abrahamic religions as an orientation system that helps to interpret reality and define human beings,[3] and thus religion, as a concept, has been applied inappropriately to non-Western cultures that are not based upon such systems, or in which these systems are a substantially simpler construct.

Etymology

Religion (from O.Fr. *religion* "religious community," from L. *religionem* (nom. *religio*) "respect for what is sacred, reverence for the gods,"[4] "obligation, the bond between man and the gods"[5]) is derived from the Latin *religiō*, the ultimate origins of which are obscure. One possibility is derivation from a reduplicated **le-ligare*, an interpretation traced to Cicero connecting *lego* "read", i.e. *re* (again) + *lego* in the sense of "choose", "go over again" or "consider carefully". Modern scholars such as Tom Harpur and Joseph Campbell favor the derivation from *ligare* "bind, connect", probably from a prefixed *re-ligare*, i.e. *re* (again) + *ligare* or "to reconnect," which was made prominent by St. Augustine, following the interpretation of Lactantius.[6][7] The medieval usage alternates with *order* in designating bonded communities like those of monastic orders: "we hear of the 'religion' of the Golden Fleece, of a knight 'of the religion of Avys'".[8]

According to the philologist Max Müller, the root of the English word "religion", the Latin *religio*, was originally used to mean only "reverence for God or the gods, careful pondering of divine things, piety" (which Cicero further derived to mean "diligence").[9][10] Max Müller characterized many other cultures around the world, including Egypt, Persia, and India, as having a similar power structure at this point in history. What is called ancient religion today, they would have only called "law".[11]

Many languages have words that can be translated as "religion", but they may use them in a very different way, and some have no word for religion at all. For example, the Sanskrit word dharma, sometimes translated as "religion", also means law. Throughout classical South Asia, the study of law consisted of concepts such as penance through piety and ceremonial as well as practical traditions. Medieval Japan at first had a similar union between "imperial law" and universal or "Buddha law", but these later became independent sources of power.[12][13]

There is no precise equivalent of "religion" in Hebrew, and Judaism does not distinguish clearly between religious, national, racial, or ethnic identities.[14] One of its central concepts is "halakha", sometimes translated as "law"", which guides religious practice and belief and many aspects of daily life.

The use of other terms, such as obedience to God or Islam are likewise grounded in particular histories and vocabularies.[15]

Religious movements

In the 19th and 20th centuries, the academic practice of comparative religion divided religious belief into philosophically defined categories called "world religions." However, some recent scholarship has argued that not all types of religion are necessarily separated by mutually exclusive philosophies, and furthermore that the utility of ascribing a practice to a certain philosophy, or even calling a given practice religious, rather than cultural, political, or social in nature, is limited.[16][17][18] The current state of

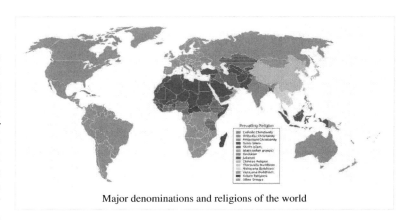

Major denominations and religions of the world

psychological study about the nature of religiousness suggests that it is better to refer to religion as a largely invariant phenomenon that should be distinguished from cultural norms (i.e. "religions").[19] The list of religious movements given here is therefore an attempt to summarize the most important regional and philosophical influences on local communities, but it is by no means a complete description of every religious community, nor does it explain the most important elements of individual religiousness.

The four largest religious groups by population, estimated to account for between 5 and 7 billion people, are Christianity, Islam, Buddhism, and Hinduism (with the relative numbers for Buddhism and Hinduism dependent on the extent of syncretism).

Four largest religions	Adherents	% of world population	Article
World population	6.96 billion[20]	Figures taken from individual articles:	
Christianity	2.1 billion – 2.2 billion	33% – 34%	Christianity by country
Islam	1.5 billion – 1.6 billion[21]	22% – 23%	Islam by country
Buddhism	500 million – 1.9 billion[22]	7% – 29%[22]	Buddhism by country
Hinduism	1.0 billion – 1.1 billion	15.2% – 16.2%	Hinduism by country
Total	5.1 billion – 6.8 billion[22]	77% – 99%[22]	

- **Abrahamic religions** are monotheistic religions which believe they descend from Abraham.

  - **Judaism** is the oldest Abrahamic religion, originating in the people of ancient Israel and Judea. Judaism is based primarily on the Torah, a text which some Jews believe was handed down to the people of Israel through the prophet Moses in 1,400 BCE. This along with the rest of the Hebrew Bible and the Talmud are the central texts of Judaism. The Jewish people were scattered after the destruction of the Temple in Jerusalem in 70 CE. Today there are about 13 million Jews, about 40 per cent living in Israel and 40 per cent in the United States.[23]

The patriarch Abraham (by József Molnár)

  - **Christianity** is based on the life and teachings of Jesus of Nazareth (1st century) as presented in the New Testament. The Christian faith is essentially faith in Jesus as the Christ, the Son of God, and as Savior and Lord. Almost all Christians believe in the Trinity, which teaches the unity of Father, Son (Jesus Christ), and Holy Spirit as three persons in one Godhead. Most Christians can describe their faith with the Nicene Creed. As the religion of Byzantine Empire in the first millennium and of Western Europe during the time of colonization, Christianity has been propagated throughout the world. The main divisions of Christianity are, according to the number of adherents:

    - **Catholic Church**, headed by the Pope in Rome, is a communion of the Western church and 22 Eastern Catholic churches.
    - **Protestantism**, separated from the Catholic Church in the 16th-century Reformation and split in many denominations,
    - **Eastern Christianity** which include Eastern Orthodoxy, Oriental Orthodoxy and the Church of the East.
      There are other smaller groups, such as Jehovah's Witnesses and the Latter Day Saint movement, whose inclusion in Christianity is sometimes disputed.

  - **Islam** refers to the religion taught by the Islamic prophet Muhammad, a major political and religious figure of the 7th century CE. Islam is the dominant religion of northern Africa, the Middle East, and South Asia. As with Christianity, there is no single orthodoxy in Islam but a multitude of traditions which are generally categorized as Sunni and Shia, although there are other minor groups as well. Wahhabi is the dominant Muslim schools of thought in the Kingdom of Saudi Arabia. There are also several Islamic republics, including Iran, which is run by a Shia Supreme Leader.

Muslims praying around Kaaba, the most sacred site in Islam

  - The **Bahá'í Faith** was founded in the 19th century in Iran and since then has spread worldwide. It teaches unity of all religious philosophies and accepts all of the prophets of Judaism, Christianity, and Islam as well as additional prophets including its founder Bahá'u'lláh.
  - Smaller regional Abrahamic groups, including Samaritanism (primarily in Israel and the West Bank), the Rastafari movement (primarily in Jamaica), and Druze (primarily in Syria and Lebanon).

- **Indian religions** are practiced or were founded in the Indian subcontinent. Concepts most of them share in common include dharma, karma, reincarnation, mantras, yantras, and darśana.

  - **Hinduism** is a synecdoche describing the similar philosophies of Vaishnavism, Shaivism, and related groups practiced or founded in the Indian subcontinent. Concepts most of them share in common include karma, caste, reincarnation, mantras, yantras, and darśana.[24] Hinduism is not a monolithic religion in the Romanic sense but a religious category containing dozens of separate philosophies amalgamated as Sanātana Dharma.

Hindu statue of Rama in Kalaram Temple (India)

  - **Jainism**, taught primarily by Parsva (9th century BCE) and Mahavira (6th century BCE), is an ancient Indian religion that prescribes a path of non-violence for all forms of living beings in this world. Jains are found mostly in India.
  - **Buddhism** was founded by Siddhattha Gotama in the 6th century BCE. Buddhists generally agree that Gotama aimed to help sentient beings end their suffering (dukkha) by understanding the true nature of phenomena, thereby escaping the cycle of suffering and rebirth (saṃsāra), that is, achieving Nirvana.

    - **Theravada Buddhism**, which is practiced mainly in Sri Lanka and Southeast Asia alongside folk religion, shares some characteristics of Indian religions. It is based in a large collection of texts called the Pali

Canon.

- Under the heading of **Mahayana** (the "Great Vehicle") fall a multitude of doctrines which began their development in China and are still relevant in Vietnam, in Korea, in Japan, and to a lesser extent in Europe and the United States. Mahayana Buddhism includes such disparate teachings as Zen, Pure Land, and Soka Gakkai.
  - **Vajrayana Buddhism**, sometimes considered a form of Mahayana, was developed in Tibet and is still most prominent there and in surrounding regions.
  - Two notable new Buddhist sects are Hòa Hảo and the Dalit Buddhist movement, which were developed separately in the 20th century.
- **Sikhism** is a monotheistic religion founded on the teachings of Guru Nanak and ten successive Sikh Gurus in 15th century Punjab. Sikhs are found mostly in India.
- There are dozens of new religious movements within Indian religions and Hindu reform movements, such as Ayyavazhi and Swaminarayan Faith.

- **Iranian religions** are ancient religions which roots predate the Islamization of the Greater Iran. Nowadays these religions are practiced only by minorities.

  Zoroastrian Fire Temple

  - **Zoroastrianism** is a religion and philosophy based on the teachings of prophet Zoroaster in the 6th century BC. The Zoroastrians worship the Creator Ahura Mazda. In Zoroastrianism good and evil have distinct sources, with evil trying to destroy the creation of Mazda, and good trying to sustain it.
  - **Mandaeism** is a monotheistic religion with a strongly dualistic worldview. Mandaeans are sometime labeled as the "Last Gnostics".
  - **Kurdish religions** include the traditional beliefs of the Yazidi, Alevi, and Ahl-e Haqq. Sometimes these are labeled Yazdânism.

- **Folk religion** is a term applied loosely and vaguely to less-organized local practices. It is also called paganism, shamanism, animism, ancestor worship, matriarchal religion, or totemism, although not all of these elements are necessarily present in local belief systems. The category of "folk religion" can generally include anything that is not part of an organization. Modern neopagan movement draws on folk religion for inspiration to varying degrees.

  Incense burner in China

  - **African traditional religion** is a category including any type of religion practiced in Africa before the arrival of Islam and Christianity, such as Yoruba religion or San religion. There are many varieties of religions developed by Africans in the Americas derived from African beliefs, including Santería, Candomblé, Umbanda, Vodou, and Oyotunji.
  - **Folk religions of the Americas** include Aztec religion, Inca religion, Maya religion, and modern Catholic beliefs such as the Virgin of Guadalupe. Native American religion is practiced across the continent of North America.
  - **Australian Aboriginal culture** contains a mythology and sacred practices characteristic of folk religion.
  - **Chinese folk religion**, practiced by Chinese people around the world, is a primarily social practice including popular elements of Confucianism and Taoism, with some remnants of Mahayana Buddhism. Most Chinese do not identify as religious due to the strong Maoist influence on the country in recent history, but adherence to religious ceremonies remains common. New religious movements include Falun Gong and I-Kuan Tao.
  - Traditional **Korean religion** is a syncretic mixture of Mahayana Buddhism and Korean shamanism. Unlike Japanese Shinto, Korean shamanism was never codified and Buddhism was never made a social necessity. In some areas these traditions remain prevalent, but Korean-influenced Christianity is also influential in society and politics in South Korea.
  - Traditional **Japanese religion** is a mixture of Mahayana Buddhism and ancient indigenous practices which were codified as Shinto in the 19th century. Japanese people retain nominal attachment to both Buddhism and Shinto through social ceremonies, but irreligion is common.

- A variety of **new religious movements** still practiced today have been founded in many other countries besides Japan and the United States, including:

  - **Shinshūkyō** is a general category for a wide variety of religious movements founded in Japan since the 19th century. These movements share almost nothing in common except the place of their founding. The largest religious movements centered in Japan include Soka Gakkai, Tenrikyo, and Seicho-No-Ie among hundreds of smaller groups.
  - **Cao Đài** is a syncretistic, monotheistic religion, established in Vietnam in 1926.
  - **Unitarian Universalism** is a religion characterized by support for a "free and responsible search for truth and meaning."
  - **Scientology** teaches that people are immortal beings who have forgotten their true nature. Its method of spiritual rehabilitation is a type of counseling known as auditing, in which practitioners aim to consciously re-experience painful or traumatic events in their past in order to free themselves of their limiting effects.
  - **Eckankar** is a religion with the purpose of making God an everyday reality in one's life.

A modern style Unitarian sanctuary

Sociological classifications of religious movements suggest that within any given religious group, a community can resemble various types of structures, including "churches", "denominations", "sects", "cults", and "institutions".

The Hindu population of South Asia comprises about 2,000 castes.[25] According to some Hindu literature, there are 330 million (including local and regional) Hindu deities.[26]

Types of religion

History of religions founding figures
Anthropology Comparative religion Development Neurotheology / God gene Origins Psychology

Prehistoric
Ancient Near East
· Ancient Egypt
· Semitic
Indo-European
· Vedic Hinduism
· Greco-Roman
· Celtic · Germanic
Axial Age
· Vedanta · Shramana
· Dharma · Tao
· Hellenism
· Monism · Dualism
· Monotheism
Christianization
Islamization
Renaissance ·
Reformation
Age of Reason
New religious
movements
· Great Awakening
· Fundamentalism
· New Age
Postmodernism
Abrahamic
· Judaism
· Christianity
· Islam
· Bahá'í Faith
Indic
· Hinduism
· Buddhism
· Jainism
· Sikhism
· Ayyavazhi
· Taoism
Neopagan
· Wicca

Further information: History of religions

Some scholars classify religions as either *universal religions* that seek worldwide acceptance and actively look for new converts, or *ethnic religions* that are identified with a particular ethnic group and do not seek converts.[27] Others reject the distinction, pointing out that all religious practices, whatever their philosophical origin, are ethnic because they come from a particular culture.[28][29][30]

Issues in religion

Interfaith cooperation

Because religion continues to be recognized in Western thought as a universal impulse, many religious practitioners have aimed to band together in interfaith dialogue and cooperation. The first major dialogue was the Parliament of the World's Religions at the 1893 Chicago World's Fair, which remains notable even today both in affirming "universal values" and recognition of the diversity of practices among different cultures. The 20th century has been especially fruitful in use of interfaith dialogue as a means of solving ethnic, political, or even religious conflict, with Christian-Jewish reconciliation representing a complete reverse in the attitudes of many Christian communities towards Jews.

Recent interfaith initiatives include "A Common Word", launched in 2007 and focused on bringing Muslim and Christian leaders together,[31] the "C1 World Dialogue",[32] the "Common Ground" initiative between Islam and Buddhism,[33] and a United Nations sponsored "World Interfaith Harmony Week".[34][35]

Secularism and irreligion

The terms "atheist" (lack of belief in any gods) and "agnostic" (belief in the unknowability of the existence of gods), though specifically contrary to theistic (e.g. Christian, Jewish, and Muslim) religious teachings, do not by definition mean the opposite of "religious". There are religions (including Buddhism and Taoism), in fact, that classify some of their followers as agnostic, atheistic, or nontheistic. The true opposite of "religious" is the word "irreligious". Irreligion describes an absence of any religion; antireligion describes an active opposition or aversion toward religions in general.

Critics of religion consider it to be to be outdated, harmful to the individual (e.g. brainwashing of children, faith healing, circumcision), harmful to society (e.g. holy wars, terrorism, wasteful distribution of resources), to impede the progress of science, and to encourage immoral acts (e.g. blood sacrifice, discrimination against homosexuals and women). A major criticism of many religions is that they require beliefs that are irrational, unscientific, or unreasonable, because religious beliefs and traditions lack scientific or rational foundations.

As religion became a more personal matter in Western culture, discussions of society found a new focus on political and scientific meaning, and religious attitudes (dominantly Christian) were increasingly seen as irrelevant for the needs of the European world. On the political side, Ludwig Feuerbach recast Christian beliefs in light of humanism, paving the way for Karl Marx's famous characterization of religion as "the opium of the people". Meanwhile, in the scientific community, T.H. Huxley in 1869 coined the term "agnostic," a term—subsequently adopted by such figures as Robert Ingersoll—that, while directly conflicting with and novel to Christian tradition, is accepted and even embraced in some other religions. Later, Bertrand Russell told the world *Why I Am Not a Christian*, which influenced several later authors to discuss their breakaway from their own religious uprbringings from Islam to Hinduism.

Some modern-day critics, such as Bryan Caplan, hold that religion lacks utility in human society; they may regard religion as irrational.[36] Nobel Peace Laureate Shirin Ebadi has spoken out against undemocratic Islamic countries justifying "oppressive acts" in the name of Islam.[37]

Related forms of thought

Religion and superstition

Further information: Superstition, Magical thinking, and Magic and religion

Superstition has been described as "the incorrect establishment of cause and effect" or a false conception of causation.[38] Religion is more complex and includes social institutions and morality. But religions may include superstitions or make use of magical thinking. Adherents of one religion sometimes think of other religions as superstition.[39][40] Some atheists, deists, and skeptics regard religious belief as superstition.

Greek and Roman pagans, who saw their relations with the gods in political and social terms, scorned the man who constantly trembled with fear at the thought of the gods (*deisidaimonia*), as a slave might fear a cruel and capricious master. The Romans called such fear of the gods *superstitio*.[41] Early Christianity was outlawed as a *superstitio Iudaica*, a "Jewish superstition", by Domitian in the 80s AD. In AD 425, when Rome had become Christian, Theodosius II outlawed pagan traditions as superstitious.

The Roman Catholic Church considers superstition to be sinful in the sense that it denotes a lack of trust in the divine providence of God and, as such, is a violation of the first of the Ten Commandments. The Catechism of the Catholic Church states that superstition "in some sense represents a perverse excess of religion" (para. #2110). "Superstition," it says, "is a deviation of religious feeling and of the practices this feeling imposes. It can even affect the worship we offer the true God, e.g., when one attributes an importance in some way magical to certain practices otherwise lawful or necessary. To attribute the efficacy of prayers or of sacramental signs to their mere external performance, apart from the interior dispositions that they demand is to fall into superstition. Cf. Matthew 23:16-22" (para. #2111)

Myth

The word *myth* has several meanings.

1. A traditional story of ostensibly historical events that serves to unfold part of the world view of a people or explain a practice, belief, or natural phenomenon;
2. A person or thing having only an imaginary or unverifiable existence; or
3. A metaphor for the spiritual potentiality in the human being.[42]

Urarina shaman, 1988

Ancient polytheistic religions, such as those of Greece, Rome, and Scandinavia, are usually categorized under the heading of mythology. Religions of pre-industrial peoples, or cultures in development, are similarly called "myths" in the anthropology of religion. The term "myth" can be used pejoratively by both religious and non-religious people. By defining another person's religious stories and beliefs as mythology, one implies that they are less real or true than one's own religious stories and beliefs. Joseph Campbell remarked, "Mythology is often thought of as *other people's* religions, and religion can be defined as mis-interpreted mythology."[43]

In sociology, however, the term *myth* has a non-pejorative meaning. There, *myth* is defined as a story that is important for the group whether or not it is objectively or provably true. Examples include the death and resurrection of Jesus, which, to Christians, explains the means by which they are freed from sin and is also ostensibly a historical event. But from a mythological outlook, whether or not the event actually occurred is unimportant. Instead, the symbolism of the death of an old "life" and the start of a new "life" is what is most significant. Religious believers may or may not accept such symbolic interpretations.

Religion and health

Mayo Clinic researchers examined the association between religious involvement and spirituality, and physical health, mental health, health-related quality of life, and other health outcomes. The authors reported that: "Most studies have shown that religious involvement and spirituality are associated with better health outcomes, including greater longevity, coping skills, and health-related quality of life (even during terminal illness) and less anxiety, depression, and suicide."[44]

Religion and violence

Charles Selengut characterizes the phrase "religion and violence" as "jarring", asserting that "religion is thought to be opposed to violence and a force for peace and reconciliation. He acknowledges, however, that "the history and scriptures of the world's religions tell stories of violence and war as they speak of peace and love."[45]

Hector Avalos argues that, because religions claim divine favor for themselves, over and against other groups, this sense of righteousness leads to violence because conflicting claims to superiority, based on unverifiable appeals to God, cannot be adjudicated objectively.[46]

Critics of religion Christopher Hitchens and Richard Dawkins go further and argue that religions do tremendous harm to society by using violence to promote their goals, in ways that are endorsed and exploited by their leaders.[47][48]

Regina Schwartz argues that all monotheistic religions are inherently violent because of an exclusivism that inevitably fosters violence against those that are considered outsiders.[49] Lawrence Wechsler asserts that Schwartz isn't just arguing that Abrahamic religions have a violent legacy, but that the legacy is actually genocidal in nature.[50]

Byron Bland asserts that one of the most prominent reasons for the "rise of the secular in Western thought" was the reaction against the religious violence of the 16th and 17th centuries. He asserts that "(t)he secular was a way of living with the religious differences that had produced so much horror. Under secularity, political entities have a warrant to make decisions independent from the need to enforce particular versions of religious orthodoxy. Indeed, they may run counter to certain strongly held beliefs if made in the interest of common welfare. Thus, one of the important goals of the secular is to limit violence."[51]

The Crusades were a series of a military campaigns fought mainly between Christian Europe and Muslims. Shown here is a battle scene from the First Crusade. They were inspired at the *jihad* of the Islam civilization.

Nonetheless, believers have used similar arguments when responding to atheists in these discussions, pointing to the widespread imprisonment and mass murder of individuals under atheist states in the twentieth century:[52][53][54]

> And who can deny that Stalin and Mao, not to mention Pol Pot and a host of others, all committed atrocities in the name of a Communist ideology that was explicitly atheistic? Who can dispute that they did their bloody deeds by claiming to be establishing a 'new man' and a religion-free utopia? These were mass murders performed with atheism as a central part of their ideological inspiration, they were not mass murders done by people who simply happened to be atheist. —Dinesh D'Souza[54]

Religion and the law

There are laws and statutes that make reference to religion.[55] This has led scholar Winnifred Sullivan to claims that religious freedom is impossible.[56] Others argue that the Western legal principle of separation of church and state tends to engender a new, more inclusive civil religion.[57]

Religion and science

Religious knowledge, according to religious practitioners, may be gained from religious leaders, sacred texts (scriptures), and/or personal revelation. Some religions view such knowledge as unlimited in scope and suitable to answer any question; others see religious knowledge as playing a more restricted role, often as a complement to knowledge gained through physical observation. Some religious people maintain that religious knowledge obtained in this way is absolute and infallible (religious cosmology).

The scientific method gains knowledge by testing hypotheses to develop theories through elucidation of facts or evaluation by experiments and thus only answers cosmological questions about the physical universe. It develops theories of the world which best fit physically observed evidence. All scientific knowledge is subject to later refinement in the face of additional evidence. Scientific theories that have an overwhelming preponderance of favorable evidence are often treated as facts (such as the theories of gravity or evolution).

Religion as a Christian concept

The social constructionists

In recent years, some academic writers have described religion according to the theory of social constructionism, which considers how ideas and social phenomena develop in a social context. Among the main proponents of this theory of religion are Timothy Fitzgerald, Daniel Dubuisson and Talal Assad. The social constructionists argue that religion is a modern concept that developed from Christianity and was then applied inappropriately to non-Western cultures.

Dubuisson, a French anthropologist, says that the idea of religion has changed a lot over time and that one cannot fully understand its development by relying on etymology, which "tends to minimize or cancel out the role of history".[58] "What the West and the history of religions in its wake have objectified under the name 'religion'", he says, " is ... something quite unique, which could be appropriate only to itself and its own history."[58] He notes that St. Augustine's definition of *religio* differed from the way we used the modern word "religion".[58] Dubuisson prefers the term "cosmographic formation" to religion. Dubuisson says that, with the emergence of religion as a category separate from culture and society, there arose religious studies. The initial purpose of religious studies was to demonstrate the superiority of the "living" or "universal" European world view to the "dead" or "ethnic" religions scattered throughout the rest of the world, expanding the teleological project of Schleiermacher and Tiele to a worldwide ideal religiousness.[59] Due to shifting theological currents, this was eventually supplanted by a liberal-ecumenical interest in searching for Western-style universal truths in every cultural tradition.[60] Clifford Geertz's definition of religion as a "cultural system" was proposed in the 20th century and continues to be widely accepted today.

According to Fitzgerald, the history of other cultures' interaction with the religious category is not about a universal constant, but rather concerns a particular idea that first developed in Europe under the influence of Christianity.[61] Fitzgerald argues that from about the 4th century CE Western Europe and the rest of the world diverged. As Christianity became commonplace, the charismatic authority identified by Augustine, a quality we might today call "religiousness", exerted a commanding influence at the local level. This system persisted in the eastern Byzantine Empire following the East-West Schism, but Western Europe regulated unpredictable expressions of charisma through the Roman Catholic Church. As the Church lost its dominance during the Protestant Reformation and Christianity became closely tied to political structures, religion was recast as the basis of national sovereignty, and religious identity gradually became a less universal sense of spirituality and more divisive, locally defined, and tied to nationality.[62] It was at this point that "religion" was dissociated with universal beliefs and moved closer to dogma in both meaning and practice. However there was not yet the idea of dogma as personal choice, only of established churches. With the Enlightenment religion lost its attachment to nationality, says Fitzgerald, but rather than becoming a universal social attitude, it now became a personal feeling or emotion.[63] Friedrich Schleiermacher in the late 18th century defined religion as *das schlechthinnige Abhängigkeitsgefühl*, commonly translated as "a feeling of absolute dependence".[64] His contemporary Hegel disagreed thoroughly, defining religion as "the Divine Spirit becoming conscious of Himself through the finite spirit."[65]

Asad argues that before the word "religion" came into common usage, Christianity was a *disciplina*, a "rule" just like that of the Roman Empire. This idea can be found in the writings of St. Augustine (354–430). Christianity was then a power structure opposing and superseding human institutions, a literal Kingdom of Heaven. It was the discipline taught by one's family, school, church, and city authorities, rather than something calling one to self-discipline through symbols.[66]

These ideas are developed by N. Balagangadhara. In the Age of Enlightenment, Balagangadhara says that the idea of Christianity as the purest expression of spirituality was supplanted by the concept of "religion" as a worldwide practice.[67] This caused such ideas as religious freedom, a reexamination of classical philosophy as an alternative to Christian thought, and more radically Deism among intellectuals such as Voltaire. Much like Christianity, the idea of "religious freedom" was exported around the world as a civilizing technique, even to regions such as India that had never treated spirituality as a matter of political identity.[16] In Japan, where Buddhism was still seen as a philosophy of natural law,[68] the concept of "religion" and "religious freedom" as separate from other power structures was unnecessary until Christian missionaries demanded free access to conversion, and when Japanese Christians refused to engage in patriotic events.[69]

Other writers

Similar views have been put forward by writers who are not social constructionists. George Lindbeck, a Lutheran and a postliberal theologian, says that religion does not refer to belief in "God" or a transcendent Absolute, but rather to "a kind of cultural and/or linguistic framework or medium that shapes the entirety of life and thought ... it is similar to an idiom that makes possible the description of realities, the formulation of beliefs, and the experiencing of inner attitudes, feelings, and sentiments."[70] Nicholas de Lange, Professor of Hebrew and Jewish Studies at Cambridge University, says that "The comparative study of religions is an academic discipline which has been developed within Christian theology faculties, and it has a tendency to force widely differing phenomena into a kind of strait-jacket cut to a Christian pattern. The problem is not only that other 'religions' may have little or nothing to say about questions which are of burning importance for Christianity, but that they may not even see themselves as religions in precisely the same way in which Christianity sees itself as a religion."[71]

Confucianism, Taoism, and Buddhism are one, a painting in the *litang style* portraying three men laughing by a river stream, 12th century, Song Dynasty

References

Notes

[1] While religion is difficult to define, one standard model of religion, used in religious studies courses, was proposed by Clifford Geertz, who simply called it a "cultural system" (Clifford Geertz, *Religion as a Cultural System*, 1973). A critique of Geertz's model by Talal Asad categorized religion as "an anthropological category." (Talal Asad, *The Construction of Religion as an Anthropological Category*, 1982.)

[2] Harvey, Graham (2000). *Indigenous Religions: A Companion.* (Ed: Graham Harvey). London and New York: Cassell. Page 06.

[3] Vergote, Antoine, *Religion, belief and unbelief: a psychological study*, Leuven University Press, 1997, p. 89

[4] Harper, Douglas. "religion" (http://www.etymonline.com/index.php?term=religion). *Online Etymology Dictionary*. .

[5] *Shorter Oxford English Dictionary*

[6] In *The Pagan Christ: Recovering the Lost Light.* Toronto. Thomas Allen, 2004. ISBN 0-88762-145-7

[7] In *The Power of Myth*, with Bill Moyers, ed. Betty Sue Flowers, New York, Anchor Books, 1991. ISBN 0-385-41886-8

[8] Johan Huizinga, *The Waning of the Middle Ages* (1919) 1924:75.

[9] Max Müller, *Natural Religion*, p.33, 1889

[10] Lewis & Short, *A Latin Dictionary* (http://www.perseus.tufts.edu/hopper/text?doc=Perseus:text:1999.04.0059:entry=#40976)

[11] Max Müller. *Introduction to the science of religion* (http://books.google.com/books?pg=PA28&id=aM0FAAAAQAAJ&as_brr=4). p. 28.

[12] Kuroda, Toshio and Jacqueline I. Stone, translator. " The Imperial Law and the Buddhist Law (http://web.archive.org/web/ 20030323095019/http://www.nanzan-u.ac.jp/SHUBUNKEN/publications/jjrs/pdf/477.pdf)." *Japanese Journal of Religious Studies* 23.3-4 (1996)

[13] Neil McMullin. *Buddhism and the State in Sixteenth-Century Japan.* Princeton, N.J. : Princeton University Press, 1984.

[14] Hershel Edelheit, Abraham J. Edelheit, History of Zionism: A Handbook and Dictionary (http://www.questia.com/library/book/ history-of-zionism-a-handbook-and-dictionary-by-abfaham-j-edelheit-hershel-edelheit.jsp), p.3, citing Solomon Zeitlin, *The Jews. Race, Nation, or Religion?* (Philadelphia: Dropsie College Press, 1936).

[15] Colin Turner. *Islam without Allah?* New York: Routledge, 2000. pp. 11-12.

[16] Brian Kemble Pennington *Was Hinduism Invented?* New York: Oxford University Press US, 2005. ISBN 0195166558

[17] Russell T. McCutcheon. *Critics Not Caretakers: Redescribing the Public Study of Religion.* Albany: SUNY Press, 2001.

[18] Nicholas Lash. *The beginning and the end of 'religion'.* Cambridge University Press, 1996. ISBN 0521566355

[19] Joseph Bulbulia. "Are There Any Religions? An Evolutionary Explanation." *Method & Theory in the Study of Religion* 17.2 (2005), pp.71-100

[20] "U.S. Census Bureau - World POPClock Projection" (http://www.census.gov/population/popclockworld.html). .

[21] Mapping the Global Muslim Population - Pew Forum on Religion & Public Life (http://pewforum.org/ Mapping-the-Global-Muslim-Population.aspx)

[22] Upper estimate includes syncretism.

[23] (http://www.cbs.gov.il/shnaton61/st02_27.pdf)

[24] Hinduism is variously defined as a "religion", "set of religious beliefs and practices", "religious tradition" etc. For a discussion on the topic, see: "Establishing the boundaries" in Gavin Flood (2003), pp. 1-17. René Guénon in his *Introduction to the Study of the Hindu Doctrines* (1921 ed.), Sophia Perennis, ISBN 0-900588-74-8, proposes a definition of the term "religion" and a discussion of its relevance (or lack of) to Hindu doctrines (part II, chapter 4, p. 58).

[25] India – Caste (http://www.britannica.com/EBchecked/topic/285248/India/46404/Caste). Encyclopædia Britannica.

[26] Jeffrey Brodd (2003). *World Religions: A Voyage of Discovery* (http://books.google.com/?id=vOzNo4MVlgMC&pg=PA45&dq="330+ million"). Saint Mary's Press. p. 45. ISBN 9780884897255. : '[..] many gods and goddesses (traditionally 330 million!) [...] Hinduism generally regards its 330 million as deities as extensions of one ultimate reality, many names for one ocean, many "masks" for one God.'

[27] Hinnells, John R. (2005). *The Routledge companion to the study of religion* (http://books.google.com/?id=IGspjXKxIf8C). Routledge. pp. 439–440. ISBN 0415333113. . Retrieved 2009-09-17.

[28] Timothy Fitzgerald. *The Ideology of Religious Studies*. New York: Oxford University Press USA, 2000.

[29] Craig R. Prentiss. *Religion and the Creation of Race and Ethnicity*. New York: NYU Press, 2003. ISBN 081476701X

[30] Tomoko Masuzawa. *The Invention of World Religions, or, How European Universalism Was Preserved in the Language of Pluralism*. Chicago: University of Chicago Press, 2005. ISBN 0226509885

[31] A Common Word (http://acommonword.com/)

[32] C1 World Dialogue (http://www.c1worlddialogue.com/)

[33] Islam and Buddhism Common Ground (http://islambuddhism.com/)

[34] World Interfaith Harmony Week (http://worldinterfaithharmonyweek.com/)

[35] UN resolution (http://worldinterfaithharmonyweek.com/world-interfaith-harmony-week-resolution/)

[36] Bryan Caplan. "Why Religious Beliefs Are Irrational, and Why Economists Should Care" (http://econfaculty.gmu.edu/bcaplan/ldebate. htm). . The article about religion and irrationality.

[37] Earth Dialogues 2006 Conference, Brisbane. "In these countries, Islamic rulers want to solve 21st century issues with laws belonging to 14 centuries ago. Their views of human rights are exactly the same as it was 1400 years ago."

[38] Kevin R. Foster and Hanna Kokko, "The evolution of superstitious and superstition-like behaviour", *Proc. R. Soc. B* (2009) 276, 31–37 (http://www.people.fas.harvard.edu/~kfoster/FosterKokko2008 Proc B superstition.pdf)

[39] Boyer (2001). "Why Belief" (http://books.google.com/books?id=wreF80OHTicC&pg=PA297&lpg=PA297&dq="fang+too+were+ quite+amazed"). *Religion Explained*. .

[40] Fitzgerald 2007

[41] Veyne 1987, p 211

[42] Joseph Campbell, *The Power of Myth*, p. 22 ISBN 0-385-24774-5

[43] Joseph Campbell, *Thou Art That: Transforming Religious Metaphor*. Ed. Eugene Kennedy. New World Library ISBN 1-57731-202-3.

[44] Paul S. Mueller, MD; David J. Plevak, MD; Teresa A. Rummans, MD. "Religious Involvement, Spirituality, and Medicine: Implications for Clinical Practice" (http://www.mayoclinicproceedings.com/content/76/12/1225.full.pdf). . Retrieved 13 November 2010. "We reviewed published studies, meta-analyses, systematic reviews, and subject reviews that examined the association between religious involvement and spirituality and physical health, mental health, health-related quality of life, and other health outcomes. We also reviewed articles that provided suggestions on how clinicians might assess and support the spiritual needs of patients. Most studies have shown that religious involvement and spirituality are associated with better health outcomes, including greater longevity, coping skills, and health-related quality of life (even during terminal illness) and less anxiety, depression, and suicide."

[45] Selengut, Charles (2008-04-28). *Sacred fury: understanding religious violence* (http://books.google.com/?id=mOqtEkGlq0cC& pg=PR7&dq="sectarian+violence"+"religious+violence"#v=onepage&q="sectarian violence" "religious violence"&f=false). p. 1. ISBN 9780742560840. .

[46] Avalos, Hector (2005). *Fighting Words: The Origins of Religious Violence*. Amherst, New York: Prometheus Books.

[47] Hitchens, Christopher (2007). *God is not Great*. Twelve.

[48] Dawkins, Richard (2006). *The God Delusion*. Bantam Books.

[49] *The Curse of Cain: The Violent Legacy of Monotheism By Regina M. Schwartz*. University of Chicago Press. 1998.

[50] Wechsler, Lawrence. "Mayhem and Monotheism" (http://faculty.plts.edu/gpence/2490/PDF/mayhem.pdf). .

[51] Bland, Byron (May 2003). "Evil Enemies: The Convergence of Religion and Politics" (http://www.law.stanford.edu/program/centers/ scicn/papers/religion_and_political_violence.pdf). p. 4. .

[52] John S. Feinberg, Paul D. Feinberg. *Ethics for a Brave New World* (http://books.google.com/books?id=Nl-f5SKq9mgC&pg=PA697& dq=Aleksandr+Solzhenitsyn+But+if+I+were+asked+today+to+formulate+as+concisely+as+possible+the+main+cause+of+the+ ruinous+revolution+that+swallowed+up+some+60+million+of+our+people,+I+could+not+put+it+more+accurately+than+to+ repeat:+'Men+have+forgotten+God;+that's+why#v=onepage&q&f=false). Crossway Books. . Retrieved 2007–10–18. "Over a half century ago, while I was still a child, I recall hearing a number of old people offer the following explanation for the great disasters that had befallen Russia: 'Men have forgotten God; that's why all this has happened.' Since then I have spend well-nigh 50 years working on the history of our revolution; in the process I have read hundreds of books, collected hundreds of personal testimonies, and have already contributed eight volumes of my own toward the effort of clearing away the rubble left by that upheaval. But if I were asked today to formulate as concisely as possible the main cause of the ruinous revolution that swallowed up some 60 million of our people, I could not put it more accurately than to repeat: 'Men have forgotten God; that's why all this has happened.'"

[53] Gregory Koukl. "The Real Murderers: Atheism or Christianity?" (http://www.str.org/site/News2?page=NewsArticle&id=5527). Stand To Reason. . Retrieved 2007–10–18.

[54] Dinesh D'Souza. "Answering Atheist's Arguments" (http://catholiceducation.org/articles/apologetics/ap0214.htm). Catholic Education Resource Center. . Retrieved 2007–10–18.

[55] An example is the Establishment Clause in the First Amendment to the United States Constitution. However the US Supreme Court has intentionally not pinned down a precise legal definition to allow for flexibility in preserving rights for what might be regarded as a religion over time. (http://legal-dictionary.thefreedictionary.com/Religion)

[56] Winnifred Fallers Sullivan, *The Impossibility of Religious Freedom*. Princeton, NJ: Princeton University Press, 2005.

[57] Ronald C. Wimberley and James A. Christenson. " Civil Religion and Church and State (http://www.jstor.org/stable/4106009)". *The Sociological Quarterly*, Vol. 21, No. 1 (Winter, 1980), pp. 35-40

[58] Daniel Dubuisson, *The Western Construction of Religion*

[59] Daniel Dubuisson. "Exporting the Local: Recent Perspectives on 'Religion' as a Cultural Category", *Religion Compass*, 1.6 (2007), p.792.

[60] Tomoko Masuzawa, *The Invention of World Religions*. Chicago: University of Chicago Press, 2007.

[61] Fitzgerald, Timothy (2007). *Discourse on Civility and Barbarity*. Oxford University Press. pp. 45–46.

[62] Fitzgerald 2007

[63] Fitzgerald 2007

[64] Hueston A. Finlay. "'Feeling of absolute dependence' or 'absolute feeling of dependence'? A question revisited". *Religious Studies* 41.1 (2005), pp.81-94.

[65] Max Müller. "Lectures on the origin and growth of religion."

[66] Talal Asad, *Genealogies of Religion*. Baltimore: Johns Hopkins Univ. Press, 1993 p.34-35.

[67] S. N. Balagangadhara. *The Heathen in His Blindness...* New York: Brill Academic Publishers, 1994. p.159.

[68] Jason Ānanda Josephson. "When Buddhism Became a 'Religion'". *Japanese Journal of Religious Studies* 33.1: 143–168.

[69] Isomae Jun'ichi. "Deconstructing 'Japanese Religion'". *Japanese Journal of Religious Studies* 32.2: 235–248.

[70] George A. Lindbeck, *Nature of Doctrine* (Louisville: Westminster/John Knox Press, 1984), 33.

[71] Nicholas de Lange, *Judaism*, Oxford University Press, 1986

Bibliography

- Saint Augustine; *The Confessions of Saint Augustine* (John K. Ryan translator); Image (1960), ISBN 0-385-02955-1.
- Descartes, René; *Meditations on First Philosophy*; Bobbs-Merril (1960), ISBN 0-672-60191-5.
- Barzilai, Gad; *Law and Religion*; The International Library of Essays in Law and Society; Ashgate (2007),ISBN 978-0-7546-2494-3
- Durant, Will (& Ariel (uncredited)); *Our Oriental Heritage*; MJF Books (1997), ISBN 1-56731-012-5.
- Durant, Will (& Ariel (uncredited)); *Caesar and Christ*; MJF Books (1994), ISBN 1-56731-014-1
- Durant, Will (& Ariel (uncredited)); *The Age of Faith*; Simon & Schuster (1980), ISBN 0-671-01200-2.
- Marija Gimbutas 1989. *The Language of the Goddess*. Thames and Hudson New York
- Gonick, Larry; *The Cartoon History of the Universe*; Doubleday, vol. 1 (1978) ISBN 0-385-26520-4, vol. II (1994) ISBN#0-385-42093-5, W. W. Norton, vol. III (2002) ISBN 0-393-05184-6.
- Haisch, Bernard *The God Theory: Universes, Zero-point Fields, and What's Behind It All* -- discussion of science vs. religion (Preface (http://www.thegodtheory.com/preface.html)), Red Wheel/Weiser, 2006, ISBN 1-57863-374-5
- Lao Tzu; *Tao Te Ching* (Victor H. Mair translator); Bantam (1998).
- Marx, Karl; "Introduction to A Contribution to the Critique of Hegel's Philosophy of Right", *Deutsch-Französische Jahrbücher*, (1844).
- Saler, Benson; "Conceptualizing Religion: Immanent Anthropologists, Transcendent Natives, and Unbounded Categories" (1990), ISBN 1-57181-219-9
- *The Holy Bible*, King James Version; New American Library (1974).
- *The Koran*; Penguin (2000), ISBN 0-14-044558-7.
- *The Origin of Live & Death*, African Creation Myths; Heinemann (1966).
- *Poems of Heaven and Hell from Ancient Mesopotamia*; Penguin (1971).
- *The World Almanac* (annual), World Almanac Books, ISBN 0-88687-964-7.
- *The Serotonin System and Spiritual Experiences* (http://ajp.psychiatryonline.org/cgi/content/full/160/11/ 1965) - American Journal of Psychiatry 160:1965-1969, November 2003.
- United States Constitution
- *Selected Work* Marcus Tullius Cicero
- *The World Almanac* (for numbers of adherents of various religions), 2005
- Religion [First Edition]. Winston King. *Encyclopedia of Religion*. Ed. Lindsay Jones. Vol. 11. 2nd ed. Detroit: Macmillan Reference USA, 2005. p7692-7701.
- *World Religions and Social Evolution of the Old World Oikumene Civilizations: A Cross-cultural Perspective* by Andrey Korotayev, Lewiston, NY: Edwin Mellen Press, 2004, ISBN 0-7734-6310-0.
- Brodd, Jefferey (2003). *World Religions*. Winona, MN: Saint Mary's Press. ISBN 978-0-88489-725-5.

On religion definition:

- The first major study: Durkheim, Emile (1976) *The Elementary Forms of the Religious Life*. London: George Allen & Unwin (in French 1912, English translation 1915).
- Wilfred Cantwell Smith *The Meaning and End of Religion* (1962) notes that the concept of religion as an ideological community and system of doctrines, developed in the 15th and 16th centuries CE.
- A distillation of the Western folk category of religion: Geertz, Clifford. 1993 [1966]. *Religion as a cultural system* (http://web.archive.org/web/20070925190332/http://resources.theology.ox.ac.uk/library/data/ pdf/THD0111.pdf). pp. 87–125 in Clifford Geertz, *The Interpretation of Cultures: Selected Essays* (http:// books.google.com/books?hl=it&lr=&id=BZ1BmKEHti0C). London: Fontana Press.
- An operational definition: Wallace, Anthony F. C. 1966. *Religion: An Anthropological View*. New York: Random House. (p. 62-66)
- A recent overview: *A Scientific Definition of Religion* (http://www.anpere.net/2007/2.pdf). By Ph.D. James W. Dow.
- Origines de l'homme - De la matière à la conscience, *Yves Coppens*, De Vive Voix, Paris, 2010
- La preistoria dell'uomo, *Yves Coppens*, Jaka Book, Milano, 2011

Studies of religion in particular geographical areas:

- A. Khanbaghi. *The Fire, the Star and the Cross: Minority Religions in Medieval and Early Modern Iran* (IB Tauris; 2006) 268 pages. Social, political and cultural history of religious minorities in Iran, c. 226-1722 AD.

External links

- Religion Statistics (http://ucblibraries.colorado.edu/govpubs/us/religion.htm) from *UCB Libraries GovPubs*
- Religion (http://www.dmoz.org/Society/Religion_and_Spirituality/) at the Open Directory Project
- Major Religions of the World Ranked by Number of Adherents (http://www.adherents.com/ Religions_By_Adherents.html) by Adherents.com August 2005
- IACSR - International Association for the Cognitive Science of Religion (http://www.iacsr.com/)
- Studying Religion (http://www.as.ua.edu/rel/studyingreligion.html) - Introduction to the methods and scholars of the academic study of religion
- A Contribution to the Critique of Hegel's Philosophy of Right (http://www.marxists.org/archive/marx/works/ 1843/critique-hpr/intro.htm#05) - Marx's original reference to religion as the *opium of the people*.
- The Complexity of Religion and the Definition of "Religion" in International Law (http://www.law.harvard. edu/students/orgs/hrj/iss16/gunn.shtml) Harvard Human Rights Journal article from the President and Fellows of Harvard College(2003)

Numinous

Numinous (🔊 /ˈnjuːmɪnəs/) is an English adjective describing the power or presence of a divinity. The word was popularised in the early twentieth century by the German theologian Rudolf Otto in his influential book *Das Heilige* (1917; translated into English as *The Idea of the Holy*, 1923). According to Otto the numinous experience has two aspects: *mysterium tremendum*, which is the tendency to invoke fear and trembling; and *mysterium fascinans*, the tendency to attract, fascinate and compel. The numinous experience also has a personal quality to it, in that the person feels to be in communion with a *wholly other*. The numinous experience can lead in different cases to belief in deities, the supernatural, the sacred, the holy, and/or the transcendent.

Etymology

The word *numinous* is derivative from the Classical Latin word *numen*.

Rudolf Otto

Otto's use of the term as referring to a characteristic of religious experience was influential among intellectuals of the subsequent generation. For example, numinous as understood by Otto was a frequently quoted concept in the writings of Carl Jung and C. S. Lewis. The notion of the numinous and the *wholly other* were also central to the religious studies of Mircea Eliade.

Mysterium tremendum et fascinans ("fearful and fascinating mystery") is a Latin phrase which Rudolf Otto uses in *The Idea of the Holy* to name the awe inspiring mystery that was the object common to all forms of religious experience.

Mysterium tremendum is described in *The Doors of Perception* by Aldous Huxley in the following terms:

> The literature of religious experience abounds in references to the pains and terrors overwhelming those who have come, too suddenly, face to face with some manifestation of the mysterium tremendum. In theological language, this fear is due to the in-compatibility between man's egotism and the divine purity, between man's self-aggravated separateness and the infinity of God.

Non-religious usage

The idea is not necessarily a religious one: noted atheists Carl Sagan,[1] Christopher Hitchens, Daniel Dennett, Richard Dawkins and Sam Harris have discussed the importance of separating the numinous from the religious.[2]

References

[1] James A. Herrick (2008). *Scientific mythologies: how science and science fiction forge new religious beliefs* (http://books.google.com.ph/ books?id=Y6TKkSFRp3YC&lpg=PA25&dq=Carl Sagan contact numinous&pg=PA25#v=onepage&q=Carl Sagan contact numinous& f=false). InterVarsity Press. p. 25. ISBN 9780830825882. .

[2] "The Four Horsemen" (http://www.youtube.com/watch?v=8PhmUyFUFyk&feature=PlayList&p=A490902178E6854D&index=1), Christopher Hitchens, Daniel Dennett, Richard Dawkins, Sam Harris, September 2007

Peine

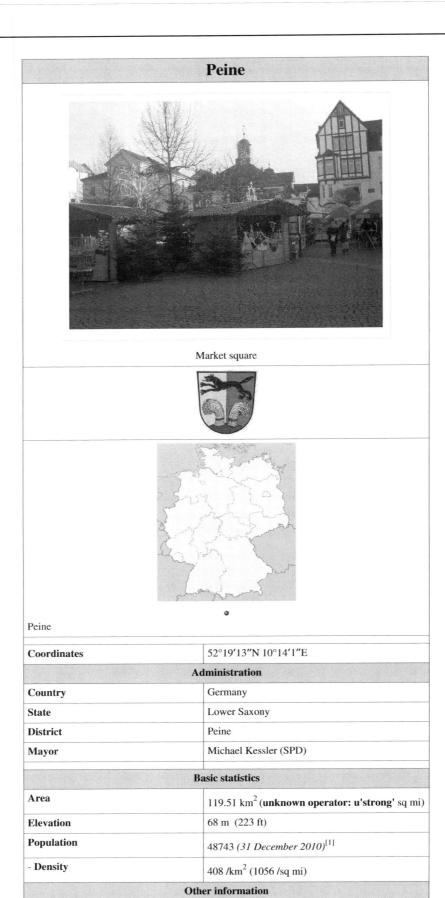

Peine	
Coordinates	52°19′13″N 10°14′1″E
Administration	
Country	Germany
State	Lower Saxony
District	Peine
Mayor	Michael Kessler (SPD)
Basic statistics	
Area	119.51 km² (**unknown operator: u'strong'** sq mi)
Elevation	68 m (223 ft)
Population	48743 *(31 December 2010)*[1]
- **Density**	408 /km² (1056 /sq mi)
Other information	

Market square

Peine

Time zone	CET/CEST (UTC+1/+2)
Licence plate	PE
Postal codes	31224–31228
Area code	05171
Website	www.peine.de [2]

Peine is a town in Lower Saxony, Germany, capital of the district Peine. It is situated on the river Fuhse and the Mittellandkanal, approx. 25 km west of Braunschweig, and 40 km east of Hanover.

History

A deed from 1130 mentions Berthold von Pagin, ministerialis of Lothair III, emperor of the Holy Roman Empire, who gave his name to the town in the form of Peine. The castle, Burg Peine, dates to this era or before.

The 1201, the Hildesheim Chronicle describes a feud between the bishop Hartbert von Hildesheim and the brothers Ekbert and Gunzelin von Wolfenbüttel. Earl Gunzelin von Wolfenbüttel was the commander-in-chief of the German army and seneschal in attendance of Otto IV, emperor of the Holy Roman Empire. Gunzelin prevailed and won control of Burg Peine and the surrounding area.

South of the castle, Gunzelin founded the town of Peine in 1218 or 1220. In 1223, the settlement gained town privileges. Gunzelin's coat of arms has been the town's symbol ever since.

In 1256, Peine was conquered by Albrecht, Duke of Braunschweig-Lüneburg, and after Gunzelin's death in 1260, his sons lost the fief of Peine to the Bishop of Hildesheim.

Otto I of Braunschweig-Lüneburg, bishop of Hildesheim, 1260–1279, gave Earl Wedekind von Poppenburg the castle, town and county of Peine as a fief. Otto later incorporated Peine as a market town.

Also in 1260, Peine earned the right to mint and issue coins and was, with a few interruptions, a mint for the bishopric of Hildesheim until 1428. In 1954 and 1956, two of the largest German medieval treasures of silver (95 pieces of round bullion, weighing 7.5 kg, dating from the 14th century) were found under the streets *Stederdorfer Straße* and *Horstweg*.

Notable natives

- Fritz Hartjenstein
- Hans-Hermann Hoppe
- Solomon Perel
- Herma Auguste Wittstock
- Rudolf Otto

Twinned cities

Peine is twinned with:

- Heywood, Greater Manchester, England.
- Aschersleben, Saxony-Anhalt (Germany) since 1990.
- Tripoli, Greece since 2000.
- Heinola, Finland

Pictures of Peine

Former City Hall from 1827 on the market square

The Burgpark

Jakobi-Kirche

Töpfers Mühle

Steel Factory

Water Tower in
southern Peine

Railway station

References

[1] "Bevölkerungsdichte der kreisfreien Städte und Landkreise - Stand 31.12.2010" (http://www.lskn.niedersachsen.de/download/59963) (in German). Landesbetrieb für Statistik und Kommunikationstechnologie Niedersachsen. July 2011. .

[2] http://www.peine.de/

University of Marburg

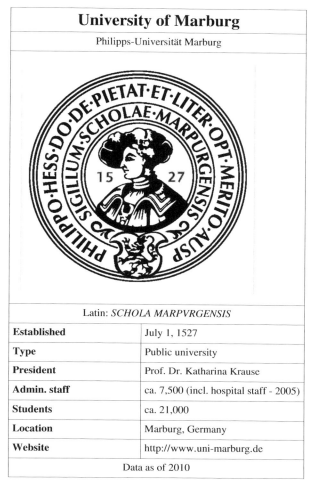

University of Marburg	
Philipps-Universität Marburg	
Latin: *SCHOLA MARPVRGENSIS*	
Established	July 1, 1527
Type	Public university
President	Prof. Dr. Katharina Krause
Admin. staff	ca. 7,500 (incl. hospital staff - 2005)
Students	ca. 21,000
Location	Marburg, Germany
Website	http://www.uni-marburg.de
Data as of 2010	

The **Philipp University of Marburg** (German: *Philipps-Universität Marburg*), was founded in 1527 by Landgrave Philip I of Hesse (usually called the Magnanimous, although the updated meaning 'haughty' is sometimes given) as the world's oldest university dating back to a Protestant foundation. As a modern state university it has no religious affiliation anymore.

It was the main university of the principality of Hesse and remains a public university of that German state. It now has about 20,000 students and 7,500 employees, making Marburg, a town of less than 80,000 inhabitants, the proverbial "university town" (*Universitätsstadt*). Though most subjects are grouped, the University of Marburg is not a campus university.

University of Marburg - Department of Social Sciences and University library

Marburg is home to one of Germany's most traditional medical faculties. The German physicians' union is called "Marburger Bund".

The department of psychology enjoys an outstanding reputation and reached Excellence Group status in the Europe-wide CHE Excellence Ranking 2009.

In 1609, the University of Marburg established the world's first professorship in chemistry.

Famous alumni and professors

Famous natural scientists who studied or taught at the University of Marburg:

- Ludwig Aschoff
- Emil von Behring
- Ferdinand Braun
- Klaus Bringmann
- Robert Bunsen
- Adolf Butenandt
- Georg Ludwig Carius
- Franz Ludwig Fick
- Hans Fischer
- Edward Frankland
- Frederick Augustus Genth
- Johann Peter Griess
- Karl Eugen Guthe
- Otto Hahn

The old university

- Johannes Hartmann
- Thomas Archer Hirst
- Erich Hückel
- Karl Hermann Knoblauch
- Hermann Kolbe
- Albrecht Kossel
- Otto Loewi
- Hans Meerwein
- Ludwig Mond
- Denis Papin
- Otto Heinrich Schindewolf
- Tawara Sunao
- John Tyndall
- Wilhelm Walcher
- Alfred Wegener
- Georg Wittig
- Alexandre Yersin
- Karl Ziegler
- Theodor Zincke

Marburg was always known as a humanities university. It retained that strength, especially in Philosophy and Theology for a long time after World War II. Famous theologians include:

- Rudolf Bultmann
- Friedrich Heiler
- Wilhelm Herrmann
- Aegidius Hunnius
- Andreas Hyperius
- Otto Kaiser
- Jacob Lorhard
- Rudolf Otto
- Kurt Rudolph
- Paul Tillich
- August Friedrich Christian Vilmar

Famous philosophers include:

- Wolfgang Abendroth, Political Science
- Ernst Cassirer
- Hermann Cohen

- Hans-Georg Gadamer
- Nicolai Hartmann
- Martin Heidegger
- Hans Jonas
- Friedrich Albert Lange
- Karl Löwith
- Paul Natorp
- Christian Wolff
- Eduard Zeller
- Karl Theodor Bayrhoffer

Other famous students:

- Hannah Arendt
- Karl Barth
- Gottfried Benn
- Gerold Bepler
- Georg Friedrich Creuzer
- T. S. Eliot (who had to quit a summer school in August 1914 - at start of World War I)
- José Ortega y Gasset
- Jacob Grimm
- Wilhelm Grimm
- Caspar Friedrich Hachenberg
- Gustav Heinemann
- Beatrice Heuser
- Kim Hwang-sik
- Helmut Koester
- Wilhelm Liebknecht
- Mikhail Vasilyevich Lomonosov
- Carlyle Ferren MacIntyre
- Ulrike Meinhof
- Boris Pasternak
- Ernst Reuter
- Isaac Rülf
- Ferdinand Sauerbruch
- Friedrich Carl von Savigny
- Annemarie Schimmel
- Heinrich Schütz
- Manfred Siebald
- Leo Strauss
- Wilhelm Röpke
- Konstantinos Simitis
- Monika Treut
- Wilhelm Viëtor - Philologist, Phonetician
- Daniel Lymperopoulos - Dentist

List of subjects

The University of Marburg has a bright spectrum of subjects with research highlights in nano sciences, material sciences, near eastern studies, and medicine.

- Law
- Economics
- Philosophy
- European Ethnology
- Political science
- Sociology
- Religious studies
- Peace and conflict studies
- Psychology
- Christian theology (Protestant)
- Christian theology (Catholic)
- History
- Archeology

- Sinology (moved to Goethe University Frankfurt)
- German language and literature
- History of art
- Graphic design
- English studies, American studies
- Language technology
- Classic and Koine (New Testament) Greek
- Classic and Medieval Latin
- Oriental studies (to be significantly enlarged in the near future), Indology, Tibetology
- Comparative Linguistics
- Celtic Studies
- Romanic languages and literature (French, Italian, Spanish, Catalan, Portuguese)
- Slavic languages and literature (moved to the University of Giessen)
- Mathematics
- Computer sciences
- Physics
- Chemistry
- Pharmacy
- Biology
- Geology (moved to Goethe University Frankfurt)
- Geography
- Medicine
- Dentistry
- Pedagogy

Collections of the University

- Alter Botanischer Garten Marburg, the university's old botanical garden
- Botanischer Garten Marburg, the university's current botanical garden
- Forschungsinstitut Lichtbildarchiv älterer Orginalurkunden bis 1250 (Collection of photographies taken from medieval charters) [1]
- Bildarchiv Foto Marburg (German national picture archive of arts) [2]
- Religionskundliche Sammlung (Collection of religious objects) [3]
- Deutscher Sprachatlas (Linguistic Atlas of Germany) [4]
- Mineralogisches Museum (Museum of Mineralogy) [5]

External links

- Philipps-Universität Marburg [6]
- T. S. Eliot [7]
- Wilhelm Viëtor [8]
- Karzer - historical detention room [9]

References

[1] http://www.uni-marburg.de/fb06/mag/lba
[2] http://www.fotomarburg.de/
[3] http://www.uni-marburg.de/relsamm
[4] http://www.uni-marburg.de/fb09/dsa
[5] http://www.uni-marburg.de/fb19/minmus?searchterm=Mineralogisches%20Museum
[6] http://www.uni-marburg.de/
[7] http://staff-www.uni-marburg.de/~nail/eliot.htm
[8] http://ww2.warwick.ac.uk/fac/soc/al/research/collect/elt_archive/halloffame/vietor/life/
[9] http://www.staff.uni-marburg.de/~nail/pdf/KarzerMappeNeu.pdf

Theology

Theology is the systematic and rational study of religion and its influences and of the nature of religious truths, or the learned profession acquired by completing specialized training in religious studies, usually at a university or school of divinity or seminary.[1]

Definition

Augustine of Hippo defined the Latin equivalent, *theologia*, as "reasoning or discussion concerning the Deity";[2] Richard Hooker defined "theology" in English as "the science of things divine".[3] The term can, however, be used for a variety of different disciplines or forms of discourse.[4] Theologians use various forms of analysis and argument (philosophical, ethnographic, historical, spiritual and others) to help understand, explain, test, critique, defend or promote any of myriad religious topics. Theology might be undertaken to help the theologian:

Albert the Great (1193/1206–1280), patron saint of Roman Catholic theologians

- understand more truly his or her own religious tradition,[5]
- understand more truly another religious tradition,[6]
- make comparisons between religious traditions,[7]
- defend or justify a religious tradition,
- facilitate reform of a particular tradition,[8]
- assist in the propagation of a religious tradition,[9] or
- draw on the resources of a tradition to address some present situation or need,[10]
- draw on the resources of a tradition to explore possible ways of interpreting the world,[11] or
- explore the nature of divinity without reference to any specific tradition.

History of the term

Theology translates into English from the Greek *theologia* (θεολογία) which derived from *theos* (θεός), meaning God, and *logia* (λόγια)[12], meaning utterances, sayings, or oracles (a word related to *logos* [λόγος], meaning word, discourse, account, or reasoning) which had passed into Latin as *theologia* and into French as *théologie*. The English equivalent "theology" (Theologie, Teologye) had evolved by 1362.[13] The sense the word has in English depends in large part on the sense the Latin and Greek equivalents had acquired in Patristic and medieval Christian usage, though the English term has now spread beyond Christian contexts.

- Greek *theologia* (θεολογια) was used with the meaning "discourse on god" in the fourth century B.C. by Plato in The Republic, Book ii, Ch. 18.[14] Aristotle divided theoretical philosophy into *mathematike, physike* and *theologike*, with the latter corresponding roughly to metaphysics, which, for Aristotle, included discourse on the nature of the divine.[15]

- Drawing on Greek Stoic sources, the Latin writer Varro distinguished three forms of such discourse: mythical (concerning the myths of the Greek gods), rational (philosophical analysis of the gods and of cosmology) and civil (concerning the rites and duties of public religious observance).[16]

- *Theologos*, closely related to theologia, appears once in some biblical manuscripts, in the heading to the book of Revelation: *apokalypsis ioannoy toy theologoy*, "the revelation of John the *theologos*." There, however, the word refers not to John the "theologian" in the modern English sense of the word but—using a slightly different sense of the root *logos*, meaning not "rational discourse" but "word" or "message"—one who speaks the words of God, *logoi toy theoy*.[17]

- Some Latin Christian authors, such as Tertullian and Augustine, followed Varro's threefold usage,[18] though Augustine also used the term more simply to mean 'reasoning or discussion concerning the deity'[2]

- In Patristic Greek Christian sources, *theologia* could refer narrowly to devout and inspired knowledge of, and teaching about, the essential nature of God.[19]

- In some medieval Greek and Latin sources, *theologia* (in the sense of "an account or record of the ways of God") could refer simply to the Bible.[20]

- The Latin author Boethius, writing in the early 6th century, used *theologia* to denote a subdivision of philosophy as a subject of academic study, dealing with the motionless, incorporeal reality (as opposed to *physica*, which deals with corporeal, moving realities).[21] Boethius' definition influenced medieval Latin usage.[22]

- In scholastic Latin sources, the term came to denote the rational study of the doctrines of the Christian religion, or (more precisely) the academic discipline which investigated the coherence and implications of the language and claims of the Bible and of the theological tradition (the latter often as represented in Peter Lombard's *Sentences*, a book of extracts from the Church Fathers).[23]

- It is in this last sense, theology as an academic discipline involving rational study of Christian teaching, that the term passed into English in the fourteenth century,[24] though it could also be used in the narrower sense found in Boethius and the Greek patristic authors, to mean rational study of the essential nature of God — a discourse now sometimes called Theology Proper.[25]

- From the 17th century onwards, it also became possible to use the term 'theology' to refer to study of religious ideas and teachings that are not specifically Christian (e.g., in the phrase 'Natural Theology' which denoted theology based on reasoning from natural facts independent of specifically Christian revelation [26]), or that are specific to another religion (see below).

- "Theology" can also now be used in a derived sense to mean "a system of theoretical principles; an (impractical or rigid) ideology."[27]

Religions other than Christianity

In academic theological circles there is some debate as to whether theology is an activity peculiar to the Christian religion, such that the word "theology" should be reserved for Christian theology, and other words used to name analogous discourses within other religious traditions.[28] It is seen by some to be a term only appropriate to the study of religions that worship a deity (a *theos*), and to presuppose belief in the ability to speak and reason about this deity (in *logia*)—and so to be less appropriate in religious contexts that are organized differently (religions without a deity, or that deny that such subjects can be studied logically). ("Hierology" has been proposed as an alternative, more generic term.[29])

Analogous discourses

Some academic inquiries within Buddhism, dedicated to the rational investigation of a Buddhist understanding of the world, prefer the designation Buddhist philosophy to the term Buddhist theology, since Buddhism lacks the same conception of a *theos*. Jose Ignacio Cabezon, who argues that the use of "theology" *is* appropriate, can only do so, he says, because "I take theology not to be restricted to discourse on God ... I take 'theology' not to be restricted to its etymological meaning. In that latter sense, Buddhism is of course *a*theological, rejecting as it does the notion of God."[30]

Within Hindu philosophy, there is a solid and ancient tradition of philosophical speculation on the nature of the universe, of God (termed "Brahman" in some schools of Hindu thought) and of the Atman (soul). The Sanskrit word for the various schools of Hindu philosophy is Darshana (meaning "view" or "viewpoint"). Vaishnava theology has been a subject of study for many devotees, philosophers and scholars in India for centuries, and in recent decades also has been taken on by a number of academic institutions in Europe, such as the Oxford Centre for Hindu Studies and Bhaktivedanta College.[31] *See also: Krishnology*

Islamic theological discussion that parallels Christian theological discussion is named "Kalam"; the Islamic analogue of Christian theological discussion would more properly be the investigation and elaboration of Islamic law, or "Fiqh". "Kalam ... does not hold the leading place in Muslim thought that theology does in Christianity. To find an equivalent for 'theology' in the Christian sense it is necessary to have recourse to several disciplines, and to the usul al-fiqh as much as to kalam." (L. Gardet)[32]

In Judaism, the historical absence of political authority has meant that most theological reflection has happened within the context of the Jewish community and synagogue, rather than within specialized academic institutions. Nevertheless, Jewish theology historically has been very active and highly significant for Christian and Islamic theology. It is sometimes claimed, however, that the Jewish analogue of Christian theological discussion would more properly be Rabbinical discussion of Jewish law and Jewish Biblical commentaries.[33]

Theology as an academic discipline

The history of the study of theology in institutions of higher education is as old as the history of such institutions themselves. For example, Taxila was an early centre of Vedic learning, possible from the 6th century BC or earlier;[34] the Platonic Academy founded in Athens in the 4th century BC seems to have included theological themes in its subject matter;[35] the Chinese Taixue delivered Confucian teaching from the 2nd century BC;[36] the School of Nisibis was a centre of Christian learning from the 4th century AD;[37] Nalanda in India was a site of Buddhist higher learning from at least the 5th or 6th century AD;[38] and the Moroccan University of Al-Karaouine was a centre of Islamic learning from the 10th century,[39] as was Al-Azhar University in Cairo.[40]

Modern Western universities evolved from the monastic institutions and (especially) cathedral schools of Western Europe during the High Middle Ages (see, for instance, the University of Bologna, Paris University and Oxford University).[41] From the beginning, Christian theological learning was therefore a central component in these institutions, as was the study of Church or Canon law): universities played an important role in training people for ecclesiastical offices, in helping the church pursue the clarification and defence of its teaching, and in supporting the legal rights of the church over against secular rulers.[42] At such universities, theological study was initially closely tied to the life of faith and of the church: it fed, and was fed by, practices of preaching, prayer and celebration of the Mass.[43]

During the High Middle Ages, theology was therefore the ultimate subject at universities, being named "The Queen of the Sciences" and serving as the capstone to the Trivium and Quadrivium that young men were expected to study. This meant that the other subjects (including Philosophy) existed primarily to help with theological thought.[44]

Christian theology's preeminent place in the university began to be challenged during the European Enlightenment, especially in Germany.[45] Other subjects gained in independence and prestige, and questions were raised about the place in institutions that were increasingly understood to be devoted to independent reason of a discipline that seemed to involve commitment to the authority of particular religious traditions.[46]

Since the early nineteenth century, various different approaches have emerged in the West to theology as an academic discipline. Much of the debate concerning theology's place in the university or within a general higher education curriculum centres on whether theology's methods are appropriately theoretical and (broadly speaking) scientific or, on the other hand, whether theology requires a pre-commitment of faith by its practitioners, and whether such a commitment conflicts with academic freedom.[47]

Theology and ministerial training

In some contexts, theology has been held to belong in institutions of higher education primarily as a form of professional training for Christian ministry. This was the basis on which Friedrich Schleiermacher, a liberal theologian, argued for the inclusion of theology in the new University of Berlin in 1810.[48]

For instance, in Germany, theological faculties at state universities are typically tied to particular denominations, Protestant or Roman Catholic, and those faculties will offer denominationally bound (konfessionsgebunden) degrees, and have denominationally bound public posts amongst their faculty; as well as contributing 'to the development and growth of Christian knowledge' they 'provide the academic training for the future clergy and teachers of religious instruction at German schools.'[49]

In the U.S.A., several prominent colleges and universities were started in order to train Christian ministers. Harvard,[50] Georgetown University,[51] Boston University,[52] Yale,[53] and Princeton[54] all had the theological training of clergy as a primary purpose at their foundation.

Seminaries and bible colleges have continued this alliance between the academic study of theology and training for Christian ministry. There are, for instance, numerous prominent US examples, including The Catholic Theological Union in Chicago,[55] the Graduate Theological Union in Berkeley,[56] Criswell College in Dallas,[57] the Southern Baptist Theological Seminary in Louisville,[58] Trinity Evangelical Divinity School in Deerfield, Illinois,[59] and Dallas Theological Seminary.[60] Assemblies of God Theological Seminary in Springfield, Missouri.

Theology as an academic discipline in its own right

In some contexts, theology is pursued as an academic discipline without formal affiliation to any particular church (though individual members of staff may well have affiliations to different churches), and without ministerial training being a central part of their purpose. This is true, for instance, of many departments in the United Kingdom, including the Department of Theology and Religion at the University of Exeter, and the Department of Theology and Religious Studies at the University of Leeds.[61] Traditional academic prizes, such as the University of Aberdeen's Lumsden and Sachs Fellowship, tend to be awarded for performance in theology (or divinity as it is known at Aberdeen) and religious studies.

Theology and religious studies

In some contemporary contexts, a distinction is made between theology, which is seen as involving some level of commitment to the claims of the religious tradition being studied, and religious studies, which is not. If contrasted with theology in this way, religious studies is normally seen as requiring the bracketing of the question of the truth of the religious traditions studied, and as involving the study of the historical or contemporary practices or ideas those traditions using intellectual tools and frameworks that are not themselves specifically tied to any religious tradition, and that are normally understood to be neutral or secular.[62] In contexts where 'religious studies' in this sense is the focus, the primary forms of study are likely to include:

- Anthropology of religion,

- Comparative religion,
- History of religions,
- Philosophy of religion,
- Psychology of religion, and
- Sociology of religion.

Theology and religious studies are sometimes seen as being in tension;[63] they are sometimes held to coexist without serious tension;[64] and it is sometimes denied that there is as clear a boundary between them as the brief description here suggests.[65]

Criticism

Whether or not reasoned discussion about the divine is possible has long been a point of contention. As early as the fifth century BC, Protagoras, who is reputed to have been exiled from Athens because of his agnosticism about the existence of the gods, said that "Concerning the gods I cannot know either that they exist or that they do not exist, or what form they might have, for there is much to prevent one's knowing: the *obscurity of the subject* and the shortness of man's life."[66]

In his two part work *The Age of Reason*, the American revolutionary Thomas Paine wrote, "The study of theology, as it stands in Christian churches, is the study of nothing; it is founded on nothing; it rests on no principles; it proceeds by no authorities; it has no data; it can demonstrate nothing; and it admits of no conclusion. Not anything can be studied as a science, without our being in possession of the principles upon which it is founded; and as this is the case with Christian theology, it is therefore the study of nothing."[67]

The atheist philosopher Ludwig Feuerbach sought to dissolve theology in his work *Principles of the Philosophy of the Future*: "The task of the modern era was the realization and humanization of God − the transformation and dissolution of theology into anthropology."[68] This mirrored his earlier work The Essence of Christianity (pub. 1841), for which he was banned from teaching in Germany, in which he had said that theology was a "web of contradictions and delusions".[69]

In his essay "Critique of Ethics and Theology" the logical-positivist A.J. Ayer sought to show that all statements about the divine are nonsensical and any divine-attribute is unprovable. He wrote: "It is now generally admitted, at any rate by philosophers, that the existence of a being having the attributes which define the god of any non-animistic religion cannot be demonstratively proved... [A]ll utterances about the nature of God are nonsensical."[70]

In his essay, "Against Theology", the philosopher Walter Kaufmann sought to differentiate theology from religion in general. "Theology, of course, is not religion; and a great deal of religion is emphatically anti-theological... An attack on theology, therefore, should not be taken as necessarily involving an attack on religion. Religion can be, and often has been, untheological or even anti-theological." However, Kaufmann found that "Christianity is inescapably a theological religion".[71]

References

[1] theology (http://wordnetweb.princeton.edu/perl/webwn?o2=&o0=1&o7=&o5=&o1=1&o6=&o4=&o3=&s=theology&h=000& j=0#c)
[2] *City of God* Book VIII. i. (http://logicmuseum.googlepages.com/civitate-8.htm) "de divinitate rationem sive sermonem"
[3] *Of the Laws of Ecclesiastical Polity*, 3.8.11 (http://anglicanhistory.org/hooker/3/368-377.pdf)
[4] McGrath, Alistair. 1998. Historical Theology: An Introduction to the History of Christian Thought. Oxford: Blackwell Publishers. pp. 1–8.
[5] See, e.g., Daniel L. Migliore, *Faith Seeking Understanding: An Introduction to Christian Theology* 2nd ed.(Grand Rapids: Eerdmans, 2004)
[6] See, e.g., Michael S. Kogan, 'Toward a Jewish Theology of Christianity' in *The Journal of Ecumenical Studies* 32.1 (Winter 1995), 89–106; available online at (http://www.icjs.org/scholars/kogan.html)
[7] See, e.g., David Burrell, *Freedom and Creation in Three Traditions* (Notre Dame: University of Notre Dame Press, 1994)
[8] See, e.g., John Shelby Spong, *Why Christianity Must Change or Die* (New York: Harper Collins, 2001)
[9] See, e.g., Duncan Dormor et al (eds), *Anglicanism, the Answer to Modernity* (London: Continuum, 2003)
[10] See, e.g., Timothy Gorringe, *Crime*, Changing Society and the Churches Series (London:SPCK, 2004)
[11] See e.g., Anne Hunt Overzee's gloss upon the view of Ricœur (1913−2005) as to the role of 'theologian': "Paul Ricœur speaks of the theologian as a hermeneut, whose task is to interpret the multivalent, rich metaphors arising from the symbolic bases of tradition so that the symbols may 'speak' once again to our existential situation." Anne Hunt Overzee *The body divine: the symbol of the body in the works of Teilhard de Chardin and Rāmānuja*, Cambridge studies in religious traditions 2 (Cambridge: Cambridge University Press, 1992), ISBN 0-521-38516-4, 9780521385169, p.4; Source: (http://books.google.com.au/books?id=EiYEktsURVAC&printsec=frontcover& source=gbs_v2_summary_r&cad=0#v=onepage&q=&f=false) (accessed: Monday April 5, 2010)
[12] The accusative plural of the neuter noun λόγιον; cf. Walter Bauer, William F. Arndt, F. Wilbur Gingrich, Frederick W. Danker, *A Greek-English Lexicon of the New Testament*, 2nd ed., (Chicago and London: University of Chicago Press, 1979), 476. For examples of λόγια in the New Testament, cf. Acts 7:38; Romans 3:2; 1 Peter 4:11.
[13] Langland, Piers Plowman A ix 136
[14] Liddell and Scott's *Greek-English Lexicon'* (http://www.perseus.tufts.edu/cgi-bin/ptext?doc=Perseus:text:1999.04. 0057;query=entry=#48216;layout=;loc=qeolo/gia1)'.
[15] Aristotle, *Metaphysics*, Book Epsilon. (http://etext.library.adelaide.edu.au/mirror/classics.mit.edu/Aristotle/metaphysics.6.vi.html)
[16] As cited by Augustine, *City of God*, Book 6 (http://www.newadvent.org/fathers/120106.htm), ch.5.

[17] This title appears quite late in the manuscript tradition for the Book of Revelation: the two earliest citations provided in David Aune's *Word Biblical Commentary 52: Revelation 1–5* (Dallas: Word Books, 1997) are both 11th century – Gregory 325/Hoskier 9 and Gregory 1006/Hoskier 215; the title was however in circulation by the 6th century – see Allen Brent 'John as theologos: the imperial mysteries and the Apocalypse', *Journal for the Study of the New Testament* 75 (1999), 87–102.

[18] See Augustine, *City of God*, Book 6 (http://www.newadvent.org/fathers/120106.htm), ch.5. and Tertullian, *Ad Nationes*, Book 2 (http://www.ccel.org/ccel/schaff/anf03.iv.viii.ii.i.html), ch.1.

[19] Gregory of Nazianzus uses the word in this sense in his fourth-century *Theological Orations* (http://www.ccel.org/fathers2/NPNF2-07/Npnf2-07-42.htm#P4178_1277213); after his death, he was called "the Theologian" at the Council of Chalcedon and thereafter in Eastern Orthodoxy—either because his *Orations* were seen as crucial examples of this kind of theology, or in the sense that he was (like the author of the Book of Revelation) seen as one who was an inspired preacher of the words of God. (It is unlikely to mean, as claimed in the *Nicene and Post-Nicene Fathers* (http://www.ccel.org/fathers2/NPNF2-07/Npnf2-07-41.htm#P4162_1255901) introduction to his *Theological Orations*, that he was a defender of the divinity of Christ the Word.) See John McGukin, *Saint Gregory of Nazianzus: An Intellectual Biography* (Crestwood, NY: St. Vladimir's Seminary Press, 2001), p.278.

[20] Hugh of St. Victor, *Commentariorum in Hierarchiam Coelestem*, Expositio to Book 9: "theologia, id est, divina Scriptura" (in Migne's *Patrologia Latina* vol.175, 1091C).

[21] De Trinitate 2 (http://pvspade.com/Logic/docs/BoethiusDeTrin.pdf)

[22] G.R. Evans, *Old Arts and New Theology: The Beginnings of Theology as an Academic Discipline* (Oxford: Clarendon Press, 1980), 31–32.

[23] See the title of Peter Abelard's *Theologia Christiana* (http://individual.utoronto.ca/pking/resources/abelard/Theologia_christiana.txt), and, perhaps most famously, of Thomas Aquinas' *Summa Theologica*

[24] See the 'note' in the Oxford English Dictionary entry for 'theology'.

[25] See, for example, Charles Hodge, *Systematic Theology*, vol. 1, part 1 (1871).

[26] Oxford English Dictionary, sense 1

[27] *Oxford English Dictionary*, 1989 edition, 'Theology' sense 1(d), and 'Theological' sense A.3; the earliest reference given is from the 1959 *Times Literary Supplement* 5 June 329/4: "The 'theological' approach to Soviet Marxism ... proves in the long run unsatisfactory."

[28] See, for example, the initial reaction of Dharmachari Nagapriya in his review (http://www.westernbuddhistreview.com/vol3/buddhisttheology.html) of Jackson and Makrasnky's *Buddhist Theology* (London: Curzon, 2000) in *Western Buddhist Review 3*

[29] E.g., by Count E. Goblet d'Alviella in 1908; see Alan H. Jones, *Independence and Exegesis: The Study of Early Christianity in the Work of Alfred Loisy (1857–1940), Charles Guignebert (1857 [i.e. 1867]–1939), and Maurice Goguel (1880–1955)* (Mohr Siebeck, 1983), p.194.

[30] Jose Ignacio Cabezon, 'Buddhist Theology in the Academy' in Roger Jackson and John J. Makransky's *Buddhist Theology: Critical Reflections by Contemporary Buddhist Scholars* (London: Routledge, 1999), pp. 25–52.

[31] See Anna S. King, 'For Love of Krishna: Forty Years of Chanting' in Graham Dwyer and Richard J. Cole, *The Hare Krishna Movement: Forty Years of Chant and Change* (London/New York: I.B. Tauris, 2006), pp. 134–167: p. 163, which describes developments in both institutions, and speaks of Hare Krishna devotees 'studying Vaishnava theology and practice in mainstream universities.'

[32] L. Gardet, ' Ilm al-kalam (http://www.muslimphilosophy.com/ei2/kalam.htm)' in *The Encyclopedia of Islam*, ed. P.J. Bearman et al (Leiden: Koninklijke Brill NV, 1999).

[33] Randi Rashkover, 'A Call for Jewish Theology' (http://findarticles.com/p/articles/mi_m2096/is_4_49/ai_58621576), *Crosscurrents*, Winter 1999, starts by saying, "Frequently the claim is made that, unlike Christianity, Judaism is a tradition of deeds and maintains no strict theological tradition. Judaism's fundamental beliefs are inextricable from their halakhic observance (that set of laws revealed to Jews by God), embedded and presupposed by that way of life as it is lived and learned."

[34] Timothy Reagan, *Non-Western Educational Traditions: Alternative Approaches to Educational Thought and Practice*, 3rd edition (Lawrence Erlbaum: 2004), p.185 and Sunna Chitnis, 'Higher Education' in Veena Das (ed), *The Oxford India Companion to Sociology and Social Anthropology* (New Delhi: Oxford University Press, 2003), pp. 1032–1056: p.1036 suggest an early date; a more cautious appraisal is given in Hartmut Scharfe, *Education in Ancient India* (Leiden: Brill, 2002), pp. 140–142.

[35] John Dillon, *The Heirs of Plato: A Study in the Old Academy, 347–274BC (Oxford: OUP, 2003)*

[36] Xinzhong Yao, *An Introduction to Confucianism* (Cambridge: CUP, 2000), p.50.

[37] Adam H. Becker, *The Fear of God and the Beginning of Wisdom: The School of Nisibis and the Development of Scholastic Culture in Late Antique Mesopotamia* (University of Pennsylvania Press, 2006); see also The School of Nisibis (http://www.nestorian.org/the_school_of_nisibis.html) at Nestorian.org

[38] Hartmut Scharfe, *Education in Ancient India* (Leiden: Brill, 2002), p.149.

[39] The Al-Qarawiyyin mosque was founded in 859 AD, but 'While instruction at the mosque must have begun almost from the beginning, it is only ... by the end of the tenth-century that its reputation as a center of learning in both religious and secular sciences ... must have begun to wax.' Y. G-M. Lulat, *A History of African Higher Education from Antiquity to the Present: A Critical Synthesis* (Greenwood, 2005), p.71

[40] Andrew Beattie, *Cairo: A Cultural History* (New York: Oxford University Press, 2005), p.101.

[41] Walter Rüegg, *A History of the University in Europe*, vol.1, ed. H. de Ridder-Symoens, *Universities in the Middle Ages* (Cambridge: Cambridge University Press, 2003).

[42] Walter Rüegg, "Themes" in Walter Rüegg, *A History of the University in Europe*, vol.1, ed. H. de Ridder-Symoens, *Universities in the Middle Ages* (Cambridge: Cambridge University Press, 2003), pp. 3–34: pp. 15–16.

[43] See Gavin D'Costa, *Theology in the Public Square: Church, Academy and Nation* (Oxford: Blackwell, 2005), ch.1.

[44] Thomas Albert Howard, *Protestant Theology and the Making of the Modern German University* (Oxford: Oxford University Press, 2006), p.56: '[P]hilosophy, the *scientia scientarum* in one sense, was, in another, portrayed as the humble "handmaid of theology".'

[45] See Thomas Albert Howard, *Protestant Theology and the Making of the Modern German University* (Oxford: Oxford University Press, 2006):

[46] See Thomas Albert Howard's work already cited, and his discussion of, for instance, Immanuel Kant's *Conflict of the Faculties* (1798), and J.G. Fichte's *Deduzierter Plan einer zu Berlin errichtenden höheren Lehranstalt* (1807).

[47] See Thomas Albert Howard, *Protestant Theology and the Making of the Modern German University* (Oxford: Oxford University Press, 2006); Hans W. Frei, *Types of Christian Theology*, ed. William C. Placher and George Hunsinger (New Haven, CT: Yale University Press, 1992); Gavin D'Costa, *Theology in the Public Square: Church, Academy and Nation* (Oxford: Blackwell, 2005); James W. McClendon, *Systematic Theology 3: Witness* (Nashville, TN: Abingdon, 2000), ch.10: 'Theology and the University'.

[48] Friedrich Schleiermacher, *Brief Outline of Theology as a Field of Study*, 2nd edition, tr. Terrence N. Tice (Lewiston, NY: Edwin Mellen, 1990); Thomas Albert Howard, *Protestant Theology and the Making of the Modern German University* (Oxford: Oxford University Press, 2006), ch.14.

[49] Reinhard G. Kratz, 'Academic Theology in Germany', *Religion* 32.2 (2002): pp.113–116.

[50] 'The primary purpose of Harvard College was, accordingly, the training of clergy.' But 'the school served a dual purpose, training men for other professions as well.' George M. Marsden, *The Soul of the American University: From Protestant Establishment to Established Nonbelief* (New York: Oxford University Press, 1994), p.41.

[51] Georgetown was a Jesuit institution founded in significant part to provide a pool of educated Catholics some of whom who could go on to full seminary training for the priesthood. See Robert Emmett Curran, Leo J. O'Donovan, *The Bicentennial History of Georgetown University: From Academy to University 1789–1889 (Georgetown: Georgetown University Press, 1961), Part One.*

[52] Boston University emerged from the Boston School of Theology, a Methodist seminary. Boston University Information Center, 'History – The Early Years' (http://www.bu.edu/dbin/infocenter/content/index.php?pageid=923&topicid=13)

[53] Yale's original 1701 charter speaks of the purpose being 'Sincere Regard & Zeal for upholding & Propagating of the Christian Protestant Religion by a succession of Learned & Orthodox' and that 'Youth may be instructed in the Arts and Sciences (and) through the blessing of Almighty God may be fitted for Publick employment both in Church and Civil State.' 'The Charter of the Collegiate School, October 1701' in Franklin Bowditch Dexter, *Documentary History of Yale University, Under the Original Charter of the Collegiate School of Connecticut 1701–1745* (New Haven, CT: Yale University Press, 1916); available online at (http://www.archive.org/stream/documentaryhisto00dextrich)

[54] At Princeton, one of the founders (probably Ebeneezer Pemberton) wrote in c.1750, 'Though our great Intention was to erect a seminary for educating Ministers of the Gospel, yet we hope it will be useful in other learned professions – Ornaments of the State as Well as the Church. Therefore we propose to make the plan of Education as extensive as our Circumstances will admit.' Quoted in Alexander Leitch, *A Princeton Companion* (http://etcweb.princeton.edu/CampusWWW/Companion/founding_princeton.html) (Princeton University Press, 1978).

[55] See 'Our Story' (http://www.ctu.edu/About_Us/Our_Story) at the Catholic Theological Union website (accessed 29 August 2009): 'lay men and women, religious sisters and brothers, and seminarians have studied alongside one another, preparing to serve God's people'.

[56] See 'About the GTU' (http://www.gtu.edu/about) at the Graduate Theological Union website (accessed 29 August 2009): 'dedicated to educating students for teaching, research, ministry, and service'.

[57] See 'About Us' (http://www.criswell.edu/news--events/about-us/) at the Criswell College website (accessed 29 August 2009): 'Criswell College exists to serve the churches of our Lord Jesus Christ by developing God-called men and women in the Word (intellectually and academically) and by the Word (professionally and spiritually) for authentic ministry leadership'.

[58] See the 'Mission Statement' (http://www.sbts.edu/about/truth/mission/) at the SBTS website (accessed 29 August 2009): 'the mission of The Southern Baptist Theological Seminary is ... to be a servant of the churches of the Southern Baptist Convention by training, educating, and preparing ministers of the gospel for more faithful service.'

[59] See 'About Trinity Evangelical Divinity School' (http://www.tiu.edu/divinity/connect/whoarewe/) at their website (accessed 29 August 2009): 'Trinity Evangelical Divinity School (TEDS) is a learning community dedicated to the development of servant leaders for the global church, leaders who are spiritually, biblically, and theologically prepared to engage contemporary culture for the sake of Christ's kingdom'

[60] See 'About DTS' (http://www.dts.edu/about/) at the Dallas Theological Seminary website (accessed 29 August 2009): 'At Dallas, the scholarly study of biblical and related subjects is inseparably fused with the cultivation of the spiritual life. All this is designed to prepare students to communicate the Word of God in the power of the Spirit of God.'

[61] See the 'Why Study Theology?' (http://huss.exeter.ac.uk/theology/undergrad/) page at the University of Exeter (accessed 1 Sep 2009), and the 'About us' (http://www.leeds.ac.uk//trs/aboutus.htm) page at the University of Leeds.

[62] See, for example, Donald Wiebe, *The Politics of Religious Studies: The Continuing Conflict with Theology in the Academy* (New York: Palgrave Macmillian, 2000).

[63] See K.L. Knoll, 'The Ethics of Being a Theologian' (http://chronicle.com/article/The-Ethics-of-Being-a/47442/?utm_source=at&utm_medium=en), *Chronicle of Higher Education*, July 27, 2009.

[64] See David Ford, 'Theology and Religious Studies for a Multifaith and Secular Society' in D.L. Bird and Simon G. Smith (eds), *Theology and Religious Studies in Higher Education* (London: Continuum, 2009).

[65] Timothy Fitzgerald, *The Ideology of Religious Studies* (Oxford: Oxford University Press, 2000).

[66] Protagoras, fr.4, from *On the Gods*, tr. Michael J. O'Brien in *The Older Sophists*, ed. Rosamund Kent Sprague (Columbia: University of South Carolina Press, 1972), 20, emphasis added. Cf. Carol Poster, "Protagoras (fl. 5th C. BCE)" (http://www.iep.utm.edu/protagor/) in *The Internet Encyclopedia of Philosophy*; accessed: October 6, 2008.

[67] Thomas Paine, The Age of Reason, from "The Life and Major Writings of Thomas Paine", ed. Philip S. Foner, (New York, The Citadel Press, 1945) p601

[68] Ludwig Feuerbach, Principles of the Philosophy of the Future, trans. Manfred H. Vogel, (Indianapolis, Hackett Publishing Company, 1986) p5

[69] Ludwig Feuerbach, The Essence of Christianity, trans. George Eliot, (Amherst, New York, Prometheus Books, 1989) Preface, XVI

[70] A.J. Ayer, Language, Truth and Logic, (New York, Dover Publications, 1936) pp. 114–115

[71] Walter Kaufmann, The Faith of a Heretic, (Garden City, New York, Anchor Books, 1963) pp. 114, 127–128, 130

Mysticism

Mysticism (pronunciation; from the Greek μυστικός, *mystikos*, meaning 'an initiate') is the knowledge of, and especially the personal experience of, states of consciousness, i.e. levels of being, beyond normal human perception, including experience and even communion with a supreme being.

Classical origins

A "mystikos" was an initiate of a mystery religion. The Eleusinian Mysteries, (Greek: Ἐλευσίνια Μυστήρια) were annual initiation ceremonies in the cults of the goddesses Demeter and Persephone, held in secret at Eleusis (near Athens) in ancient Greece.[1] The mysteries began in about 1600 B.C. in the Mycenean period and continued for two thousand years, becoming a major festival during the Hellenic era, and later spreading to Rome.[2]

Modern understanding

The present meaning of the term *mysticism* arose via Platonism and Neoplatonism—which referred to the Eleusinian initiation as a metaphor for the "initiation" to spiritual truths and experiences—and is the pursuit of communion with, identity with, or conscious awareness of an ultimate reality, divinity, spiritual truth, or God through direct experience, intuition, instinct or insight. Mysticism usually centers on practices intended to nurture those experiences. Mysticism may be dualistic, maintaining a distinction between the self and the divine, or may be nondualistic. [3]

Many if not all of the world's great religions have arisen around the teachings of mystics (including Buddha, Jesus, Lao Tze, and Krishna); and most religious traditions describe fundamental mystical experience, at least esoterically. *Enlightenment* or *Illumination* are generic English terms for the phenomenon, derived from the Latin *illuminatio* (applied to Christian prayer in the 15th century) and adopted in English translations of Buddhist texts, but used loosely to describe the state of mystical attainment regardless of faith. [4]

The goddess Persephone, from the great Eleusinian relief in the National Archaeological Museum in Athens

Conventional religions, by definition, have strong institutional structures, including formal hierarchies and mandated sacred texts and/or creeds. Adherents of the faith are expected to respect or follow these closely, so mysticism is often deprecated or persecuted.[5]

The following table briefly summarizes the major forms of mysticism within world religions and their basic concepts.

An all-seeing Eye of Providence that appears on
the tower of Aachen Cathedral.

*The Appearance of the Holy Spirit before Saint
Teresa of Ávila,* Peter Paul Rubens

"The Temple of the Rose Cross," Teophilus
Schweighardt Constantiens, 1618.

a Buddha-statue

Mysticism in World Religions

Host Religion	Form of Mysticism	Basic Concept	Sources of Information
Buddhism	Shingon, Tibetan, Zen	attainment of Nirvana, Satori: connection to ultimate reality	[6] [7]
Christianity	Catholic spirituality, Quaker tradition, Christian mysticism, Gnosticism	Spiritual enlightenment, Spiritual vision, the Love of God, union with God (Theosis)	[8] [9] [10]
Freemasonry	-	Enlightenment	[11]
Hinduism	Vedanta, Yoga, Bhakti, Kashmir Shaivism	liberation from cycles of Karma, non-identification (Kaivalya), experience of ultimate reality (Samadhi), Innate Knowledge (Sahaja and Svabhava)	[12]
Islam	Sufism, Irfan	Innate knowledge, union with God (fana)	[13]
Jainism	Moksha	liberation from cycles of Karma	[14]
Judaism	Kabbalah, Hassidic Judaism	abnegation of the ego, Ein Sof	[15]
Rosicrucianism	-	-	[16]
Sikhism	-	liberation from cycles of Karma	[17] [18]
Taoism	-	Te: connection to ultimate reality	[19]

Literary Forms used by Spiritual Teachers

Since, by definition, mystical knowledge cannot be directly written down or spoken of (but must be experienced), numerous literary forms that allude to such knowledge - often with contradictions or even jokes - have developed, for example:

Aphorisms, poetry

Aphorisms and poetry include artistic efforts to crystallize some particular description or aspect of the mystical experience in words:

- *God is Love* (Christian and Sufi in particular)
- *Atman is Brahman* (Advaitan)
- *God and me, me and God, are One* (Kundalini Yoga, Sikhism)
- Zen haiku
- Rumi's love poems[20] (Sufism)

Koans, riddles, contradictions

Zen koans, riddles, and metaphysical contradictions are intentionally irresolvable tasks or lines of thought, designed to direct one away from intellectualism and effort towards direct experience. [21]

- "What is the sound of one hand (clapping)?" (Zen)
- "How many angels can stand on the head of a pin?" (Christian).

These can be meant as humorous phrases (see humour, below); or as serious questions with significant mystical answers. Others believe that the most edifying understanding of these riddles is that excessive effort contemplating the impossible can give an individual the opportunity to stop trying to 'achieve' and start just 'being'.

- The evocative Taoist phrase—*To yield is to be preserved whole, to be bent is to become straight, to be empty is to be full, to have little is to possess*[22] —is another example of a metaphysical contradiction describing the path of emptying the learned self.

Jokes

Jokes and humorous stories can be used in spiritual teaching to make simple yet profound metaphysical points:

- Some examples are the Nasrudin tales[23], e.g. someone shouts at Nasrudin sitting on a river bank, "How do I get across?" "You are across." he replies;
- Bektashi jokes[24] within Orthodox Islam;
- the Trickster or Animal Spirit stories passed down in Native American, Australian Aboriginal, and African Tribal folklore, and even the familiar "Br'er Rabbit and the Tar Baby"[25].

Stories, parables, metaphors

Parables and metaphor include stories that have a deeper meaning to them:

- Jesus makes use of parables and metaphors when teaching his followers. See Parables of Jesus.

Some Passages seem to be aphorisms, riddles and parables all at once. For instance, Yunus Emre's famous passage:

> I climbed into the plum tree
>
> and ate the grapes I found there.
>
> The owner of the garden called to me,
>
> "Why are you eating my walnuts?"

A perennial philosophy

The centuries-old idea of a perennial philosophy, popularized by Aldous Huxley in his 1945 book: *The Perennial Philosophy*, states one view of what mysticism is all about:

> [W]ith the one, divine reality substantial to the manifold world of things and lives and minds. But the nature of this one reality is such that it cannot be directly or immediately apprehended except by those who have chosen to fulfill certain conditions, making themselves loving, pure in heart, and poor in spirit.[26]

The unknowable

According to Schopenhauer,[27] mystics arrive at a condition in which there is no knowing subject and known object:

> ... we see all religions at their highest point end in mysticism and mysteries, that is to say, in darkness and veiled obscurity. These really indicate merely a blank spot for knowledge, the point where all knowledge necessarily ceases. Hence for thought this can be expressed only by negations, but for sense-perception it is indicated by symbolical signs, in temples by dim light and silence, in Brahmanism even by the required suspension of all thought and perception for the purpose of entering into the deepest communion with one's own self, by mentally uttering the mysterious *Om*. In the widest sense, mysticism is every guidance to the immediate awareness of what is not reached by either perception or conception, or generally by any knowledge. The mystic is opposed to the philosopher by the fact that he begins from within, whereas the philosopher begins from without. The mystic starts from his inner, positive, individual experience, in which he finds himself as the eternal and only being, and so on. But nothing of this is communicable except the assertions that we have to accept on his word; consequently he is unable to convince.
>
> — Schopenhauer, *The World as Will and Representation*, Vol. II, Ch. XLVIII

References and footnotes

[1] Kerényi, Karoly, "Kore," in C.G. Jung and C. Kerényi, *Essays on a Science of Mythology: The Myth of the Divine Child and the Mysteries of Eleusis*. Princeton: Princeton University Press, 1963: pages 101-55.

[2] Eliade, Mircea, A History of Religious Ideas: From the Stone Age to the Eleusinian Mysteries. Chicago: University of Chicago Press, 1978.

[3] W.F. Cobb. Mysticism and the Creed. BiblioBazaar, 2009. ISBN 978-1113209375

[4] Evelyn Underhill. Practical Mysticism. Wilder Publications, new edition 2008. ISBN 978-1604595086

[5] David Steindl-Rast. The Mystical Core of Organized Religion. ReVision, Summer 1989. 12 (1):11-14. Council on Spiritual Practices (http://csp.org/experience/docs/steindl-mystical.html) Retrieved 29 October 2011

[6] D.T. Suzuki. Mysticism: Christian and Buddhist. Routledge, 2002. ISBN 978-0415285865

[7] Shunryu Suzuki. Zen Mind, Beginner's Mind. Shambhala. New edition 2011.

[8] Louth, Andrew., The Origins of the Christian Mystical Tradition. Oxford: Oxford University Press, 2007. ISBN 978-0-19-929140-3.

[9] King, Ursula. Christian Mystics: Their Lives and Legacies Throughout the Ages. London: Routledge 2004.

[10] Fanning, Steven., Mystics of the Christian Tradition. New York: Routledge Press, 2001.

[11] Michael R. Poll. Masonic Enlightenment - The Philosophy, History And Wisdom Of Freemasonry. Michael Poll Publishing, 2006.

[12] S. N. Dasgupta. Hindu Mysticism. BiblioBazaar, 2009. ISBN 978-0559069895

[13] Reynold A. Nicholson. Studies in Islamic Mysticism. Routledge. New edition 2001. ISBN 978-0700702787

[14] T.K. Tukol. Yoga, Meditation & Mysticism in Jainism (Shri Raj Krishen Jain memorial lectures). Shri Raj Krishen Jain Charitable Trust, 1978.

[15] Elior, Rachel, Jewish Mysticism: The Infinite Expression of Freedom, Oxford. Portland, Oregon: The Littman Library of Jewish Civilization, 2007.

[16] A.E. Waite. Rosicrucian Rites and Ceremonies of the Fellowship of the Rosy Cross by Founder of the Holy Order of the Golden Dawn. Ishtar, 2008. ISBN 978-0978388348

[17] Mohan Singh Uberoi. Sikh Mysticism. 1964.

[18] Krishna Chattopadhyay. The world of mystics: A comparative study of Baul, Sufi and Sikh mysticism. R.K. Prakashan, 1993.

[19] Harold D Roth. Original Tao: Inward Training (Nei-yeh) and the Foundations of Taoist Mysticism. Columbia University Press. New Edition, 2004. ISBN 978-0231115650

[20] Jalaluddin Rumi: Poems (http://www.poemhunter.com/i/ebooks/pdf/mewlana_jalaluddin_rumi_2004_9.pdf)

[21] Koun Yamada. The Gateless Gate: The Classic Book of Zen Koans. Wisdom Publications. New edition, 2005. ISBN 978-0861713820

[22] Tao Te Ching. LinYutan version. Chapter 22, sentence 1. For other versions see *TTC Compared* (http://wayist.org/ttc compared/chap22.htm)

[23] Nasruddin stories (http://en.wikibooks.org/wiki/Sufism/Nasrudin)

[24] * Bektashi jokes (http://www.bektashi.net/beliefs-jokes1.html)

[25] Brer Rabbit and the Tar Baby (http://americanfolklore.net/folklore/2010/07/brer_rabbit_meets_a_tar_baby.html) retold by S.E. Schlosser as 'A Georgia Folktale'. Retrieved 29 October 2011.

[26] Huxley, Aldous (1945). *The Perennial Philosophy*. Perennial. ISBN 0-06-057058-X.

[27] Schopenhauer, Arthur (1844). *Die Welt als Wille und Vorstellung*. **2**.

Further reading

• Daniels, P., Horan A., (1987) "*Mystic Places*". Alexandria, Time-Life Books, ISBN 0-8094-6312-1.

• Fanning, Steven., *Mystics of the Christian Tradition*. New York: Routledge Press, 2001.

• Louth, Andrew., *The Origins of the Christian Mystical Tradition*. Oxford: Oxford University Press, 2007. ISBN 978-0-19-929140-3.

• McGinn, Bernard, *The Presence of God: A History of Western Christian Mysticism'.' Vol. 1 - 4. (*The Foundations of Mysticism*;* The Growth of Mysticism*;* The Flowering of Mysticism*) New York: Crossroad, 1997-2005.*

• "Buried Memories on the Acropolis. Freud's Relation to Mysticism and Anti-Semitism", International Journal of Psycho-Analysis, Volume 59 (1978): 199-208. (Jeffrey Masson and Terri C. Masson)

• Chronicle Books. *Mysticism, the Experience of the Devine: Medieval Wisdom*. Labyrinth, 2004.

• Underhill, Evelyn. *Mysticism: A Study in the Nature and Development of Spiritual Consciousness* (http://www.ccel.org/ccel/underhill/mysticism.html). 1911

• Stace, W. T. *Mysticism and Philosophy*. 1960.

• Stace, W. T. *The Teachings of the Mystics*, 1960.

• King, Ursula. Christian Mystics: Their Lives and Legacies Throughout the Ages. London: Routledge 2004.

• Langer, Otto. Christliche Mystik im Mittelalter. Mystik und Rationalisierung − Stationen eines Konflikts. Darmstadt: 2004.

• Kroll, Jerome, Bernard Bachrach, The Mystic Mind: The Psychology of Medieval Mystics and Ascetics, New York and London: Routledge, 2005.

• Elior, Rachel, *Jewish Mysticism: The Infinite Expression of Freedom*, Oxford. Portland, Oregon: The Littman Library of Jewish Civilization, 2007.

• Louth, Andrew, *The Origins of the Christian Mystical Tradition* (Oxford: 2007).

• Harmless, William, *Mystics*. (Oxford: 2008).

• Otto, Rudolf (author); Bracy, Bertha L. (translator) & Payne, Richenda C. (1932, 1960). *Mysticism East and West: A Comparative Analysis of the Nature of Mysticism*. New York, N. Y., USA: The Macmillan Company

• Dinzelbacher, Peter (hg), *Mystik und Natur. Zur Geschichte ihres Verhältnisses vom Altertum bis zur Gegenwart* (Berlin: 2009) (Theophrastus Paracelsus Studien, 1).

• Merton, Thomas, *An Introduction to Christian Mysticism: Initiation into the Monastic Tradition, 3.* (Kalamazoo: 2008) (Monastic Wisdom series).

- Nelstrop, Louise, Kevin Magill and Bradley B. Onishi, *Christian Mysticism: An Introduction to Contemporary Theoretical Approaches* (Aldershot: 2009).
- Baba, Meher (1995). Discourses (http://www.discoursesbymeherbaba.org). Myrtle Beach, S.C.: Sheriar Foundation. ISBN 1-880619-09-1.

External links

- Resources > Medieval Jewish History > Jewish Mysticism (http://www.dinur.org/resources/resourceCategoryDisplay.aspx?categoryid=450&rsid=478) The Jewish History Resource Center, The Hebrew University of Jerusalem
- "Mysticism" (http://plato.stanford.edu/entries/mysticism/) *Stanford Encyclopedia of Philosophy*
- "Mysticism" (http://hirr.hartsem.edu/ency/Mysticism.htm) *Encyclopedia of Religion and Society*
- "Self-transcendence enhanced by removal of portions of the parietal-occipital cortex" (http://ibcsr.org/index.php?option=com_content&view=article&id=147:removal-of-portions-of-the-parietal-occipital-cortex-enhances-self-transcendence&catid=25:research-news&Itemid=59) Article from the Institute for the Biocultural Study of Religion (http://ibcsr.org/)

Paul Tillich

Paul Tillich	
Region	Western philosophy
Born	Starzeddel, Germany
Died	October 22, 1965 (aged 79) New Harmony, Indiana, US
Occupation	Theologian
Language	English, German
Period	20th-century philosophy
Tradition or movement	Christian existentialism
Main interests	Ontology, Ground of Being
Notable ideas	God above God, New Being
Notable works	*The Courage to Be* (1952), *Systematic Theology* (1951–63)
Influences	Origen, René Descartes, Johann Gottlieb Fichte, Friedrich Schleiermacher, Søren Kierkegaard, Martin Heidegger
Influenced	Rollo May, Thomas J. J. Altizer, Martin Luther King, Robert Cummings Neville, Ernest Becker, John Shelby Spong

Paul Johannes Tillich (August 20, 1886 – October 22, 1965) was a German-American theologian and Christian existentialist philosopher. Tillich was one of the most influential Protestant theologians of the 20th century.[1] Among the general populace, he is best known for his works *The Courage to Be* (1952) and *Dynamics of Faith* (1957), which introduced issues of theology and modern culture to a general readership. Theologically, he is best known for his major three-volume work *Systematic Theology* (1951–63), in which he developed his "method of correlation": an approach of exploring the symbols of Christian revelation as answers to the problems of human existence raised by contemporary existential philosophical analysis.[2][3]

Biography

Tillich was born on August 20, 1886, in the small village of Starzeddel which was then part of Germany. He was the oldest of three children, with two sisters: Johanna (b. 1888, d. 1920) and Elisabeth (b. 1893). Tillich's Prussian father Johannes Tillich was a conservative Lutheran pastor of the Evangelical State Church of Prussia's older Provinces; his mother Mathilde Dürselen was from the Rhineland and was more liberal. When Tillich was four, his father became superintendent of a diocese in Schönfliess, a town of three thousand, where Tillich began elementary school. In 1898, Tillich was sent to Königsberg to begin *gymnasium*. At Königsberg, he lived in a boarding house and experienced loneliness that he sought to overcome by reading the Bible. Simultaneously, however, he was exposed to humanistic ideas at school.[3]

In 1900, Tillich's father was transferred to Berlin, Tillich switching in 1901 to a Berlin school, from which he graduated in 1904. Before his graduation, however, his mother died of cancer in September 1903, when Tillich was 17. Tillich attended several universities – the University of Berlin beginning in 1904, the University of Tübingen in 1905, and the University of Halle in 1905-07. He received his Doctor of Philosophy degree at the University of Breslau in 1911 and his Licentiate of Theology degree at the University of Halle in 1912.[3] During his time at university, he became a member of the Wingolf.

That same year, 1912, Tillich was ordained as a Lutheran minister in the province of Brandenburg. On 28 September 1914 he married Margarethe ("Grethi") Wever (1888–1968), and in October he joined the German army as a chaplain. Grethi deserted Tillich in 1919 after an affair that produced a child not fathered by Tillich; the two then divorced.[4] Tillich's academic career began after the war; he became a Privatdozent of Theology at the University of Berlin, a post he held from 1919 to 1924. On his return from the war he had met Hannah Werner Gottswchow, then married and pregnant.[5] In March 1924 they married; it was the second marriage for both.

During 1924-25, he was a Professor of Theology at the University of Marburg, where he began to develop his systematic theology, teaching a course on it during the last of his three terms. From 1925 until 1929, Tillich was a Professor of Theology at the University of Dresden and the University of Leipzig. He held the same post at the University of Frankfurt during 1929-33.

While at Frankfurt, Tillich gave public lectures and speeches throughout Germany that brought him into conflict with the Nazi movement. When Hitler became German Chancellor in 1933, Tillich was dismissed from his position.

Reinhold Niebuhr visited Germany in the summer of 1933 and, already impressed with Tillich's writings, contacted Tillich upon learning of Tillich's dismissal. Niebuhr urged Tillich to join the faculty at New York City's Union Theological Seminary; Tillich accepted.[4][6]

At the age of 47, Tillich moved with his family to America. This meant learning English, the language in which Tillich would eventually publish works such as the *Systematic Theology*. From 1933 until 1955 he taught at Union, where he began as a Visiting Professor of Philosophy of Religion. During 1933-34 he was also a Visiting Lecturer in Philosophy at Columbia University. Tillich acquired tenure at Union in 1937, and in 1940 he was promoted to Professor of Philosophical Theology and became an American citizen.[3]

At the Union Theological Seminary, Tillich earned his reputation, publishing a series of books that outlined his particular synthesis of Protestant Christian theology and existential philosophy. He published *On the Boundary* in 1936; *The Protestant Era*, a collection of his essays, in 1948; and *The Shaking of the Foundations*, the first of three volumes of his sermons, also in 1948. His collections of sermons would give Tillich a broader audience than he had yet experienced. His most heralded achievements though, were the 1951 publication of volume one of *Systematic Theology* which brought Tillich academic acclaim, and the 1952 publication of *The Courage to Be*. The first volume of the systematic theology series prompted an invitation to give the prestigious Gifford lectures during 1953–54 at the University of Aberdeen. The latter book, called "his masterpiece" in the Paucks's biography of Tillich (p. 225), was based on his 1950 Dwight H. Terry Lectureship and reached a wide general readership.[3]

Tillich's gravestone in the Paul Tillich Park, New Harmony, Indiana

These works led to an appointment at the Harvard Divinity School in 1955, where he became one of the University's five University Professors − the five highest ranking professors at Harvard. Tillich's Harvard career lasted until 1962. During this period he published volume 2 of *Systematic Theology*[7] and also published the popular book *Dynamics of Faith* (1957).

In 1962, Tillich moved to the University of Chicago, where he was a Professor of Theology until his death in Chicago in 1965. Volume 3 of *Systematic Theology* was published in 1963. In 1964 Tillich became the first theologian to be honored in Kegley and Bretall's *Library of Living Theology*. They wrote: "The adjective 'great,' in our opinion, can be applied to very few thinkers of our time, but Tillich, we are far from alone in believing, stands unquestionably amongst these few." (Kegley and Bretall, 1964, pp. ix-x) A widely quoted critical assessment of his importance was Georgia Harkness' comment, "What Whitehead was to American philosophy, Tillich has been to American theology."[8][9]

Tillich died on October 22, 1965, ten days after experiencing a heart attack. In 1966 his ashes were interred in the Paul Tillich Park in New Harmony, Indiana.

Theology

Method of correlation

The key to understanding Tillich's theology is what he calls the "method of correlation." It is an approach that correlates insights from Christian revelation with the issues raised by existential, psychological, and philosophical analysis.[2]

Tillich states in the introduction to the *Systematic Theology*:

> Philosophy formulates the questions implied in human existence, and theology formulates the answers implied in divine self-manifestation under the guidance of the questions implied in human existence. This is a circle which drives man to a point where question and answer are not separated. This point, however, is not a moment in time.[10]

> The Christian message provides the answers to the questions implied in human existence. These answers are contained in the revelatory events on which Christianity is based and are taken by systematic theology from the sources, through the medium, under the norm. Their content cannot be derived from questions that would come from an analysis of human existence. They are 'spoken' to human existence from beyond it, in a sense. Otherwise, they would not be answers, for the question is human existence itself.[11]

For Tillich, the existential questions of human existence are associated with the field of philosophy and, more specifically, ontology (the study of being). This is because, according to Tillich, a lifelong pursuit of philosophy reveals that the central question of every philosophical inquiry always comes back to the question of being, or what it means to be, to exist, to be a finite human being.[12] To be correlated with these questions are the theological answers, themselves derived from Christian revelation. The task of the philosopher primarily involves developing the questions, whereas the task of the theologian primarily involves developing the answers to these questions. However, it should be remembered that the two tasks overlap and include one another: the theologian must be somewhat of a philosopher and vice versa, for Tillich's notion of faith as "ultimate concern" necessitates that the theological answer be correlated with, compatible with, and in response to the general ontological question which must be developed independently from the answers.[13][14] Thus, on one side of the correlation lies an ontological analysis of the human situation, whereas on the other is a presentation of the Christian message as a response to this existential dilemma. For Tillich, no formulation of the question can contradict the theological answer. This is because the Christian message claims, *a priori*, that the *logos* "who became flesh" is also the universal *logos* of the Greeks.[15]

In addition to the intimate relationship between philosophy and theology, another important aspect of the method of correlation is Tillich's distinction between form and content in the theological answers. While the nature of revelation determines the actual content of the theological answers, the character of the questions determines the form of these answers. This is because, for Tillich, theology must be an answering theology, or apologetic theology. God is called the "ground of being" because God is the answer to the ontological threat of non-being, and this characterization of the theological answer in philosophical terms means that the answer has been conditioned (insofar as its form is considered) by the question.[16] Throughout the *Systematic Theology*, Tillich is careful to maintain this distinction between form and content without allowing one to be inadvertently conditioned by the other. Many criticisms of Tillich's methodology revolve around this issue of whether the integrity of the Christian message is really maintained when its form is conditioned by philosophy.[17]

The theological answer is also determined by the sources of theology, our experience, and the norm of theology. Though the form of the theological answers are determined by the character of the question, these answers (which "are contained in the revelatory events on which Christianity is based") are also "taken by systematic theology from the sources, through the medium, under the norm."[16] There are three main sources of systematic theology: the Bible, Church history, and the history of religion and culture. Experience is not a source but a medium through which the sources speak. And the norm of theology is that by which both sources and experience are judged with regard to the content of the Christian faith.[18] Thus, we have the following as elements of the method and structure of systematic theology:

- Sources of theology[19]
  - Bible[20]
  - Church history
  - History of religion and culture
- Medium of the sources
  - Collective Experience of the Church
- Norm of theology (determines use of sources)
  - Content of which is the biblical message itself, for example:
    - Justification through faith
    - New Being in Jesus as the Christ

- The Protestant Principle
- The criterion of the cross

As McKelway explains, the sources of theology contribute to the formation of the norm, which then becomes the criterion through which the sources and experience are judged.[21] The relationship is circular, as it is the present situation which conditions the norm in the interaction between church and biblical message. The norm is then subject to change, but Tillich insists that its basic content remains the same: that of the biblical message.[22] It is tempting to conflate revelation with the norm, but we must keep in mind that revelation (whether original or dependent) is not an element of the structure of systematic theology per se, but an event.[23] For Tillich, the present day norm is the "New Being in Jesus as the Christ as our Ultimate Concern".[24] This is because the present question is one of estrangement, and the overcoming of this estrangement is what Tillich calls the "New Being". But since Christianity answers the question of estrangement with "Jesus as the Christ", the norm tells us that we find the New Being in Jesus as the Christ.

There is also the question of the validity of the method of correlation. Certainly one could reject the method on the grounds that there is no a priori reason for its adoption. But Tillich claims that the method of any theology and its system are interdependent. That is, an absolute methodological approach cannot be adopted because the method is continually being determined by the system and the objects of theology.[25]

The use of "Being" in systematic theology

Tillich used the concept of "being" in systematic theology. There are 3 roles :

...[The concept of Being] appears in the present system in three places: in the doctrine of God, where God is called the being as being or the ground and the power of being;

in the doctrine of man, where the distinction is carried through between man's essential and his existential being;

and finally, in the doctrine of the Christ, where he is called the manifestation of the New Being, the actualization of which is the work of the divine Spirit.

— Tillich, *Systematic Theology Vol. 2*, p.10

...It is the expression of the experience of being over against non-being. Therefore, it can be described as the power of being which resists non-being. For this reason, the medieval philosophers called being the basic *transcendentale*, beyond the universal and the particular...

The same word, the emptiest of all concepts when taken as an abstraction, becomes the most meaningful of all concepts when it is understood as the power of being in everything that has being.

— Tillich, *Systematic Theology Vol. 2*, p.11

Life and the Spirit

This is part four of Tillich's *Systematic Theology*. In this part, Tillich talks about life and the divine Spirit.

Life remains ambiguous as long as there is life. The question implied in the ambiguities of life derives to a new question, namely, that of the direction in which life moves. This is the question of history. Systematically speaking, history, characterized as it as by its direction toward the future, is the dynamic quality of life. Therefore, the "riddle of history" is a part of the problem of life.

— Tillich , *Systematic Theology, Vol.2* , p.4

Absolute faith

Tillich stated the courage to take meaninglessness into oneself presupposes a relation to the ground of being: absolute faith.[26] Absolute faith can transcend the theistic idea of God, and has three elements.

… The first element is the experience of the power of being which is present even in the face of the most radical manifestation of non being. If one says that in this experience vitality resists despair, one must add that vitality in man is proportional to intentionality.

The vitality that can stand the abyss of meaninglessness is aware of a hidden meaning within the destruction of meaning.

— Tillich , *The Courage to Be*, p.177

The second element in absolute faith is the dependence of the experience of nonbeing on the experience of being and the dependence of the experience of meaninglessness on the experience of meaning. Even in the state of despair one has enough being to make despair possible.

— Tillich , *The Courage to Be*, p.177

There is a third element in absolute faith, the acceptance of being accepted. Of course, in the state of despair there is nobody and nothing that accepts. But there is the power of acceptance itself which is experienced. Meaninglessness, as long as it is experienced, includes an experience of the "power of acceptance". To accept this power of acceptance consciously is the religious answer of absolute faith, of a faith which has been deprived by doubt of any concrete content, which nevertheless is faith and the source of the most paradoxical manifestation of the courage to be.

— Tillich , *The Courage to Be*, p.177

Faith as ultimate concern

According to the Stanford Encyclopedia of Philosophy, Tillich believes the essence of religious attitudes is what he calls "ultimate concern". Separate from all profane and ordinary realities, the object of the concern is understood as sacred, numinous or holy. The perception of its reality is felt as so overwhelming and valuable that all else seems insignificant, and for this reason requires total surrender.[27] In 1957, Tillich defined his conception of faith more explicitly in his work, *Dynamics of Faith.*

… "Man, like every living being, is concerned about many things, above all about those which condition his very existence...If [a situation or concern] claims ultimacy it demands the total surrender of him who accepts this claim...it demands that all other concerns...be sacrificed."

— Tillich , *Dynamics of Faith*, p.1-2

Tillich further refined his conception of faith by stating that

… "Faith as ultimate concern is an act of the total personality. It is the most centered act of the human mind...it participates in the dynamics of personal life."

— Tillich , *Dynamics of Faith*, p.5

An arguably central component of Tillich's concept of faith is his notion that faith is "ecstatic". That is to say that

… "It transcends both the drives of the nonrational unconsciousness and the structures of the rational conscious...the ecstatic character of faith does not exclude its rational character although it is not identical with it, and it includes nonrational strivings without being identical with them. 'Ecstasy' means 'standing outside of oneself' - without ceasing to be oneself - with all the elements which are united in the personal center."

— Tillich , *Dynamics of Faith*, p.8-9

In short, for Tillich, faith does not stand opposed to rational or nonrational elements (reason and emotion respectively), as some philosophers would maintain. Rather, it *transcends* them in an ecstatic passion for the ultimate.[28]

It should also be noted that Tillich does not exclude atheists in his exposition of faith. Everyone has an ultimate concern, and this concern can be in an act of faith, "even if the act of faith includes the denial of God. Where there is ultimate concern, God can be denied only in the name of God"[29]

God Above God

Throughout most of his works Paul Tillich provides an apologetic and alternative ontological view of God. Traditional medieval philosophical theology in the work of figures such as St. Anselm, Thomas Aquinas, Duns Scotus, and William of Ockham tended to understand God as the highest existing Being, to which predicates such as omnipotence, omniscience, omnipresence, goodness, righteousness, holiness, etc. may be ascribed. Arguments for and against the existence of God presuppose such an understanding of God. Tillich is critical of this mode of discourse which he refers to as "theological theism," and argues that if God is a Being [das Seiende], even if the highest Being, God cannot be properly called the source of all being, and the question can of course then be posed as to why God exists, who created God, when God's beginning is, and so on. To put the issue in traditional language: if God is a being [das Seiende], then God is a creature, even if the highest one, and thus cannot be the Creator. Rather, God must be understood as the "ground of Being-Itself." The problem persists in the same way when attempting to determine whether God is an eternal essence, or an existing being, neither of which are adequate, as traditional theology was well aware.[30] When God is understood in this way, it becomes clear that not only is it impossible to argue for the "existence" of God, since God is beyond the distinction between essence and existence, but it is also foolish: one cannot deny that there is being, and thus there is a Power of Being. The question then becomes whether and in what way personal language about God and humanity's relationship to God is appropriate. In distinction to "theological theism," Tillich refers to another kind of theism as that of the "divine-human encounter." Such

Bust of Tillich by James Rosati in New Harmony, Indiana

is the theism of the encounter with the "Holy Other," as in the work of Karl Barth and Rudolf Otto, and implies a personalism with regard to God's self revelation. Tillich is quite clear that this is both appropriate and necessary, as it is the basis of the personalism of Biblical Religion altogether and the concept of the "Word of God",[31] but can become falsified if the theologian tries to turn such encounters with God as the Holy Other into an understanding of God as a being.[32] In other words, God is both personal *and* transpersonal.[33]

Tillich's ontological view of God is not without precedent in the history of Christian theology. Many theologians, especially in the period denoted by scholars as the Hellenistic or Patristic period of Christian theology, that of the Church Fathers, understood God as the "unoriginate source" (agennetos) of all being.[34] This was the view, in particular, of the theologian Origen, one among the crowd of thinkers by whom Tillich was deeply influenced, and who themselves had shown notable influences from middle Platonism.

Tillich further argues that theological theism is not only logically problematic, but is unable to speak into the situation of radical doubt and despair about meaning in life, which is the primary problem typical of the modern age, as opposed to a fundamental anxiety about fate and death or guilt and condemnation.[35] This is because the state of finitude entails by necessity anxiety, and that it is our finitude as human beings, our being a mixture of being and nonbeing, that is at the ultimate basis of anxiety. If God is not the ground of being itself, then God cannot provide an answer to the question of finitude; God would also be finite in some sense. The term "God Above God," then, means to indicate the God who appears, who is the ground of being itself, when the "God" of theological theism has disappeared in the anxiety of doubt.[36] While on the one hand this God goes beyond the God of theological theism, it is nevertheless rooted in the religious symbols of Christian faith, particularly that of the crucified Christ, and is, according to Tillich, the possibility of the recovery of religious symbols which may otherwise have become ineffective in contemporary society.

Tillich argues that the God of theological theism is at the root of much revolt against theism and religious faith in the modern period. Tillich states, sympathetically, that the God of theological theism

> deprives me of my subjectivity because he is all-powerful and all-knowing. I revolt and make *him* into an object, but the revolt fails and becomes desperate. God appears as the invincible tyrant, the being in contrast with whom all other beings are without freedom and subjectivity. He is equated with the recent tyrants who with the help of terror try to transform everything into a mere object, a thing among things, a cog in a machine they control. He becomes the model of everything against which Existentialism revolted. This is the God Nietzsche said had to be killed because nobody can tolerate being made into a mere object of absolute knowledge and absolute control. This is the deepest root of atheism. It is an atheism which is justified as the reaction against theological theism and its disturbing implications.[37]

Another reason Tillich criticized theological theism was because it placed God into the subject-object dichotomy. This is the basic distinction made in Epistemology, that branch of Philosophy which deals with human knowledge, how it is possible, what it is, and its limits. *Epistemologically*, God cannot be made into an object, that is, an object of the knowing subject. Tillich deals with this question under the rubric of the relationality of God. The question is "whether there are external relations between God and the creature."[38] Traditionally Christian theology has always understood the doctrine of creation to mean precisely this external relationality between God, the Creator, and the creature as separate and not identical realities. Tillich reminds us of the point, which can be found in Luther, that "there is no place to which man can withdraw from the divine thou, because it includes the ego and is nearer to the ego than the ego to itself."[39] Tillich goes further to say that the desire to draw God into the subject-object dichotomy is an "insult" to the divine holiness.[40] Similarly, if God were made into the subject rather than the object of knowledge (The Ultimate Subject), then the rest of existing entities then become subjected to the absolute knowledge and scrutiny of God, and the human being is "reified," or made into a mere object. It would deprive the person of his or her own subjectivity and creativity. According to Tillich, theological theism has provoked the rebellions found in atheism and Existentialism, although other social factors such as the industrial revolution have also contributed to the "reification" of the human being. The modern man could no longer tolerate the idea of being an "object" completely subjected to the absolute knowledge of God. Tillich argued, as mentioned, that theological theism is "bad theology".

> The God of the theological theism is a being besides others and as such a part of the whole reality. He is certainly considered its most important part, but as a part and therefore as subjected to the structure of the whole. He is supposed to be beyond the ontological elements and categories which constitute reality. But every statement subjects him to them. He is seen as a self which has a world, as an ego which relates to a thought, as a cause which is separated from its effect, as having a definite space and endless time. He is a being, not being-itself"[41]

Alternatively, Tillich presents the above mentioned ontological view of God as Being-Itself, Ground of Being, Power of Being, and occasionally as Abyss or God's "Abysmal Being." What makes Tillich's ontological view of God different from theological theism is that it transcends it by being the foundation or ultimate reality that "precedes" all beings. Just as Being for Heidegger is ontologically *prior* to conception, Tillich views God to be beyond Being-Itself, manifested in the structure of beings.[42] God is not a supernatural entity among other entities. Instead, God is the ground upon which all beings exist. We cannot perceive God as an object which is related to a subject because God *precedes* the subject-object dichotomy.[42]

Thus Tillich dismisses a literalistic Biblicism. Instead of completely rejecting the notion of personal God, however, Tillich sees it as a symbol that points directly to the Ground of Being.[43] Since the Ground of Being ontologically precedes reason, it cannot be comprehended since comprehension presupposes the subject-object dichotomy. Tillich disagreed with any literal philosophical and religious statements that can be made about God. Such literal statements attempt to define God and lead not only to anthropomorphism but also to a philosophical mistake that Immanuel Kant warned against, that setting limits against the transcendent inevitably leads to contradictions. Any statements about God are simply symbolic, but these symbols are sacred in the sense that they function to participate or point to the Ground of Being. Tillich insists that anyone who participates in these symbols is empowered by the Power of Being, which overcomes and conquers nonbeing and meaninglessness.

Tillich also further elaborated the thesis of the God above the God of theism in his Systematic Theology.

> … (the God above the God of theism) This has been misunderstood as a dogmatic statement of a pantheistic or mystical character. First of all, it is not a dogmatic, but an apologetic, statement. It takes seriously the radical doubt experienced by many people. It gives one the courage of self-affirmation even in the extreme state of radical doubt.
>
> — Tillich , *Systematic Theology Vol. 2* , p.12

> … In such a state the God of both religious and theological language disappears. But something remains, namely, the seriousness of that doubt in which meaning within meaninglessness is affirmed. The source of this affirmation of meaning within meaninglessness, of certitude within doubt, is not the God of traditional theism but the "God above God," the power of being, which works through those who have no name for it, not even the name God.
>
> — Tillich , *Systematic Theology Vol. 2* , p.12

> …This is the answer to those who ask for a message in the nothingness of their situation and at the end of their courage to be. But such an extreme point is not a space with which one can live. The dialectics of an extreme situation are a criterion of truth but not the basis on which a whole structure of truth can be built.
>
> — Tillich , *Systematic Theology Vol. 2* , p.12

Popular works by Tillich

Two of Tillich's works, *The Courage to Be* (1952) and *Dynamics of Faith* (1957), were read widely, even by people who do not normally read religious books. In *The Courage to Be*, he lists three basic anxieties: anxiety about our biological finitude, i.e. that arising from the knowledge that we will eventually die; anxiety about our moral finitude, linked to guilt; and anxiety about our existential finitude, a sense of aimlessness in life. Tillich related these to three different historical eras: the early centuries of the Christian era; the Reformation; and the 20th century. Tillich's popular works have influenced psychology as well as theology, having had an influence on Rollo May, whose "The Courage to Create" was inspired by "The Courage to Be".

Reception

Today Tillich's most observable legacy may well be that of a spiritually-oriented public intellectual and teacher with a broad and continuing range of influence. Tillich's chapel sermons (especially at Union) were enthusiastically received (Tillich was known as the only faculty member of his day at Union willing to attend the revivals of Billy Graham). When Tillich was University Professor at Harvard he was chosen as keynote speaker from among an auspicious gathering of many who had appeared on the cover of Time Magazine during its first four decades. Tillich along with his student, psychologist Rollo May, was an early leader at the Esalen Institute. Contemporary New Age catchphrases describing God (spatially) as the "Ground of Being" and (temporally) as the "Eternal Now,"[44] in tandem with the view that God is not an entity among entities but rather is "Being-Itself" - notions which Eckhart Tolle, for example, has invoked repeatedly throughout his career[45] - were pioneered by Tillich. The introductory philosophy course taught by the person Tillich considered to be his best student, John E. Smith, "probably turned more undergraduates to the study of philosophy at Yale than all the other philosophy courses put together. His courses in philosophy of religion and American philosophy defined those fields for many years. Perhaps most important of all, he has educated a younger generation in the importance of the public life in philosophy and in how to practice philosophy publicly."[46] In the 1980s and '90s the Boston University Institute for Philosophy and Religion, a leading forum dedicated to the revival of the American public tradition of philosophy and religion, flourished under the leadership of Tillich's student and expositor Leroy S. Rouner.

Criticism

- Martin Buber criticized Tillich's "transtheistic position" as a reduction of God to the impersonal "necessary being" of Thomas Aquinas.[47]
- Tillich is not held in high regard by biblical literalists many of whom think of him not as a Christian, but a pantheist or atheist.[48] The Elwell Evangelical Dictionary states, "At best Tillich was a pantheist, but his thought borders on atheism."[49]

Bibliography

- *The Religious Situation* (1925, *Die religiose Lage der Gegenwart*), Holt 1932, Meridian Press 1956, online edition [50]
- *The Socialist Decision* (1933, New York : Harper & Row, c1977)
- *The Interpretation of History* (1936), online edition [51]
- *The Protestant Era* (1948), The University of Chicago Press, online edition [52]
- *The Shaking of the Foundations* (1948), Charles Scribner's Sons, a sermon collection, online edition [53]
- *Systematic Theology*, 1951–63 (3 volumes), University of Chicago Press
    - *Volume 1* (1951). ISBN 0-226-80337-6
    - *Volume 2: Existence and the Christ* (1957). ISBN 0-226-80338-4
    - *Volume 3: Life and the Spirit: History and the Kingdom of God* (1963). ISBN 0-226-80339-2
- *The Courage to Be* (1952), Yale University Press, ISBN 0-300-08471-4 (2nd ed)
- *Love, Power, and Justice: Ontological Analysis and Ethical Applications* (1954), Oxford University Press, ISBN 0-19-500222-9
- *Biblical Religion and the Search for Ultimate Reality* (1955), University Of Chicago Press, ISBN 0-226-80341-4
- *The New Being* (1955), Charles Scribner's Sons, ISBN 0-684-71908-8, a sermon collection, online edition [54], 2006 Bison Press edition with introduction by Mary Ann Stenger: ISBN 0-8032-9458-1
- *Dynamics of Faith* (1957), Harper and Row, ISBN 0-06-093713-0
- *Theology of Culture* (1959), Oxford University Press, ISBN 0-19-500711-5
- *Christianity and the Encounter of the World Religions* (1963), Columbia University Press, online edition [55]
- *Morality and Beyond* (1963), Harper and Row, 1995 edition: Westminster John Knox Press, ISBN 0-664-25564-7

- *The Eternal Now* (1963), Charles Scribner's Sons, 2003 SCM Press: ISBN 0-334-02875-2, university sermons 1955–63, online edition [56]
- *Ultimate Concern: Tillich in Dialogue* (1965), editor D. Mackenzie Brown, Harper & Row, online edition [57]
- *On the Boundary*, 1966 New York: Charles Scribner's
- *My Search for Absolutes* (1967, posthumous), ed. Ruth Nanda Anshen, Simon & Schuster, 1984 reprint: ISBN 0-671-50585-8 (includes autobiographical chapter) online edition [58]
- "The Philosophy of Religion", in *What Is Religion?* (1969), ed. James Luther Adams. New York: Harper & Row
  - "The Conquest of the Concept of Religion in the Philosophy of Religion" in *What is Religion?*
  - "On the Idea of a Theology of Culture" in *What is Religion?*
- *My Travel Diary 1936: Between Two Worlds* (1970), Harper & Row, (edited and published posthumously by J.C. Brauer) online edition [59]
- *A History of Christian Thought: From its Judaic and Hellenistic Origins to Existentialism* (1972), Simon and Schuster, (edited from his lectures and published posthumously by C. E. Braaten), ISBN 0-671-21426-8;
  - *A History of Christian Thought* (1968), Harper & Row, online edition [60] contains the first part of the two part 1972 edition (comprising the 38 New York lectures)
- *The System of the Sciences* (1981), Translated by Paul Wiebe. London: Bucknell University Press. (originally published in German in 1923)
- *The Essential Tillich* (1987), (anthology) F. Forrester Church, editor; (Macmillan): ISBN 0-02-018920-6; 1999 (U. of Chicago Press): ISBN 0-226-80343-0

References

[1] Ted Peters (1995), Carl E. Braaten, ed., *A map of twentieth-century theology: readings from Karl Barth to radical pluralism* (http://books. google.com/books?id=Xax15MpLyjYC&lpg=PA392), Fortress Press, , retrieved 2011-01-01, "Backjacket review by Ted Peters: "The current generation of students has heard only the names of Barth, Brunner, Bultmann, Bonhoeffer, Tillich, and the Niebuhrs.""
[2] "Tillich, Paul Johannes Oskar", *The Concise Oxford Dictionary of World Religions*. Ed. John Bowker. Oxford University Press, 2000. Oxford Reference Online. Oxford University Press.
[3] "Tillich, Paul." *Encyclopædia Britannica*. 2008. Encyclopædia Britannica Online. retrieved 17 February 2008 (http://search.eb.com/eb/article-7265).
[4] *Paul Tillich: His Life & Thought–Volume 1: Life*, Pauck, Wilhelm & Marion. New York: Harper & Row, 1976
[5] Paul Tillich, Lover (http://www.time.com/time/magazine/article/0,9171,908007-1,00.html), *Time*, October 8, 1973
[6] (Tillich, 1964, p. 16).
[7] (1957)
[8] "Dr. Paul Tillich, Outstanding Protestant Theologian", *The Times*, Oct 25, 1965
[9] *Tillich*, John Heywood Thomas, Continuum International Publishing Group, 2002, ISBN 0-8264-5082-2
[10] |Paul Tillich|*Systematic Theology*, vol. 1, p 61
[11] Tillich|*Systematic Theology*, vol. 1, p. 64
[12] Paul Tillich, "Biblical Religion and the Search for Ultimate Reality," University of Chicago Press: Chicago, 1955, 11-20
[13] Tillich, *Systematic Theology*, vol. 1, pp 23ff.
[14] Tillich, *Biblical Religion and the Search for Ultimate Reality*, pp 58ff.
[15] Tillich, *Systematic Theology*, vol. 1, p 28.
[16] Tillich, *Systematic Theology*, vol. 1, p 64.
[17] McKelway, *The Systematic Theology of Paul Tillich*, p 47.
[18] Tillich, *Systematic Theology*, vol. 1, p 47.
[19] Systematic Theology, vol 1, University of Chicago Press: Chicago, 1951, 40.
[20] Systematic Theology, vol 1, University of Chicago Press: Chicago, 1951, 35.
[21] McKelway, *The Systematic Theology of Paul Tillich*, pp 55-56.
[22] Tillich, *Systematic Theology*, vol. 1, p 52.
[23] McKelway, *The Systematic Theology of Paul Tillich*, p 80.
[24] Tillich, *Systematic Theology*, vol. 1, p 50.
[25] Tillich, *Systematic Theology*, vol. 1, p 60.
[26] The Courage to Be, page 182
[27] Wainwright, William (2010-09-29), "Concepts of God" (http://plato.stanford.edu/entries/concepts-god/), *Stanford Encyclopedia of Philosophy*, Stanford University, , retrieved 2011-01-01
[28] Tillich Interview part 12 (http://www.youtube.com/watch?v=KR7QAjm3yxU&feature=related)
[29] Tillich, *Dynamics of Faith*, p. 52
[30] Systematic Theology, vol 1, University of Chicago Press: Chicago, 1951, 236.
[31] Biblical Religion and the Search for Ultimate Reality, University of Chicago Press: Chicago, 1955, 21-62.
[32] The Courage to Be, Yale: New Haven, 2000, 184.
[33] The Courage to Be, Yale: New Haven, 2000, 187.
[34] J.N.D. Kelly, Early Christian Doctrines, HarperCollins: New York, 1978, 128.
[35] Tillich, Courage To Be, p 184.
[36] The Courage to Be, Yale: New Haven, 2000, 190.
[37] Tillich, *Courage To Be*, p 185.
[38] *Systematic Theology*, vol 1, University of Chicago Press: Chicago, 1951, 271
[39] *Systematic Theology*, vol 1, University of Chicago Press: Chicago, 1951, 271.
[40] *Systematic Theology*, vol 1, University of Chicago Press: Chicago, 1951, 272.
[41] Tillich, *Courage To Be*, p 184.
[42] Tillich, *Theology of Culture*, p 15.
[43] Tillich, *Theology of Culture*, p 127-132.

[44] "There is no present in the mere stream of time; but the present is real, as our experience witnesses. And it is real because eternity breaks into time and gives it a real present. We could not even say now, if eternity did not elevate that moment above the ever-passing time. Eternity is always present; and its presence is the cause of our having the present at all. When the psalmist looks at God, for Whom a thousand years are like one day, he is looking at that eternity which alone gives him a place on which he can stand, a now which has infinite reality and infinite significance. In every moment that we say now, something temporal and something eternal are united. Whenever a human being says, 'Now I am living; now I am really present,' resisting the stream which drives the future into the past, eternity is. In each such Now eternity is made manifest; in every real now, eternity is present." (Tillich, "The Mystery of Time," in *The Shaking of Foundations*).

[45] In his September 2010 Live Meditation (https://www.eckharttolletv.com/), e.g., Tolle expounds at length on "the dimension of depth."

[46] *The Chronicle of Higher Education* (Jan. 24, 2010)

[47] David Novak, Buber and Tillich, Journal of Ecumenical Studies, Vol. 29, 1992 (reprinted in: Talking With Christians: Musings of A Jewish Theologian, 2005)

[48] Tillich held an equally low opinion of biblical literalism: "When fundamentalism is combined with an antitheological bias, as it is, for instance, in its biblicistic-evangelical form, the theological truth of yesterday is defended as an unchangeable message against the theological truth of today and tomorrow. Fundamentalism fails to make contact with the present situation, not because it speaks from beyond every situation, but because it speaks from a situation from the past. It elevates something finite and transitory to infinite and eternal validity. In this sense fundamentalism has demonic traits." (This quotation is located at the heart of the first paragraph of Volume I of *Systematic Theology*).

[49] S N Gundry, "Death of God Theology" (http://mb-soft.com/believe/txn/deathgod.htm), in Walter A. Elwell, *Evangelical Dictionary of Theology*, ISBN 9780801020759, , retrieved 2011-01-01

[50] http://www.religion-online.org/showbook.asp?title=376

[51] http://www.religion-online.org/showbook.asp?title=377

[52] http://www.religion-online.org/showbook.asp?title=380

[53] http://www.religion-online.org/showbook.asp?title=378

[54] http://www.religion-online.org/showbook.asp?title=375

[55] http://www.religion-online.org/showbook.asp?title=1557

[56] http://www.religion-online.org/showbook.asp?title=1630

[57] http://www.religion-online.org/showbook.asp?title=538

[58] http://www.religion-online.org/showbook.asp?title=1628

[59] http://www.religion-online.org/showbook.asp?title=3181

[60] http://www.religion-online.org/showbook.asp?title=2310

Further reading

- Adams, James Luther. 1965. *Paul Tillich's Philosophy of Culture, Science, and Religion*. New York: New York University Press
- Armbruster, Carl J. 1967. *The Vision of Paul Tillich*. New York: Sheed and Ward
- Breisach, Ernst. 1962. *Introduction to Modern Existentialism*. New York: Grove Press
- Bruns, Katja. 2011. *Anthropologie zwischen Theologie und Naturwissenschaft bei Paul Tillich und Kurt Goldstein. Historische Grundlagen und systematische Perspektiven.* Kontexte. Neue Beiträge zur historischen und systematischen Theologie, Vol. 41. Goettingen: Edition Ruprecht, ISBN 978-3-7675-7143-3
- Carey, Patrick W., and Lienhard, Joseph. 2002. "Biographical Dictionary of Christian Theologians". Mass: Hendrickson
- Ford, Lewis S. 1966. "Tillich and Thomas: The Analogy of Being." *Journal of Religion* 46:2 (April)
- Freeman, David H. 1962. *Tillich*. Philadelphia: Presbyterian and Reformed Publishing Co.
- Grenz, Stanley, and Olson, Roger E. 1997. *20th Century Theology God & the World in a Transitional Age*
- Hamilton, Kenneth. 1963. *The System and the Gospel: A Critique of Paul Tillich*. New York: Macmillan
- Hammond, Guyton B. 1965. *Estrangement: A Comparison of the Thought of Paul Tillich and Erich Fromm*. Nashville: Vanderbilt University Press.
- Hegel, G. W. F. 1967. *The Phenomenology of Mind*, trans. With intro. J. B. Baillie, Torchbook intro. by George Lichtheim. New York: Harper Torchbooks
- Hook, Sidney, ed. 1961 *Religious Experience and Truth: A Symposium* (New York: New York University Press)
- Hopper, David. 1968. *Tillich: A Theological Portrait*. Philadelphia: Lippincott
- Howlett, Duncan. 1964. *The Fourth American Faith*. New York: Harper & Row
- Kaufman, Walter. 1961a. *The Faith of a Heretic*. New York: Doubleday
- — 1961b. *Critique of Religion and Philosophy*. Garden City, NY: Anchor Books, Doubleday
- Kegley, Charles W., and Bretall, Robert W., eds. 1964. *The Theology of Paul Tillich*. New York: Macmillan
- Kelsey, David H. 1967 *The Fabric of Paul Tillich's Theology*. New Haven: Yale University Press
- MacIntyre, Alasdair. 1963. "God and the Theologians," *Encounter* 21:3 (September)
- Martin, Bernard. 1963. *The Existentialist Theology of Paul Tillich*. New Haven: College and University Press
- Marx, Karl. n.d. *Capital*. Ed. Frederick Engels. trans. from 3rd German ed. by Samuel Moore and Edward Aveling. New York: The Modern Library
- May, Rollo. 1973. *Paulus: Reminiscences of a Friendship*. New York: Harper & Row
- McKelway, Alexander J. 1964. *The Systematic Theology of Paul Tillich: A Review and Analysis*. Richmond: John Knox Press
- Modras, Ronald. 1976. *Paul Tillich 's Theology of the Church: A Catholic Appraisal*. Detroit: Wayne State University Press, 1976.
- Palmer, Michael. 1984. *Paul Tillich's Philosophy of Art*. New York: Walter de Gruyter
- Pauck, Wilhelm & Marion. 1976. *Paul Tillich: His Life & Thought—Volume 1: Life*. New York: Harper & Row

- Re Manning, Russell, ed. 2009. *The Cambridge Companion to Paul Tillich.* Cambridge: Cambridge University Press
- Rowe, William L. 1968. *Religious Symbols and God: A Philosophical Study of Tillich's Theology.* Chicago: University of Chicago Press
- Scharlemann, Robert P. 1969. *Reflection and Doubt in the Theology of Paul Tillich.* New Haven: Yale University Press
- Schweitzer, Albert. 1961. *The Quest of the Historical Jesus,* trans. W. Montgomery. New York: Macmillan
- Soper, David Wesley. 1952. *Major Voices in American Theology: Six Contemporary Leaders* Philadelphia: Westminster
- Tavard, George H. 1962. *Paul Tillich and the Christian Message.* New York: Charles Scribner's Sons
- Taylor, Mark Kline, ed. 1991. "Paul Tillich: Theologian of the Boundaries". Minneapolis: Fortress Press.
- Thomas, George F. 1965. *Religious Philosophies of the West.* New York: Scribner's, 1965.
- Thomas, J. Heywood. 1963. *Paul Tillich: An Appraisal.* Philadelphia, Westminster
- Tillich, Hannah. 1973. *From Time to Time.* New York: Stein and Day
- Tucker, Robert. 1961. *Philosophy and Myth in Karl Marx.* Cambridge: Cambridge University Press
- Wheat, Leonard F. 1970. *Paul Tillich's Dialectical Humanism: Unmasking the God above God.* Baltimore: The Johns Hopkins Press

External links

- Paul Tillich (1886-1965) (http://people.bu.edu/wwildman/bce/tillich.htm) An article in the Boston Collaborative Encyclopedia of Western Theology (http://people.bu.edu/wwildman/bce/index.htm) edited by Derek Michaud incorporating material by James Wu and Wilfredo Tangunan.
- Tillich profile, and synopsis (http://www.giffordlectures.org/Author.asp?AuthorID=169) of Gifford Lectures
- North American Paul Tillich Society (http://www.napts.org/)
- Werner Schüßler (1997). Bautz, Traugott. ed (in German). *Tillich, Paul* (http://www.bautz.de/bbkl/t/tillich_p.shtml). Biographisch-Bibliographisches Kirchenlexikon (BBKL). **12**. Herzberg. cols. 85–123. ISBN 3-88309-068-9. with further reading
- James Rosati's sculpture of Tillich's head (http://faculty.evansville.edu/ck6/bstud/tillich.jpg) in the Paul Tillich Park in New Harmony, Indiana
- Tillich Park Finger Labyrinth. (http://www.billressl.us/tillichparklabyrinth.pdf) Walk Tillich Park while discerning Tillich's theology. Created by Rev. Bill Ressl after an inspirational walk in Tillich Park in New Harmony, Indiana.
- Sermons and lectures (http://gargoyle.union-psce.edu/tutorial/IRC/Pages/TillichCDs.htm) – audio recordings on Compact Disc
- Paul Tillich television interview (http://www.youtube.com/watch?v=g-tqfnt7An0&feature=related) Paul Tillich in four separate interviews entitled (1) philosophy and religion, (2) religion in the philosophy of life, (3) religion and psychotherapy, and (4) philosophy and art. It is conducted by members of the faculty of Pittsburgh Theological Seminary and produced as part of the WQED of Pittsburgh "Heritage" series on NET. The date is unclear. 1st of 12 YouTube segments.
- The Courage to Be (http://www.archive.org/details/courageofbe011129mbp) in the Internet Archive
- Dynamics of faith (http://ishare.iask.sina.com.cn/f/11760419.html) at sina-ishare.

Mircea Eliade

Mircea Eliade	
Born	March 13, 1907 Bucharest, Romania
Died	April 22, 1986 (aged 79) Chicago, Illinois, United States
Occupation	Historian, philosopher, short story writer, journalist, essayist, novelist
Nationality	Romanian
Period	1921–1986
Genres	fantasy, autobiography, travel literature
Subjects	history of religion, philosophy of religion, cultural history, political history
Literary movement	Modernism *Criterion* *Trăirism*

Mircea Eliade (Romanian pronunciation: ['mirt͡ʃea eli'ade]; March 13 [O.S. February 28] 1907 – April 22, 1986) was a Romanian historian of religion, fiction writer, philosopher, and professor at the University of Chicago. He was a leading interpreter of religious experience, who established paradigms in religious studies that persist to this day. His theory that *hierophanies* form the basis of religion, splitting the human experience of reality into sacred and profane space and time, has proved influential.[1] One of his most influential contributions to religious studies was his theory of *Eternal Return*, which holds that myths and rituals do not simply commemorate hierophanies, but, at least to the minds of the religious, actually participate in them.[1]

His literary works belong to the fantasy and autobiographical genres. The best known are the novels *Maitreyi* ("La Nuit Bengali" or "Bengal Nights"), *Noaptea de Sânziene* ("The Forbidden Forest"), *Isabel și apele diavolului* ("Isabel and the Devil's Waters") and the *Novel of the Nearsighted Adolescent*, the novellas *Domnișoara Christina* ("Miss Christina") and *Tinerețe fără tinerețe* ("Youth Without Youth"), and the short stories *Secretul doctorului Honigberger* ("The Secret of Dr. Honigberger") and *La Țigănci* ("With the Gypsy Girls").

Early in his life, Eliade was a noted journalist and essayist, a disciple of Romanian far right philosopher and journalist Nae Ionescu, and member of the literary society *Criterion*. He also served as cultural attaché to the United Kingdom and Portugal. Several times during the late 1930s, Eliade publicly expressed his support for the Iron Guard, a fascist and antisemitic political organization. His political involvement at the time, as well as his other far right connections, were the frequent topic of criticism after World War II.

Noted for his vast erudition, Eliade had fluent command of five languages (Romanian, French, German, Italian, and English) and a reading knowledge of three others (Hebrew, Persian, and Sanskrit). He was elected a posthumous member of the Romanian Academy.

Biography

Childhood

Born in Bucharest, he was the son of Romanian Land Forces officer Gheorghe Eliade (whose original surname was Ieremia)[2][3] and Jeana *née* Vasilescu.[4] An Orthodox believer, Gheorghe Eliade registered his son's birth four days before the actual date, to coincide with the liturgical calendar feast of the Forty Martyrs of Sebaste.[3] Mircea Eliade had a sister, Corina, the mother of semiologist Sorin Alexandrescu.[5][6] His family moved between Tecuci and Bucharest, ultimately settling in the capital in 1914,[2] and purchasing a house on Melodiei Street, near Piața Rosetti, where Mircea Eliade resided until late in his teens.[6]

Eliade kept a particularly fond memory of his childhood and, later in life, wrote about the impact various unusual episodes and encounters had on his mind. In one instance during the World War I Romanian Campaign, when Eliade was about ten years of age, he witnessed the bombing of Bucharest by German zeppelins and the patriotic fervor in the occupied capital at news that Romania was able to stop the Central Powers' advance into Moldavia.[7] He notably described this stage in his life as marked by an unrepeatable epiphany.[8][9] Recalling his entrance into a drawing room that an "eerie iridescent light" had turned into "a fairy-tale palace", he wrote,

I practiced for many years [the] exercise of recapturing that epiphanic moment, and I would always find again the same plenitude. I would slip into it as into a fragment of time devoid of duration—without beginning, middle, or end. During my last years of lycée, when I struggled with profound attacks of melancholy, I still succeeded at times in returning to the golden green light of that afternoon. [...] But even though the beatitude was the same, it was now impossible to bear because it aggravated my sadness too much. By this time I knew the world to which the drawing room belonged [...] was a world forever lost.[10]

Robert Ellwood, a professor of religion who did his graduate studies under Mircea Eliade,[11] saw this type of nostalgia as one of the most characteristic themes in Eliade's life and academic writings.[9]

Adolescence and literary debut

After completing his primary education at the school on Mântuleasa Street,[2] Eliade attended the Spiru Haret National College in the same class as Arşavir Acterian, Haig Acterian, and Petre Viforeanu (and several years the senior of Nicolae Steinhardt, who eventually became a close friend of Eliade's).[12] Among his other colleagues was future philosopher Constantin Noica[3] and Noica's friend, future art historian Barbu Brezianu.[13]

As a child, Eliade was fascinated with the natural world, which formed the setting of his very first literary attempts,[3] as well as with Romanian folklore and the Christian faith as expressed by peasants.[6] Growing up, he aimed to find and record what he believed was the common source of all religious traditions.[6] The young Eliade's interest in physical exercise and adventure led him to pursue mountaineering and sailing,[6] and he also joined the Romanian Boy Scouts.[14] With a group of friends, he designed and sailed a boat on the Danube, from Tulcea to the Black Sea.[15] In parallel, Eliade grew estranged from the educational environment, becoming disenchanted with the discipline required and obsessed with the idea that he was uglier and less virile than his colleagues.[3] In order to cultivate his willpower, he would force himself to swallow insects[3] and only slept four to five hours a night.[7] At one point, Eliade was flunking four subjects, among which was the study of Romanian language.[3]

Instead, he became interested in natural science and chemistry, as well as the occult,[3] and wrote short pieces on entomological subjects.[7] Despite his father's concern that he was in danger of losing his already weak eyesight, Eliade read passionately.[3] One of his favorite authors was Honoré de Balzac, whose work he studied carefully.[3][7] Eliade also became acquainted with the modernist short stories of Giovanni Papini and social anthropology studies by James George Frazer.[7] His interest in the two writers led him to learn Italian and English in private, and he also began studying Persian and Hebrew.[2][7] At the time, Eliade became acquainted with Saadi's poems and the ancient Mesopotamian *Epic of Gilgamesh*.[7] He was also interested in philosophy—studying, among others, Socrates, Vasile Conta, and the Stoics Marcus Aurelius and Epictetus, and read works of history—the two Romanian historians who influenced him from early on were Bogdan Petriceicu Hasdeu and Nicolae Iorga.[7] His first published work was the 1921 *Inamicul viermelui de mătase* ("The Silkworm's Enemy"),[2] followed by *Cum am găsit piatra filosofală* ("How I Found the Philosophers' Stone").[7] Four years later, Eliade completed work on his debut volume, the autobiographical *Novel of the Nearsighted Adolescent*.[7]

University studies and Indian sojourn

Between 1925 and 1928, he attended the University of Bucharest's Faculty of Philosophy and Letters in 1928, earning his diploma with a study on Early Modern Italian philosopher Tommaso Campanella.[2] In 1927, Eliade traveled to Italy, where he met Papini[2] and collaborated with the scholar Giuseppe Tucci.

It was during his student years that Eliade met Nae Ionescu, who lectured in Logic, becoming one of his disciples and friends.[3][6][16] He was especially attracted to Ionescu's radical ideas and his interest in religion, which signified a break with the rationalist tradition represented by senior academics such as Constantin Rădulescu-Motru, Dimitrie Gusti, and Tudor Vianu (all of whom owed inspiration to the defunct literary society *Junimea*, albeit in varying degrees).[3]

Eliade's scholarly works began after a long period of study in British India, at the University of Calcutta. Finding that the Maharaja of Kassimbazar sponsored European scholars to study in India, Eliade applied and was granted an allowance for four years, which was later doubled by a Romanian scholarship.[17] In autumn 1928, he sailed for Calcutta to study Sanskrit and philosophy under Surendranath Dasgupta, a Bengali Cambridge alumnus and professor at Calcutta University, the author of a five volume *History of Indian Philosophy*. Before reaching the Indian subcontinent, Eliade also made a brief visit to Egypt.[2] Once there, he visited large areas of the region, and spent a short period at a Himalayan *ashram*.[18]

He studied the basics of Indian philosophy, and, in parallel, learned Sanskrit, Pali and Bengali under Dasgupta's direction.[17] At the time, he also became interested in the actions of Mahatma Gandhi, whom he met personally,[19] and the *Satyagraha* as a phenomenon; later, Eliade adapted Gandhist ideas in his discourse on spirituality and Romania.[19] In 1930, while living with Dasgupta, Eliade fell in love with his host's daughter, Maitreyi Devi, later writing a barely disguised autobiographical novel *Maitreyi* (also known as "La Nuit Bengali" or "Bengal Nights"), in which he claimed that he carried on a physical relationship with her.[20]

Eliade received his PhD in 1933, with a thesis on Yoga practices.[3][6][21][22] The book, which was translated into French three years later,[17] had significant impact in academia, both in Romania and abroad.[6] He later recalled that the book was an early step for understanding not just Indian religious practices, but also Romanian spirituality.[23] During the same period, Eliade began a correspondence with the Ceylonese-born philosopher Ananda Coomaraswamy.[24] In 1936–1937, he functioned as honorary assistant for Ionescu's course, lecturing in Metaphysics.[25]

In 1933, Mircea Eliade had a physical relationship with the actress Sorana Țopa, while falling in love with Nina Mareș, whom he ultimately married.[5][6][26] The latter, introduced to him by his new friend Mihail Sebastian, already had a daughter, Giza, from a man who had divorced her.[6] Eliade subsequently adopted Giza,[27] and the three of them moved to an apartment at 141 Dacia Boulevard.[6] He left his residence in 1936, during a trip he made to the United Kingdom and Nazi Germany, when he first visited London, Oxford and Berlin.[2]

Criterion and *Cuvântul*

After contributing various and generally polemical pieces in university magazines, Eliade came to the attention of journalist Pamfil Șeicaru, who invited him to collaborate on the nationalist paper *Cuvântul*, which was noted for its harsh tones.[3] By then, *Cuvântul* was also hosting articles by Ionescu.[3]

As one of the figures in the *Criterion* literary society (1933–1934), Eliade's initial encounter with the traditional far right was polemical: the group's conferences were stormed by members of A. C. Cuza's National-Christian Defense League, who objected to what they viewed as pacifism and addressed antisemitic insults to several speakers, including Sebastian;[28] in 1933, he was among the signers of a manifesto opposing Nazi Germany's state-enforced racism.[29] In 1934, at a time when Sebastian was publicly insulted by Nae Ionescu, who

Eliade's home in Bucharest (1934-1940)

prefaced his book (*De două mii de ani...*) with thoughts on the "eternal damnation" of Jews, Mircea Eliade spoke out against this perspective, and commented that Ionescu's references to the verdict "Outside the Church there is no salvation" contradicted the notion of God's omnipotence.[30][31] However, he contended that Ionescu's text was not evidence of antisemitism.[32]

In 1936, reflecting on the early history of the Romanian Kingdom and its Jewish community, he deplored the expulsion of Jewish savants from Romanian soil, making specific references to Moses Gaster, Heimann Hariton Tiktin and Lazăr Șăineanu.[33] Eliade's views at the time focused on innovation—in the summer of 1933, he replied to an anti-modernist critique written by George Călinescu:

> All I wish for is a deep change, a complete transformation. But, for God's sake, in any direction other than spirituality.[34]

He and friends Emil Cioran and Constantin Noica were by then under the influence of *Trăirism*, a school of thought that was formed around the ideals expressed by Ionescu. A form of existentialism, *Trăirism* was also the synthesis of traditional and newer right-wing beliefs.[35] Early on, a public polemic was sparked between Eliade and Camil Petrescu: the two eventually reconciled and later became good friends.[27] Like Mihail Sebastian, who was himself becoming influenced by Ionescu, he maintained contacts with intellectuals from all sides of the political spectrum: their entourage included the right-wing Dan Botta and Mircea Vulcănescu, the non-political Petrescu and Ionel Jianu, and Belu Zilber, who was a member of the illegal Romanian Communist Party.[36] The group also included Haig Acterian, Mihail Polihroniade, Petru Comarnescu, Marietta Sadova and Floria Capsali.[30]

He was also close to Marcel Avramescu, a former Surrealist writer whom he introduced to the works of René Guénon.[37] A doctor in the Kabbalah and future Romanian Orthodox cleric, Avramescu joined Eliade in editing the short-lived esoteric magazine *Memra* (the only one of its kind in Romania).[38] Among the intellectuals who attended his lectures were Mihail Șora (whom he deemed his favorite student), Eugen Schileru and Miron Constantinescu—known later as, respectively, a philosopher, an art critic, and a sociologist and political figure of the communist regime.[27] Mariana Klein, who became Șora's wife, was one of Eliade's female students, and later authored works on his scholarship.[27]

Eliade later recounted that he had himself enlisted Zilber as a *Cuvântul* contributor, in order for him to provide a Marxist perspective on the issues discussed by the journal.[36] Their relation soured in 1935, when the latter publicly accused Eliade of serving as an agent for the secret police, *Siguranţa Statului* (Sebastian answered to the statement by alleging that Zilber was himself a secret agent, and the latter eventually retracted his claim).[36]

1930s political transition

Eliade's articles before and after his adherence to the principles of the Iron Guard (or, as it was usually known at the time, the *Legionary Movement*), beginning with his famous *Itinerar spiritual* ("Spiritual Itinerary", serialized in *Cuvântul* in 1927), center on several political ideals advocated by the far right. They displayed his rejection of liberalism and the modernizing goals of the 1848 Wallachian revolution (perceived as "an abstract apology of Mankind"[39] and "ape-like imitation of [Western] Europe"),[40] as well as for democracy itself (accusing it of "managing to crush all attempts at national renaissance",[41] and later praising Benito Mussolini's Fascist Italy on the grounds that, according to Eliade, "[in Italy,] he who thinks for himself is promoted to the highest office in the shortest of times").[41] He approved of an ethnic nationalist state centered on the Orthodox Church (in 1927, despite his still-vivid interest in Theosophy, he recommended young intellectuals "the return to the Church"),[42] which he opposed to, among others, the secular nationalism of Constantin Rădulescu-Motru;[43] referring to this particular ideal as "Romanianism", Eliade was, in 1934, still viewing it as "neither fascism, nor chauvinism".[44] Eliade was especially dissatisfied with the incidence of unemployment among intellectuals, whose careers in state-financed institutions had been rendered uncertain by the Great Depression.[45]

In 1936, Eliade was the focus of a campaign in the far right press, being targeted for having authored "pornography" in his *Domnişoara Christina* and *Isabel şi apele diavolului* (similar accusations were aimed at other cultural figures, including Tudor Arghezi and Geo Bogza).[46] Assessments of Eliade's work were in sharp contrast to one another: also in 1936, Eliade accepted an award from the Romanian Writers' Society, of which he had been a member since 1934.[47] In summer 1937, through an official decision which came as a result of the accusations, and despite student protests, he was stripped of his position at the University.[48] Eliade decided to sue the Ministry of Education, asking for a symbolic compensation of 1 leu.[49] He won the trial, and regained his position as Nae Ionescu's assistant.[49]

Nevertheless, by 1937, he gave his intellectual support to the Iron Guard, in which he saw "a Christian revolution aimed at creating a new Romania",[50] and a group able "to reconcile Romania with God".[50] His articles of the time, published in Iron Guard papers such as *Sfarmă Piatră* and *Buna Vestire*, contain ample praises of the movement's leaders (Corneliu Zelea Codreanu, Ion Moţa, Vasile Marin, and Gheorghe Cantacuzino-Grănicerul).[51][52] The transition he went through was similar to that of his fellow generation members and close collaborators—among the notable exceptions to this rule were Petru Comarnescu, sociologist Henri H. Stahl and future dramatist Eugène Ionesco, as well as Sebastian.[53]

He eventually enrolled in the *Totul pentru Ţară* ("Everything for the Fatherland" Party), the political expression of the Iron Guard,[3][54] and contributed to its 1937 electoral campaign in Prahova County—as indicated by his inclusion on a list of party members with county-level responsibilities (published in *Buna Vestire*).[54]

Internment and diplomatic service

The stance taken by Eliade resulted in his arrest on July 14, 1938 after a crackdown on the Iron Guard authorized by King Carol II. At the time of his arrest, he had just interrupted a column on *Provincia şi legionarismul* ("The Province and Legionary Ideology") in *Vremea*, having been singled out by Prime Minister Armand Călinescu as an author of Iron Guard propaganda.[55]

Eliade was kept for three weeks in a cell at the *Siguranţa Statului* Headquarters, in an attempt to have him sign a "declaration of dissociation" with the Iron Guard, but he refused to do so.[56] In the first week of August he was transferred to a makeshift camp at Miercurea-Ciuc. When Eliade began coughing blood in October 1938, he was taken to a clinic in Moroeni.[56] Eliade was simply released on November 12, and subsequently spent his time writing his play *Iphigenia* (also known as *Ifigenia*).[30] In April 1940, with the help of Alexandru Rosetti, became the Cultural Attaché to the United Kingdom, a posting cut short when Romanian-British foreign relations were broken.[56]

After leaving London he was assigned the office of Counsel and Press Officer (later Cultural Attaché) to the Romanian Embassy in Portugal,[26][57][58][59] where he was kept on as diplomat by the National Legionary State (the Iron Guard government) and, ultimately, by Ion Antonescu's regime. His office involved disseminating propaganda in favor of the Romanian state.[26] In February 1941, weeks after the bloody Legionary Rebellion was crushed by Antonescu, *Iphigenia* was staged by the National Theater Bucharest—the play soon raised doubts that it owed inspiration to the Iron Guard's ideology, and even that its inclusion in the program was a Legionary attempt at subversion.[30]

In 1942, Eliade authored a volume in praise of the *Estado Novo*, established in Portugal by António de Oliveira Salazar,[59][60][61] claiming that "The Salazarian state, a Christian and totalitarian one, is first and foremost based on love".[60] On July 7 of the same year, he was received by Salazar himself, who assigned Eliade the task of warning Antonescu to withdraw the Romanian Army from the Eastern Front ("[In his place], I would not be grinding it in

Russia").[62] Eliade also claimed that such contacts with the leader of a neutral country had made him the target for Gestapo surveillance, but that he had managed to communicate Salazar's advice to Mihai Antonescu, Romania's Foreign Minister.[19][62]

In autumn 1943, he traveled to occupied France, where he rejoined Emil Cioran, also meeting with scholar Georges Dumézil and the collaborationist writer Paul Morand.[26] At the same time, he applied for a position of lecturer at the University of Bucharest, but withdrew from the race, leaving Constantin Noica and Ion Zamfirescu to dispute the position, in front of a panel of academics comprising Lucian Blaga and Dimitrie Gusti (Zamfirescu's eventual selection, going against Blaga's recommendation, was to be the topic of a controversy).[63] In his private notes, Eliade wrote that he took no further interest in the office, because his visits abroad had convinced him that he had "something great to say", and that he could not function within the confines of "a minor culture".[26] Also during the war, Eliade traveled to Berlin, where he met and conversed with controversial political theorist Carl Schmitt,[61][26] and frequently visited Francoist Spain, where he notably attended the 1944 Lusitano-Spanish scientific congress in Córdoba.[26][64][65] It was during his trips to Spain that Eliade met philosophers José Ortega y Gasset and Eugeni d'Ors. He maintained a friendship with d'Ors, and met him again on several occasions after the war.[64]

Nina Eliade fell ill with uterine cancer and died during their stay in Lisbon, in late 1944. As the widower later wrote, the disease was probably caused by an abortion procedure she had undergone at an early stage of their relationship.[26] He came to suffer with clinical depression, which increased as Romania and her Axis allies suffered major defeats on the Eastern Front.[26][65] Contemplating a return to Romania as a soldier or a monk,[26] he was on a continuous search for effective antidepressants, medicating himself with passion flower extract, and, eventually, with methamphetamine.[65] This was probably not his first experience with drugs: vague mentions in his notebooks have been read as indication that Mircea Eliade was taking opium during his travels to Calcutta.[65] Later, discussing the works of Aldous Huxley, Eliade wrote that the British author's use of mescaline as a source of inspiration had something in common with his own experience, indicating 1945 as a date of reference and adding that it was "needless to explain why that is".[65]

Early exile

At signs that the Romanian communist regime was about to take hold, Eliade opted not to return to the country. On September 16, 1945, he moved to France with his adopted daughter Giza.[2][26] Once there, he resumed contacts with Dumézil, who helped him recover his position in academia.[6] On Dumézil's recommendation, he taught at the *École Pratique des Hautes Études* in Paris.[27] It was estimated that, at the time, it was not uncommon for him to work 15 hours a day.[22] Eliade married a second time, to the Romanian exile Christinel Cotescu.[6][66] His second wife, the descendant of boyars, was the sister-in-law of prestigious conductor Ionel Perlea.[66]

Together with Emil Cioran and other Romanian expatriates, Eliade rallied with the former diplomat Alexandru Busuioceanu, helping him publicize anti-communist opinion to the Western European public.[67] He was also briefly involved in publishing a Romanian-language magazine, titled *Luceafărul* ("The Morning Star"),[67] and was again in contact with Mihail Şora, who had been granted a scholarship to study in France, and by Şora's wife Mariana.[27] In 1947, he was facing material constraints, and Ananda Coomaraswamy found him a job as a French-language teacher in the United States, at a school in Arizona; the arrangement ended upon Coomaraswamy's death in September.[24]

Beginning in 1948, he wrote for the journal *Critique*, edited by French thinker Georges Bataille.[2] The following year, he went on a visit to Italy, where he wrote the first 300 pages of his novel *Noaptea de Sânziene* (he visited the country a third time in 1952).[2] He collaborated with Carl Jung and the *Eranos* circle after Henry Corbin recommended him in 1949,[24] and wrote for the *Antaios* magazine (edited by Ernst Jünger).[22] In 1950, Eliade began attending *Eranos* conferences, meeting Jung, Olga Fröbe-Kapteyn, Gershom Scholem and Paul Radin.[68] He described *Eranos* as "one of the most creative cultural experiences of the modern Western world."[69]

In October 1956, he moved to the United States, settling in Chicago the following year.[2][6] He had been invited by Joachim Wach to give a series of lectures at Wach's home institution, the University of Chicago.[69] Eliade and Wach are generally admitted to be the founders of the "Chicago school" that basically defined the study of religions for the second half of the 20th century.[70] Upon Wach's death before the lectures were delivered, Eliade was appointed as his replacement, becoming, in 1964, the *Sewell Avery Distinguished Service Professor of the History of Religions*.[2] Beginning in 1954, with the first edition of his volume on *Eternal Return*, Eliade also enjoyed commercial success: the book went through several editions under different titles, which sold over 100,000 copies.[71]

In 1966, Mircea Eliade became a member of the American Academy of Arts and Sciences.[2] He also worked as editor-in-chief of Macmillan Publishers' *Encyclopedia of Religion*, and, in 1968, lectured in religious history at the University of California, Santa Barbara.[72] It was also during that period that Mircea Eliade completed his voluminous and influential *History of Religious Ideas*, which grouped together the overviews of his main original interpretations of religious history.[6] He occasionally traveled out of the United States, notably attending the Congress for the History of Religions in Marburg (1960) and visiting Sweden and Norway (1970).[2]

Final years and death

Initially, Eliade was attacked with virulence by the Romanian Communist Party press, chiefly by *România Liberă*—which described him as "the Iron Guard's ideologue, enemy of the working class, apologist of Salazar's dictatorship".[73] However, the regime also made secretive attempts to enlist his and Cioran's support: Haig Acterian's widow, theater director Marietta Sadova, was sent to Paris in order to re-establish contacts with the two.[74] Although the move was planned by Romanian officials, her encounters were to be used as evidence incriminating her at a February 1960 trial for treason (where Constantin Noica and Dinu Pillat were the main defendants).[74] Romania's secret police, the Securitate, also portrayed Eliade as a spy for the British Secret Intelligence Service and a former agent of the Gestapo.[75]

He was slowly rehabilitated at home beginning in the early 1960s, under the rule of Gheorghe Gheorghiu-Dej.[76] In the 1970s, Eliade was approached by the Nicolae Ceauşescu regime in several ways, in order to have him return.[6] The move was prompted by the officially sanctioned nationalism and Romania's claim to independence from the Eastern Bloc, as both phenomena came to see Eliade's prestige as an asset. An unprecedented event occurred with the interview that was granted by Mircea Eliade to poet Adrian Păunescu, during the latter's 1970 visit to Chicago; Eliade complimented both Păunescu's activism and his support for official tenets, expressing a belief that

> the youth of Eastern Europe is clearly superior to that of Western Europe. [...] I am convinced that, within ten years, the young revolutionary generation shan't be behaving as does today the noisy minority of Western contesters. [...] Eastern youth have seen the abolition of traditional institutions, have accepted it [...] and are not yet content with the structures enforced, but rather seek to improve them.[77]

Păunescu's visit to Chicago was followed by those of the nationalist official writer Eugen Barbu and by Eliade's friend Constantin Noica (who had since been released from jail).[52] At the time, Eliade contemplated returning to Romania, but was eventually persuaded by fellow Romanian intellectuals in exile (including Radio Free Europe's Virgil Ierunca and Monica Lovinescu) to reject Communist proposals.[52] In 1977, he joined other exiled Romanian intellectuals in signing a telegram protesting the repressive measures newly enforced by the Ceauşescu regime.[3] Writing in 2007, Romanian anthropologist Andrei Oişteanu recounted how, around 1984, the Securitate unsuccessfully pressured to become an agent of influence in Eliade's Chicagoan circle.[78]

During his later years, Eliade's fascist past was progressively exposed publicly, the stress of which probably contributed to the decline of his health.[3] By then, his writing career was hampered by severe arthritis.[27] The last academic honors bestowed upon him were the French Academy's Bordin Prize (1977) and the title of *Doctor Honoris Causa*, granted by the University of Washington (1985).[2]

Mircea Eliade died at the Bernard Mitchell Hospital in April 1986. Eight days previously, he suffered a stroke while reading Emil Cioran's *Exercises of Admiration*, and had subsequently lost his speech function.[8] Four months before, a fire had destroyed part of his office at the Meadville Lombard Theological School (an event which he had interpreted as an omen).[3][8] Eliade's Romanian disciple Ioan Petru Culianu, who recalled the scientific community's reaction to the news, described Eliade's death as "a *mahaparanirvana*", thus comparing it to the passing of Gautama Buddha.[8] His body was cremated in Chicago, and the funeral ceremony was held on University grounds, at the Rockefeller Chapel.[2][8] It was attended by 1,200 people, and included a public reading of Eliade's text in which he recalled the epiphany of his childhood—the lecture was given by novelist Saul Bellow, Eliade's colleague at the University.[8]

Work

The general nature of religion

In his work on the history of religion, Eliade is most highly regarded for his writings on Shamanism, Yoga and what he called the eternal return—the implicit belief, supposedly present in religious thought in general, that religious behavior is not only an imitation of, but also a participation in, sacred events, and thus restores the mythical time of origins. Eliade's thinking was in part influenced by Rudolf Otto, Gerardus van der Leeuw, Nae Ionescu and the writings of the Traditionalist School (René Guénon and Julius Evola).[37] For instance, Eliade's *The Sacred and the Profane* partially builds on Otto's *The Idea of the Holy* to show how religion emerges from the experience of the sacred, and myths of time and nature.

Eliade is noted for his attempt to find broad, cross-cultural parallels and unities in religion, particularly in myths. Wendy Doniger, Eliade's colleague from 1978 until his death, notes that "Eliade argued boldly for universals where he might more safely have argued for widely prevalent patterns".[79] His *Treatise on the History of Religions* was praised by French philologist Georges Dumézil for its coherence and ability to synthesize diverse and distinct mythologies.[80]

Robert Ellwood describes Eliade's approach to religion as follows. Eliade approaches religion by imagining an ideally "religious" person, whom he calls *homo religiosus* in his writings. Eliade's theories basically describe how this *homo religiosus* would view the world.[81] This does not mean that all religious practitioners actually think and act like *homo religiosus*. Instead, it means that religious behavior "says through its own language" that the world is as *homo religiosus* would see it, whether or not the real-life participants in religious behavior are aware of it.[82] However, Ellwood notes that Eliade "tends to slide over that last qualification", implying that traditional societies actually thought like *homo religiosus*.[82]

Sacred and profane

Eliade argues that religious thought in general rests on a sharp distinction between the Sacred and the profane;[83] whether it takes the form of God, gods, or mythical Ancestors, the Sacred contains all "reality", or value, and other things acquire "reality" only to the extent that they participate in the sacred.[84]

Eliade's understanding of religion centers on his concept of hierophany (manifestation of the Sacred)—a concept that includes, but is not limited to, the older and more restrictive concept of theophany (manifestation of a god).[85] From the perspective of religious thought, Eliade argues, hierophanies give structure and orientation to the world, establishing a sacred order. The "profane" space of nonreligious experience can only be divided up geometrically: it has no "qualitative differentiation and, hence, no orientation [is] given by virtue of its inherent structure".[86] Thus, profane space gives man no pattern for his behavior. In contrast to profane space, the site of a hierophany has a sacred structure to which religious man conforms himself. A hierophany amounts to a "revelation of an absolute reality, opposed to the non-reality of the vast surrounding expanse".[87] As an example of "sacred space" demanding a certain response from man, Eliade gives the story of Moses halting before Yahweh's manifestation as a burning bush (*Exodus* 3:5) and taking off his shoes.[88]

Moses taking off his shoes in front of the burning bush (illustration from a 16th century edition of the *Speculum Humanae Salvationis*).

Origin myths and sacred time

Eliade notes that, in traditional societies, myth represents the absolute truth about primordial time.[89] According to the myths, this was the time when the Sacred first appeared, establishing the world's structure—myths claim to describe the primordial events that made society and the natural world be that which they are. Eliade argues that all myths are, in that sense, origin myths: "myth, then, is always an account of a *creation*".[90]

Many traditional societies believe that the power of a thing lies in its origin.[91] If origin is equivalent to power, then "it is the first manifestation of a thing that is significant and valid"[92] (a thing's reality and value therefore lies only in its first appearance).

According to Eliade's theory, only the Sacred has value, only a thing's first appearance has value and, therefore, only the Sacred's first appearance has value. Myth describes the Sacred's first appearance; therefore, the mythical age is sacred time,[89] the only time of value: "primitive man was interested only in the *beginnings* [...] to him it mattered little what had happened to himself, or to others like him, in more or less distant times".[93] Eliade postulated this as the reason for the "nostalgia for origins" that appears in many religions, the desire to return to a primordial Paradise.[93]

Eternal return and "Terror of history"

Eliade argues that traditional man attributes no value to the linear march of historical events: only the events of the mythical age have value. To give his own life value, traditional man performs myths and rituals. Because the Sacred's essence lies only in the mythical age, only in the Sacred's first appearance, any later appearance is actually the first appearance; by recounting or re-enacting mythical events, myths and rituals "re-actualize" those events.[94] Eliade often uses the term "archetypes" to refer to the mythical models that established by the Sacred, although Eliade's use of the term should be distinguished from the use of the term in Jungian psychology.[95]

Thus, argues Eliade, religious behavior does not only commemorate, but also participates in, sacred events:

> In *imitating* the exemplary acts of a god or of a mythical hero, or simply by recounting their adventures, the man of an archaic society detaches himself from profane time and magically re-enters the Great Time, the sacred time.[89]

Eliade called this concept the "eternal return" (distinguished from the philosophical concept of "eternal return"). Wendy Doniger noted that Eliade's theory of the eternal return "has become a truism in the study of religions".[1]

Eliade attributes the well-known "cyclic" vision of time in ancient thought to belief in the eternal return. For instance, the New Year ceremonies among the Mesopotamians, the Egyptians, and other Near Eastern peoples re-enacted their cosmogonic myths. Therefore, by the logic of the eternal return, each New Year ceremony *was* the beginning of the world for these peoples. According to Eliade, these peoples felt a need to return to the Beginning at regular intervals, turning time into a circle.[96]

Eliade argues that yearning to remain in the mythical age causes a "terror of history": traditional man desires to escape the linear succession of events (which, Eliade indicated, he viewed as empty of any inherent value or sacrality). Eliade suggests that the abandonment of mythical thought and the full acceptance of linear, historical time, with its "terror", is one of the reasons for modern man's anxieties.[97] Traditional societies escape this anxiety to an extent, as they refuse to completely acknowledge historical time.

Coincidentia oppositorum

Eliade claims that many myths, rituals, and mystical experiences involve a "coincidence of opposites", or *coincidentia oppositorum*. In fact, he calls the *coincidentia oppositorum* "the mythical pattern".[98] Many myths, Eliade notes, "present us with a twofold revelation":

> they express on the one hand the diametrical opposition of two divine figures sprung from one and the same principle and destined, in many versions, to be reconciled at some *illud tempus* of eschatology, and on the other, the *coincidentia oppositorum* in the very nature of the divinity, which shows itself, by turns or even simultaneously, benevolent and terrible, creative and destructive, solar and serpentine, and so on (in other words, actual and potential).[99]

Eliade argues that "Yahweh is both kind and wrathful; the God of the Christian mystics and theologians is terrible and gentle at once".[100] He also thought that the Indian and Chinese mystic tried to attain "a state of perfect indifference and neutrality" that resulted in a coincidence of opposites in which "pleasure and pain, desire and repulsion, cold and heat [...] are expunged from his awareness".[100]

According to Eliade, the *coincidentia oppositorum*'s appeal lies in "man's deep dissatisfaction with his actual situation, with what is called the human condition".[101] In many mythologies, the end of the mythical age involves a "fall", a fundamental "ontological change in the structure of the World".[102] Because the *coincidentia oppositorum* is a contradiction, it represents a denial of the world's current logical structure, a reversal of the "fall".

Also, traditional man's dissatisfaction with the post-mythical age expresses itself as a feeling of being "torn and separate".[101] In many mythologies, the lost mythical age was a Paradise, "a paradoxical state in which the contraries exist side by side without conflict, and the multiplications form aspects of a mysterious Unity".[102] The *coincidentia oppositorum* expresses a wish to recover the lost unity of the mythical Paradise, for it presents a reconciliation of opposites and the unification of diversity:

> On the level of pre-systematic thought, the mystery of totality embodies man's endeavor to reach a perspective in which the contraries are abolished, the Spirit of Evil reveals itself as a stimulant of Good, and Demons appear as the night aspect of the Gods.[102]

Exceptions to the general nature

Eliade acknowledges that not all religious behavior has all the attributes described in his theory of sacred time and the eternal return. The Zoroastrian, Jewish, Christian, and Muslim traditions embrace linear, historical time as sacred or capable of sanctification, while some Eastern traditions largely reject the notion of sacred time, seeking escape from the cycles of time.

Because they contain rituals, Judaism and Christianity necessarily—Eliade argues—retain a sense of cyclic time:

> by the very fact that it is a religion, Christianity had to keep at least one mythical aspect—liturgical Time, that is, the periodic rediscovery of the *illud tempus* of the beginnings [and] an *imitation* of the Christ as *exemplary pattern*.[103]

However, Judaism and Christianity do not see time as a circle endlessly turning on itself; nor do they see such a cycle as desirable, as a way to participate in the Sacred. Instead, these religions embrace the concept of linear history progressing toward the Messianic Age or the Last Judgment, thus initiating the idea of "progress" (humans are to work for a Paradise in the future).[104] However, Eliade's understanding of Judaeo-Christian

The Last Judgment (detail) in the 12th century Byzantine mosaic at Torcello.

eschatology can also be understood as cyclical in that the "end of time" is a return to God: "The final catastrophe will put an end to history, hence will restore man to eternity and beatitude".[105]

The pre-Islamic Persian religion of Zoroastrianism, which made a notable "contribution to the religious formation of the West",[106] also has a linear sense of time. According to Eliade, the Hebrews had a linear sense of time before being influenced by Zoroastrianism.[106] In fact, Eliade identifies the Hebrews, not the Zoroastrians, as the first culture to truly "valorize" historical time, the first to see all major historical events as episodes in a continuous divine revelation.[107] However, Eliade argues, Judaism elaborated its mythology of linear time by adding elements borrowed from Zoroastrianism—including ethical dualism, a savior figure, the future resurrection of the body, and the idea of cosmic progress toward "the final triumph of Good".[106]

The Dharmic religions of the East generally retain a cyclic view of time—for instance, the Hindu doctrine of *kalpas*. According to Eliade, most religions that accept the cyclic view of time also embrace it: they see it as a way to return to the sacred time. However, in Buddhism, Jainism, and some forms of Hinduism, the Sacred lies outside the flux of the material world (called *maya*, or "illusion"), and one can only reach it by escaping from the cycles of time.[108] Because the Sacred lies outside cyclic time, which conditions humans, people can only reach the Sacred by escaping the human condition. According to Eliade, Yoga techniques aim at escaping the limitations of the body, allowing the soul (*atman*) to rise above *maya* and reach the Sacred (*nirvana, moksha*). Imagery of "freedom", and of death to one's old body and rebirth with a new body, occur frequently in Yogic texts, representing escape from the bondage of the temporal human condition.[109] Eliade discusses these themes in detail in *Yoga: Immortality and Freedom*.

Symbolism of the Center

A recurrent theme in Eliade's myth analysis is the *axis mundi*, the Center of the World. According to Eliade, the Cosmic Center is a necessary corollary to the division of reality into the Sacred and the profane. The Sacred contains all value, and the world gains purpose and meaning only through hierophanies:

> In the homogeneous and infinite expanse, in which no point of reference is possible and hence no orientation is established, the hierophany reveals an absolute fixed point, a center.[87]

Because profane space gives man no orientation for his life, the Sacred must manifest itself in a hierophany, thereby establishing a sacred site around which man can orient himself. The site of a hierophany establishes a "fixed point, a center".[110] This Center abolishes the "homogeneity and relativity of profane space",[86] for it becomes "the central axis for all future orientation".[87]

A manifestation of the Sacred in profane space is, by definition, an example of something breaking through from one plane of existence to another. Therefore, the initial hierophany that establishes the Center must be a point at which there is contact between different planes—this, Eliade argues, explains the frequent mythical imagery of a Cosmic Tree or Pillar joining Heaven, Earth, and the underworld.[111]

Eliade noted that, when traditional societies found a new territory, they often perform consecrating rituals that reenact the hierophany that established the Center and founded the world.[112] In addition, the designs of traditional buildings, especially temples, usually imitate the mythical image of the *axis mundi* joining the different cosmic levels. For instance, the Babylonian ziggurats were built to resemble cosmic mountains passing through the heavenly spheres, and the rock of the Temple in Jerusalem was supposed to reach deep into the *tehom*, or primordial waters.[113]

According to the logic of the eternal return, the site of each such symbolic Center will actually be the Center of the World:

> It may be said, in general, that the majority of the sacred and ritual trees that we meet with in the history of religions are only replicas, imperfect copies of this exemplary archetype, the Cosmic Tree. Thus, all these sacred trees are thought of as situated at the Centre of the World, and all the ritual trees or posts [...] are, as it were, magically projected into the Centre of the World.[114]

The Cosmic Tree *Yggdrasill*, as depicted in a 17th century Icelandic miniature.

According to Eliade's interpretation, religious man apparently feels the need to live not only near, but *at*, the mythical Center as much as possible, given that the Center is the point of communication with the Sacred.[115]

Thus, Eliade argues, many traditional societies share common outlines in their mythical geographies. In the middle of the known world is the sacred Center, "a place that is sacred above all";[116] this Center anchors the established order.[86] Around the sacred Center lies the known world, the realm of established order; and beyond the known world is a chaotic and dangerous realm, "peopled by ghosts, demons, [and] 'foreigners' (who are [identified with] demons and the souls of the dead)".[117] According to Eliade, traditional societies place their known world at the Center because (from their perspective) their known world is the realm that obeys a recognizable order, and it therefore must be the realm in which the Sacred manifests itself; the regions beyond the known world, which seem strange and foreign, must lie far from the Center, outside the order established by the Sacred.[118]

The High God

According to some "evolutionistic" theories of religion, especially that of Edward Burnett Tylor, cultures naturally progress from animism and polytheism to monotheism.[119] According to this view, more advanced cultures should be more monotheistic, and more primitive cultures should be more polytheistic. However, many of the most "primitive", pre-agricultural societies believe in a supreme sky-god.[120] Thus, according to Eliade, post-19th-century scholars have rejected Tylor's theory of evolution from animism.[121] Based on the discovery of supreme sky-gods among "primitives", Eliade suspects that the earliest humans worshiped a heavenly Supreme Being.[122] In *Patterns in Comparative Religion*, he writes, "The most popular prayer in the world is addressed to 'Our Father who art in heaven.' It is possible that man's earliest prayers were addressed to the same heavenly father."[123]

However, Eliade disagrees with Wilhelm Schmidt, who thought the earliest form of religion was a strict monotheism. Eliade dismisses this theory of "primordial monotheism" (*Urmonotheismus*) as "rigid" and unworkable.[124] "At most," he writes, "this schema [Schmidt's theory] renders an account of human [religious] evolution since the Paleolithic era".[125] If an *Urmonotheismus* did exist, Eliade adds, it probably differed in many ways from the conceptions of God in many modern monotheistic faiths: for instance, the primordial High God could manifest himself as an animal without losing his status as a celestial Supreme Being.[126]

According to Eliade, heavenly Supreme Beings are actually less common in more advanced cultures.[127] Eliade speculates that the discovery of agriculture brought a host of fertility gods and goddesses into the forefront, causing the celestial Supreme Being to fade away and eventually vanish from many ancient religions.[128] Even in primitive hunter-gatherer societies, the High God is a vague, distant figure, dwelling high above the world.[129] Often he has no cult and receives prayer only as a last resort, when all else has failed.[130] Eliade calls the distant High God a *deus otiosus* ("idle god").[131]

In belief systems that involve a *deus otiosus*, the distant High God is believed to have been closer to humans during the mythical age. After finishing his works of creation, the High God "forsook the earth and withdrew into the highest heaven".[132] This is an example of the Sacred's distance from "profane" life, life lived after the mythical age: by escaping from the profane condition through religious behavior, figures such as the shaman return to the conditions of the mythical age, which include nearness to the High God ("by his *flight* or ascension, the shaman [...] meets the God of Heaven face to face and speaks directly to him, as man sometimes did *in illo tempore*").[133] The shamanistic behaviors surrounding the High God are a particularly clear example of the eternal return.

Shamanism

Overview

Eliade's scholarly work includes a well-known study of shamanism, *Shamanism: Archaic Techniques of Ecstasy*, a survey of shamanistic practices in different areas. His *Myths, Dreams and Mysteries* also addresses shamanism in some detail.

In *Shamanism*, Eliade argues for a restrictive use of the word *shaman*: it should not apply to just any magician or medicine man, as that would make the term redundant; at the same time, he argues against restricting the term to the practitioners of the sacred of Siberia and Central Asia (it is from one of the titles for this function, namely, *šamán*, considered by Eliade to be of Tungusic origin, that the term itself was introduced into Western languages).[134] Eliade defines a shaman as follows:

> he is believed to cure, like all doctors, and to perform miracles of the fakir type, like all magicians [...] But beyond this, he is a psychopomp, and he may also be a priest, mystic, and poet.[135]

A shaman performing a ceremonial in Tuva.

If we define shamanism this way, Eliade claims, we find that the term covers a collection of phenomena that share a common and unique "structure" and "history".[135] (When thus defined, shamanism tends to occur in its purest forms in hunting and pastoral societies like those of Siberia and Central Asia, which revere a celestial High God "on the way to becoming a *deus otiosus*".[136] Eliade takes the shamanism of those regions as his most representative example.)

In his examinations of shamanism, Eliade emphasizes the shaman's attribute of regaining man's condition before the "Fall" out of sacred time: "The most representative mystical experience of the archaic societies, that of shamanism, betrays the *Nostalgia for Paradise*, the desire to recover the state of freedom and beatitude before 'the Fall'."[133] This concern—which, by itself, is the concern of almost all religious behavior, according to Eliade—manifests itself in specific ways in shamanism.

Death, resurrection and secondary functions

According to Eliade, one of the most common shamanistic themes is the shaman's supposed death and resurrection. This occurs in particular during his initiation.[137] Often, the procedure is supposed to be performed by spirits who dismember the shaman and strip the flesh from his bones, then put him back together and revive him. In more than one way, this death and resurrection represents the shaman's elevation above human nature.

First, the shaman dies so that he can rise above human nature on a quite literal level. After he has been dismembered by the initiatory spirits, they often replace his old organs with new, magical ones (the shaman dies to his profane self so that he can rise again as a new, sanctified, being).[138] Second, by being reduced to his bones, the shaman experiences rebirth on a more symbolic level: in many hunting and herding societies, the bone represents the source of life, so reduction to a skeleton "is equivalent to re-entering the womb of this primordial life, that is, to a complete renewal, a mystical rebirth".[139] Eliade considers this return to the source of life essentially equivalent to the eternal return.[140]

Third, the shamanistic phenomenon of repeated death and resurrection also represents a transfiguration in other ways. The shaman dies not once but many times: having died during initiation and risen again with new powers, the shaman can send his spirit out of his body on errands; thus, his whole career consists of repeated deaths and resurrections. The shaman's new ability to die and return to life shows that he is no longer bound by the laws of profane time, particularly the law of death: "the ability to 'die' and come to life again [...] denotes that [the shaman] has surpassed the human condition".[141]

Having risen above the human condition, the shaman is not bound by the flow of history. Therefore, he enjoys the conditions of the mythical age. In many myths, humans can speak with animals; and, after their initiations, many shamans claim to be able to communicate with animals. According to Eliade, this is one manifestation of the shaman's return to "the *illud tempus* described to us by the paradisiac myths".[142]

The shaman can descend to the underworld or ascend to heaven, often by climbing the World Tree, the cosmic pillar, the sacred ladder, or some other form of the *axis mundi*.[143] Often, the shaman will ascend to heaven to speak with the High God. Because the gods (particularly the High God, according to Eliade's *deus otiosus* concept) were closer to humans during the mythical age, the shaman's easy communication with the High God represents an abolition of history and a return to the mythical age.[133]

Because of his ability to communicate with the gods and descend to the land of the dead, the shaman frequently functions as a psychopomp and a medicine man.[135]

Eliade's philosophy

Early contributions

In addition to his political essays, the young Mircea Eliade authored others, philosophical in content. Connected with the ideology of *Trăirism*, they were often prophetic in tone, and saw Eliade being hailed as a herald by various representatives of his generation.[7] When Eliade was 21 years old and publishing his *Itinerar spiritual*, literary critic Şerban Cioculescu described him as "the column leader of the spiritually mystical and Orthodox youth."[7] Cioculescu discussed his "impressive erudition", but argued that it was "occasionally plethoric, poetically inebriating itself through abuse".[7] Cioculescu's colleague Perpessicius saw the young author and his generation as marked by "the specter of war", a notion he connected to various essays of the 1920s and 30s in which Eliade threatened the world with the verdict that a new conflict was looming (while asking that young people be allowed to manifest their will and fully experience freedom before perishing).[7]

One of Eliade's noted contributions in this respect was the 1932 *Soliloquii* ("Soliloquies"), which explored existential philosophy. George Călinescu who saw in it "an echo of Nae Ionescu's lectures",[144] traced a parallel with the essays of another of Ionescu's disciples, Emil Cioran, while noting that Cioran's were "of a more exulted tone and written in the aphoristic form of Kierkegaard".[145] Călinescu recorded Eliade's rejection of objectivity, citing the author's stated indifference towards any "naïveté" or "contradictions" that the reader could possibly reproach him, as well as his dismissive thoughts of "theoretical data" and mainstream philosophy in general (Eliade saw the latter as "inert, infertile and pathogenic").[144] Eliade thus argued, "a sincere brain is unassailable, for it denies itself to any relationship with outside truths."[146]

The young writer was however careful to clarify that the existence he took into consideration was not the life of "instincts and personal idiosyncrasies", which he believed determined the lives of many humans, but that of a distinct set comprising "personalities".[146] He described "personalities" as characterized by both "purpose" and "a much more complicated and dangerous alchemy".[146] This differentiation, George Călinescu believed, echoed Ionescu's metaphor of man, seen as "the only animal who can fail at living", and the duck, who "shall remain a duck no matter what it does".[147] According to Eliade, the purpose of personalities is infinity: "consciously and gloriously bringing [existence] to waste, into as many skies as possible, continuously fulfilling and polishing oneself, seeking ascent and not circumference."[146]

In Eliade's view, two roads await man in this process. One is glory, determined by either work or procreation, and the other the asceticism of religion or magic—both, Călinescu believed, where aimed at reaching the absolute, even in those cases where Eliade described the latter as an "abyssal experience" into which man may take the plunge.[144] The critic pointed out that the addition of "a magical solution" to the options taken into consideration seemed to be Eliade's own original contributions to his mentor's philosophy, and proposed that it may have owed inspiration to Julius Evola and his disciples.[144] He also recorded that Eliade applied this concept to human creation, and specifically to artistic creation, citing him describing the latter as "a magical joy, the victorious break of the iron circle" (a reflection of *imitatio dei*, having salvation for its ultimate goal).[144]

Philosopher of religion

Anti-reductionism and the "transconscious"

By profession, Eliade was a historian of religion. However, his scholarly works draw heavily on philosophical and psychological terminology. In addition, they contain a number of philosophical arguments about religion. In particular, Eliade often implies the existence of a universal psychological or spiritual "essence" behind all religious phenomena.[148] Because of these arguments, some have accused Eliade of over-generalization and "essentialism", or even of promoting a theological agenda under the guise of historical scholarship. However, others argue that Eliade is better understood as a scholar who is willing to openly discuss sacred experience and its consequences.[149]

In studying religion, Eliade rejects certain "reductionist" approaches.[150] Eliade thinks a religious phenomenon cannot be reduced to a product of culture and history. He insists that, although religion involves "the social man, the economic man, and so forth", nonetheless "all these conditioning factors together do not, of themselves, add up to the life of the spirit".[151]

Using this anti-reductionist position, Eliade argues against those who accuse him of overgeneralizing, of looking for universals at the expense of particulars. Eliade admits that every religious phenomenon is shaped by the particular culture and history that produced it:

> When the Son of God incarnated and became the Christ, he had to speak Aramaic; he could only conduct himself as a Hebrew of his times [...] His religious message, however universal it might be, was conditioned by the past and present history of the Hebrew people. If the Son of God had been born in India, his spoken language would have had to conform itself to the structure of the Indian languages.[151]

However, Eliade argues against those he calls "historicist or existentialist philosophers" who do not recognize "man in general" behind particular men produced by particular situations[151] (Eliade cites Immanuel Kant as the likely forerunner of this kind of "historicism").[152] He adds that human consciousness transcends (is not reducible to) its historical and cultural conditioning,[153] and even suggests the possibility of a "transconscious".[154] By this, Eliade does not necessarily mean anything supernatural or mystical: within the "transconscious", he places religious motifs, symbols, images, and nostalgias that are supposedly universal and whose causes therefore cannot be reduced to historical and cultural conditioning.[155]

Platonism and "primitive ontology"

According to Eliade, traditional man feels that things "acquire their reality, their identity, only to the extent of their participation in a transcendent reality".[84] To traditional man, the profane world is "meaningless", and a thing rises out of the profane world only by conforming to an ideal, mythical model.[156]

Eliade describes this view of reality as a fundamental part of "primitive ontology" (the study of "existence" or "reality").[156] Here he sees a similarity with the philosophy of Plato, who believed that physical phenomena are pale and transient imitations of eternal models or "Forms" (*see Theory of forms*). He argued:

> Plato could be regarded as the outstanding philosopher of 'primitive mentality,' that is, as the thinker who succeeded in giving philosophic currency and validity to the modes of life and behavior of archaic humanity.[156]

Eliade thinks the Platonic *Theory of forms* is "primitive ontology" persisting in Greek philosophy. He claims that Platonism is the "most fully elaborated" version of this primitive ontology.[157]

In *The Structure of Religious Knowing: Encountering the Sacred in Eliade and Lonergan*, John Daniel Dadosky argues that, by making this statement, Eliade was acknowledging "indebtedness to Greek philosophy in general, and to Plato's theory of forms specifically, for his own theory of archetypes and repetition".[158] However, Dadosky also states that "one should be cautious when trying to assess Eliade's indebtedness to Plato".[159] Dadosky quotes Robert Segal, a professor of religion, who draws a distinction between Platonism and Eliade's "primitive ontology": for Eliade, the ideal models are patterns that a person or object may or may not imitate; for Plato, there is a Form for everything, and everything imitates a Form by the very fact that it exists.[160]

Existentialism and secularism

Behind the diverse cultural forms of different religions, Eliade proposes a universal: traditional man, he claims, "always believes that there is an absolute reality, *the sacred*, which transcends this world but manifests itself in this world, thereby sanctifying it and making it real".[161] Furthermore, traditional man's behavior gains purpose and meaning through the Sacred: "By imitating divine behavior, man puts and keeps himself close to the gods—that is, in the real and the significant."[162]

According to Eliade, "modern nonreligious man assumes a new existential situation".[161] For traditional man, historical events gain significance by imitating sacred, transcendent events. In contrast, nonreligious man lacks sacred models for how history or human behavior should be, so he must decide on his own how history should proceed—he "regards himself solely as the subject and agent of history, and refuses all appeal to transcendence".[163] From the standpoint of religious thought, the world has an objective purpose established by mythical events, to which man should conform himself: "Myth teaches [religious man] the primordial 'stories' that have constituted him existentially."[164] From the standpoint of secular thought, any purpose must be invented and imposed on the world by man. Because of this new "existential situation", Eliade argues, the Sacred becomes the primary obstacle to nonreligious man's "freedom". In viewing himself as the proper maker of history, nonreligious man resists all notions of an externally (for instance, divinely) imposed order or model he must obey: modern man "*makes himself*, and he only makes himself completely in proportion as he desacralizes himself and the world. [...] He will not truly be free until he has killed the last god".[163]

Religious survivals in the secular world

Eliade says that secular man cannot escape his bondage to religious thought. By its very nature, secularism depends on religion for its sense of identity: by resisting sacred models, by insisting that man make history on his own, secular man identifies himself only through opposition to religious thought: "He [secular man] recognizes himself in proportion as he 'frees' and 'purifies' himself from the 'superstitions' of his ancestors."[165] Furthermore, modern man "still retains a large stock of camouflaged myths and degenerated rituals".[166] For example, modern social events still have similarities to traditional initiation rituals, and modern novels feature mythical motifs and themes.[167] Finally, secular man still participates in something like the eternal return: by reading modern literature, "modern man succeeds in obtaining an 'escape from time' comparable to the 'emergence from time' effected by myths".[168]

Eliade sees traces of religious thought even in secular academia. He thinks modern scientists are motivated by the religious desire to return to the sacred time of origins:

> One could say that the anxious search for the origins of Life and Mind; the fascination in the 'mysteries of Nature'; the urge to penetrate and decipher the inner structure of Matter—all these longings and drives denote a sort of nostalgia for the primordial, for the original universal *matrix*. Matter, Substance, represents the *absolute origin*, the beginning of all things.[169]

Eliade believes the rise of materialism in the 19th century forced the religious nostalgia for "origins" to express itself in science. He mentions his own field of History of Religions as one of the fields that was obsessed with origins during the 19th century:

> The new discipline of History of Religions developed rapidly in this cultural context. And, of course, it followed a like pattern: the positivistic approach to the facts and the search for origins, for the very beginning of religion.

> All Western historiography was during that time obsessed with the quest of *origins*. [...] This search for the origins of human institutions and cultural creations prolongs and completes the naturalist's quest for the origin of species, the biologist's dream of grasping the origin of life, the geologist's and the astronomer's endeavor to understand the origin of the Earth and the Universe. From a psychological point of view, one can decipher here the same nostalgia for the 'primordial' and the 'original'.[170]

In some of his writings, Eliade describes modern political ideologies as secularized mythology. According to Eliade, Marxism "takes up and carries on one of the great eschatological myths of the Middle Eastern and Mediterranean world, namely: the redemptive part to be played by the Just (the 'elect', the 'anointed', the 'innocent', the 'missioners', in our own days the proletariat), whose sufferings are invoked to change the ontological status of the world."[171] Eliade sees the widespread myth of the Golden Age, "which, according to a number of traditions, lies at the beginning and the end of History", as the "precedent" for Karl Marx's vision of a classless society.[172] Finally, he sees Marx's belief in the final triumph of the good (the proletariat) over the evil (the bourgeoisie) as "a truly messianic Judaeo-Christian ideology".[172] Despite Marx's hostility toward religion, Eliade implies, his ideology works within a conceptual framework inherited from religious mythology.

Likewise, Eliade notes that Nazism involved a pseudo-pagan mysticism based on ancient Germanic religion. He suggests that the differences between the Nazis' pseudo-Germanic mythology and Marx's pseudo-Judaeo-Christian mythology explain their differing success:

In comparison with the vigorous optimism of the communist myth, the mythology propagated by the national socialists seems particularly inept; and this is not only because of the limitations of the racial myth (how could one imagine that the rest of Europe would voluntarily accept submission to the master-race?), but above all because of the fundamental pessimism of the Germanic mythology. [...] For the eschaton prophesied and expected by the ancient Germans was the ragnarok--that is, a catastrophic end of the world.[172]

Modern man and the "Terror of history"

According to Eliade, modern man displays "traces" of "mythological behavior" because he intensely needs sacred time and the eternal return.[173] Despite modern man's claims to be nonreligious, he ultimately cannot find value in the linear progression of historical events; even modern man feels the "Terror of history": "Here too [...] there is always the struggle against Time, the hope to be freed from the weight of 'dead Time,' of the Time that crushes and kills."[174]

According to Eliade, this "terror of history" becomes especially acute when violent and threatening historical events confront modern man—the mere fact that a terrible event has happened, that it is part of history, is of little comfort to those who suffer from it. Eliade asks rhetorically how modern man can "tolerate the catastrophes and horrors of history—from collective deportations and massacres to atomic bombings—if beyond them he can glimpse no sign, no transhistorical meaning".[175]

Eliade indicates that, if repetitions of mythical events provided sacred value and meaning for history in the eyes of ancient man, modern man has denied the Sacred and must therefore invent value and purpose on his own. Without the Sacred to confer an absolute, objective value upon historical events, modern man is left with "a relativistic or nihilistic view of history" and a resulting "spiritual aridity".[176] In chapter 4 ("The Terror of History") of *The Myth of the Eternal Return* and chapter 9 ("Religious Symbolism and the Modern Man's Anxiety") of *Myths, Dreams, and Mysteries*, Eliade argues at length that the rejection of religious thought is a primary cause of modern man's anxieties.

Inter-cultural dialogue and a "new humanism"

Eliade argues that modern man may escape the "Terror of history" by learning from traditional cultures. For example, Eliade thinks Hinduism has advice for modern Westerners. According to many branches of Hinduism, the world of historical time is illusory, and the only absolute reality is the immortal soul or *atman* within man. According to Eliade, Hindus thus escape the terror of history by refusing to see historical time as the true reality.[177]

Eliade notes that a Western or Continental philosopher might feel suspicious toward this Hindu view of history:

> One can easily guess what a European historical and existentialist philosopher might reply [...] You ask me, he would say, to 'die to History'; but man is not, and he *cannot be* anything else but History, for his very essence is temporality. You are asking me, then, to give up my authentic existence and to take refuge in an abstraction, in pure Being, in the *atman*: I am to sacrifice my dignity as a creator of History in order to live an a-historic, inauthentic existence, empty of all human content. Well, I prefer to put up with my anxiety: at least, it cannot deprive me of a certain heroic grandeur, that of becoming conscious of, and accepting, the human condition.[178]

However, Eliade argues that the Hindu approach to history does not necessarily lead to a rejection of history. On the contrary, in Hinduism historical human existence is not the "absurdity" that many Continental philosophers see it as.[178] According to Hinduism, history is a divine creation, and one may live contentedly within it as long as one maintains a certain degree of detachment from it: "One is devoured by Time, by History, not because one lives in them, but because one thinks them *real* and, in consequence, one forgets or undervalues eternity."[179]

Furthermore, Eliade argues that Westerners can learn from non-Western cultures to see something besides absurdity in suffering and death. Traditional cultures see suffering and death as a rite of passage. In fact, their initiation rituals often involve a symbolic death and resurrection, or symbolic ordeals followed by relief. Thus, Eliade argues, modern man can learn to see his historical ordeals, even death, as necessary initiations into the next stage of one's existence.[180]

Eliade even suggests that traditional thought offers relief from the vague anxiety caused by "our obscure presentiment of the end of the world, or more exactly of the end of *our* world, our *own* civilization".[180] Many traditional cultures have myths about the end of their world or civilization; however, these myths do not succeed "in paralysing either Life or Culture".[180] These traditional cultures emphasize cyclic time and, therefore, the inevitable rise of a new world or civilization on the ruins of the old. Thus, they feel comforted even in contemplating the end times.[181]

Eliade argues that a Western spiritual rebirth can happen within the framework of Western spiritual traditions.[182] However, he says, to start this rebirth, Westerners may need to be stimulated by ideas from non-Western cultures. In his *Myths, Dreams, and Mysteries*, Eliade claims that a "genuine encounter" between cultures "might well constitute the point of departure for a new humanism, upon a world scale".[183]

Christianity and the "salvation" of History

Mircea Eliade sees the Abrahamic religions as a turning point between the ancient, cyclic view of time and the modern, linear view of time, noting that, in their case, sacred events are not limited to a far-off primordial age, but continue throughout history: "time is no longer [only] the circular Time of the Eternal Return; it has become linear and irreversible Time".[184] He thus sees in Christianity the ultimate example of a religion embracing linear, historical time. When God is born as a man, into the stream of history, "all history becomes a theophany".[185] According to Eliade, "Christianity strives to *save* history".[186] In Christianity, the Sacred enters a human being (Christ) to save humans, but it also enters history to "save" history and turn otherwise ordinary, historical events into something "capable of transmitting a trans-historical message".[186]

From Eliade's perspective, Christianity's "trans-historical message" may be the most important help that modern man could have in confronting the terror of history. In his book *Mito* ("Myth"), Italian researcher Furio Jesi argues that Eliade denies man the position of a true protagonist in history: for Eliade, true human experience lies not in intellectually "making history", but in man's experiences of joy and grief. Thus, from Eliade's perspective, the Christ story becomes the perfect myth for modern man.[187] In Christianity, God willingly entered historical time by being born as Christ, and accepted the suffering that followed. By identifying with Christ, modern man can learn to confront painful historical events.[187] Ultimately, according to Jesi, Eliade sees Christianity as the only religion that can save man from the "Terror of history".[188]

In Eliade's view, traditional man sees time as an endless repetition of mythical archetypes. In contrast, modern man has abandoned mythical archetypes and entered linear, historical time—in this context, unlike many other religions, Christianity attributes value to historical time. Thus, Eliade concludes, "Christianity incontestably proves to be the religion of 'fallen man'", of modern man who has lost "the paradise of archetypes and repetition".[189]

"Modern gnosticism", Romanticism and Eliade's nostalgia

In analyzing the similarities between the "mythologists" Eliade, Joseph Campbell and Carl Jung, Robert Ellwood concluded that the three modern mythologists, all of whom believed that myths reveal "timeless truth",[190] fulfilled the role "gnostics" had in antiquity. The diverse religious movements covered by the term "gnosticism" share the basic doctrines that the surrounding world is fundamentally evil or inhospitable, that we are trapped in the world through no fault of our own, and that we can be saved from the world only through secret knowledge (*gnosis*).[191] Ellwood claimed that the three mythologists were "modern gnostics through and through",[192] remarking,

> Whether in Augustan Rome or modern Europe, democracy all too easily gave way to totalitarianism, technology was as readily used for battle as for comfort, and immense wealth lay alongside abysmal poverty. [...] Gnostics past and present sought answers not in the course of outward human events, but in knowledge of the world's beginning, of what lies above and beyond the world, and of the secret places of the human soul. To all this the mythologists spoke, and they acquired large and loyal followings.[193]

According to Ellwood, the mythologists believed in gnosticism's basic doctrines (even if in a secularized form). Ellwood also believes that Romanticism, which stimulated the modern study of mythology,[194] strongly influenced the mythologists. Because Romantics stress that emotion and imagination have the same dignity as reason, Ellwood argues, they tend to think political truth "is known less by rational considerations than by its capacity to fire the passions" and, therefore, that political truth is "very apt to be found [...] in the distant past".[194]

As modern gnostics, Ellwood argues, the three mythologists felt alienated from the surrounding modern world. As scholars, they knew of primordial societies that had operated differently than the modern world. And as people influenced by Romanticism, they saw myths as a saving *gnosis* that offered "avenues of eternal return to simpler primordial ages when the values that rule the world were forged".[195]

In addition, Ellwood identifies Eliade's personal sense of nostalgia as a source for his interest in, or even his theories about, traditional societies.[196] He cites Eliade himself claiming to desire an "eternal return" like that by which traditional man returns to the mythical paradise: "My essential preoccupation is precisely the means of escaping History, of saving myself through symbol, myth, rite, archetypes".[197]

In Ellwood's view, Eliade's nostalgia was only enhanced by his exile from Romania: "In later years Eliade felt about his own Romanian past as did primal folk about mythic time. He was drawn back to it, yet he knew he could not live there, and that all was not well with it."[198] He suggests that this nostalgia, along with Eliade's sense that "exile is among the profoundest metaphors for all human life",[199] influenced Eliade's theories. Ellwood sees evidence of this in Eliade's concept of the "Terror of history" from which modern man is no longer shielded.[200] In this concept, Ellwood sees an "element of nostalgia" for earlier times "when the sacred was strong and the terror of history had barely raised its head".[201]

Criticism of Eliade's scholarship

Overgeneralization

Eliade cites a wide variety of myths and rituals to support his theories. However, he has been accused of making over-generalizations: many scholars think he lacks sufficient evidence to put forth his ideas as universal, or even general, principles of religious thought. According to one scholar, "Eliade may have been the most popular and influential contemporary historian of religion", but "many, if not most, specialists in anthropology, sociology, and even history of religions have either ignored or quickly dismissed" Eliade's works.[202]

The classicist G. S. Kirk criticizes Eliade's insistence that Australian Aborigines and ancient Mesopotamians had concepts of "being", "non-being", "real", and "becoming", although they lacked words for them. Kirk also believes that Eliade overextends his theories: for example, Eliade claims that the modern myth of the "noble savage" results from the religious tendency to idealize the primordial, mythical age.[203] According to Kirk, "such extravagances, together with a marked repetitiousness, have made Eliade unpopular with many anthropologists and sociologists".[203] In Kirk's view, Eliade derived his theory of eternal return from the functions of Australian Aboriginal mythology and then proceeded to apply the theory to other mythologies to which it did not apply. For example, Kirk argues that the eternal return does not accurately describe the functions of Native American or Greek mythology.[204] Kirk concludes, "Eliade's idea is a valuable perception about certain myths, not a guide to the proper understanding of all of them".[205]

Even Wendy Doniger, Eliade's successor at the University of Chicago, claims (in an introduction to Eliade's own *Shamanism*) that the eternal return does not apply to all myths and rituals, although it may apply to many of them.[1] However, although Doniger agrees that Eliade made over-generalizations, she notes that his willingness to "argue boldly for universals" allowed him to see patterns "that spanned the entire globe and the whole of human history".[206] Whether they were true or not, she argues, Eliade's theories are still useful "as starting points for the comparative study of religion". She also argues that Eliade's theories have been able to accommodate "new data to which Eliade did not have access".[207]

Lack of empirical support

Several researchers have criticized Eliade's work as having no empirical support. Thus, he is said to have "failed to provide an adequate methodology for the history of religions and to establish this discipline as an empirical science",[208] though the same critics admit that "the history of religions should not aim at being an empirical science anyway".[208] Specifically, his claim that the sacred is a structure of human consciousness is distrusted as not being empirically provable: "no one has yet turned up the basic category *sacred*".[209] Also, there has been mention of his tendency to ignore the social aspects of religion.[52] Anthropologist Alice Kehoe is highly critical of Eliade's work on Shamanism, namely because he was not an anthropologist but a historian. She contends that Eliade never did any field work or contacted any indigenous groups that practiced Shamanism, and that his work was synthesized from various sources without being supported by direct field research.[210]

In contrast, Professor Kees W. Bolle of the University of California, Los Angeles argues that "Professor Eliade's approach, in all his works, is empirical":[211] Bolle sets Eliade apart for what he sees as Eliade's particularly close "attention to the various particular motifs" of different myths.[211] French researcher Daniel Dubuisson places doubt on Eliade's scholarship and its scientific character, citing the Romanian academic's alleged refusal to accept the treatment of religions in their historical and cultural context, and proposing that Eliade's notion of *hierophany* refers to the actual existence of a supernatural level.[59]

Ronald Inden, a historian of India and University of Chicago professor, criticized Mircea Eliade, alongside other intellectual figures (Carl Jung and Joseph Campbell among them), for an encouraging a "romantic view" of Hinduism.[212] He argued that their approach to the subject relied mainly on an Orientalist approach, and made Hinduism seem like "a private realm of the imagination and the religious which modern, Western man lacks but needs."[212]

Far right and nationalist influences

Although his scholarly work was never subordinated to his early political beliefs, the school of thought he was associated with in interwar Romania, namely *Trăirism*, as well as the works of Julius Evola he continued to draw inspiration from, have thematic links to fascism.[37][59][213] Writer and academic Marcel Tolcea has argued that, through Evola's particular interpretation of Guénon's works, Eliade kept a traceable connection with far right ideologies in his academic contributions.[37] Daniel Dubuisson singled out Eliade's concept of *homo religiosus* as a reflection of fascist elitism, and argued that the Romanian scholar's views of Judaism and the Old Testament, which depicted Hebrews as the enemies of an ancient cosmic religion, were ultimately the preservation of an antisemitic discourse.[59]

A piece authored in 1930 saw Eliade defining Julius Evola as a great thinker and offering praise to the controversial intellectuals Oswald Spengler, Arthur de Gobineau, Houston Stewart Chamberlain and the Nazi ideologue Alfred Rosenberg.[59] Evola, who continued to defend the core principles of mystical fascism, once protested to Eliade about the latter's failure to cite him and Guénon. Eliade replied that his works were written for a contemporary public, and not to initiates of esoteric circles.[214] After the 1960s, he, together with Evola, Louis Rougier, and other intellectuals, offered support to Alain de Benoist's controversial *Groupement de recherche et d'études pour la civilisation européenne*, part of the *Nouvelle Droite* intellectual trend.[215]

Notably, Eliade was also preoccupied with the cult of Zalmoxis and its supposed monotheism.[216][217] This, like his conclusion that Romanization had been superficial inside Roman Dacia, was a view celebrated by contemporary partisans of Protochronist nationalism.[52][216] According to historian Sorin Antohi, Eliade may have actually encouraged Protochronists such as Edgar Papu to carry out research which resulted in the claim that medieval Romanians had anticipated the Renaissance.[218]

In his study of Eliade, Jung, and Campbell, Ellwood also discusses the connection between academic theories and controversial political involvements, noting that all three mythologists have been accused of reactionary political positions. Ellwood notes the obvious parallel between the conservatism of myth, which speaks of a primordial golden age, and the conservatism of far right politics.[219] However, Ellwood argues that the explanation is more complex than that. Wherever their political sympathies may have sometimes been, he claims, the three mythologists were often "apolitical if not antipolitical, scorning any this-worldly salvation".[220] Moreover, the connection between mythology and politics differs for each of the mythologists in question: in Eliade's case, Ellwood believes, a strong sense of nostalgia ("for childhood, for historical times past, for cosmic religion, for paradise"),[81] influenced not only the scholar's academic interests, but also his political views.

Because Eliade stayed out of politics during his later life, Ellwood tries to extract an implicit political philosophy from Eliade's scholarly works. Ellwood argues that the later Eliade's nostalgia for ancient traditions did not make him a political reactionary, even a quiet one. He concludes that the later Eliade was, in fact, a "radical modernist".[221] According to Ellwood,

> Those who see Eliade's fascination with the primordial as merely reactionary in the ordinary political or religious sense of the word do not understand the mature Eliade in a sufficiently radical way. [...] Tradition was not for him exactly Burkean 'prescription' or sacred trust to be kept alive generation after generation, for Eliade was fully aware that tradition, like men and nations, lives only by changing and even occultation. The tack is not to try fruitlessly to keep it unchanging, but to discover where it is hiding.[221]

According to Eliade, religious elements survive in secular culture, but in new, "camouflaged" forms.[222] Thus, Ellwood believes that the later Eliade probably thought modern man should preserve elements of the past, but should not try to restore their original form through reactionary politics.[223] He suspects that Eliade would have favored "a minimal rather than a maximalist state" that would allow personal spiritual transformation without enforcing it.[224]

Many scholars have accused Eliade of "essentialism", a type of over-generalization in which one incorrectly attributes a common "essence" to a whole group—in this case, all "religious" or "traditional" societies. Furthermore, some see a connection between Eliade's essentialism with regard to religion and fascist essentialism with regard to races and nations.[225] To Ellwood, this connection "seems rather tortured, in the end amounting to little more than an *ad hominem* argument which attempts to tar Eliade's entire [scholarly] work with the ill-repute all decent people feel for storm troopers and the Iron Guard".[225] However, Ellwood admits that common tendencies in "mythological thinking" may have caused Eliade, as well as Jung and Campbell, to view certain groups in an "essentialist" way, and that this may explain their purported antisemitism: "A tendency to think in generic terms of peoples, races, religions, or parties, which as we shall see is undoubtedly the profoundest flaw in mythological thinking, including that of such modern mythologists as our three, can connect with nascent anti-Semitism, or the connection can be the other way."[226]

Literary works

Generic traits

Many of Mircea Eliade's literary works, in particular his earliest ones, are noted for their eroticism and their focus on subjective experience. Modernist in style, they have drawn comparisons to the contemporary writings of Mihail Sebastian,[227] I. Valerian,[228] and Ion Biberi.[229] Alongside Honoré de Balzac and Giovanni Papini, his literary passions included Aldous Huxley and Miguel de Unamuno,[27] as well as André Gide.[7] Eliade also read with interest the prose of Romain Rolland, Henrik Ibsen, and the Enlightenment thinkers Voltaire and Denis Diderot.[7] As a youth, he read the works of Romanian authors such as Liviu Rebreanu and Panait Istrati; initially, he was also interested in Ionel Teodoreanu's prose works, but later rejected them and criticized their author.[7]

Investigating the works' main characteristics, George Călinescu stressed that Eliade owed much of his style to the direct influence of French author André Gide, concluding that, alongside Camil Petrescu and a few others, Eliade was among Gide's leading disciples in Romanian literature.[4] He commented that, like Gide, Eliade believed that the artist "does not take a stand, but experiences good and evil while setting himself free from both, maintaining an intact curiosity."[4] A specific aspect of this focus on experience is sexual experimentation—Călinescu notes that Eliade's fiction works tend to depict a male figure "possessing all practicable women in [a given] family".[230] He also considered that, as a rule, Eliade depicts woman as "a basic means for a sexual experience and repudiated with harsh egotism."[230]

For Călinescu, such a perspective on life culminated in "banality", leaving authors gripped by the "cult of the self" and "a contempt for literature".[4] Polemically, Călinescu proposed that Mircea Eliade's supposed focus on "aggressive youth" and served to instill his interwar Romanian writers with the idea that they had a common destiny as a generation apart.[4] He also commented that, when set in Romania, Mircea Eliade's stories lacked the "perception of immediate reality", and, analyzing the non-traditional names the writer tended to ascribe to his Romanian characters, that they did not depict "specificity".[231] Additionally, in Călinescu's view, Eliade's stories were often "sensationalist compositions of the illustrated magazine kind."[232] Mircea Eliade's assessment of his own pre-1940 literary contributions oscillated between expressions of pride[26] and the bitter verdict that they were written for "an audience of little ladies and high school students".[58]

A secondary but unifying feature present in most of Eliade's stories is their setting, a magical and part-fictional Bucharest.[6] In part, they also serve to illustrate or allude to Eliade's own research in the field of religion, as well as to the concepts he introduced.[6] Thus, commentators such as Matei Călinescu and Carmen Muşat have also argued that a main characteristic of Eliade's fantasy prose is a substitution between the supernatural and the mundane: in this interpretation, Eliade turns the daily world into an incomprehensible place, while the intrusive supernatural aspect promises to offer the sense of life.[233] The notion was in turn linked to Eliade's own thoughts on transcendence, and in particular his idea that, once "camouflaged" in life or history, miracles become "unrecognizable".[233]

Oriental themed novels

One of Eliade's earliest fiction writings, the controversial first-person narrative *Isabel şi apele diavolului*, focused on the figure of a young and brilliant academic, whose self-declared fear is that of "being common".[234] The hero's experience is recorded in "notebooks", which are compiled to form the actual narrative, and which serve to record his unusual, mostly sexual, experiences in British India—the narrator describes himself as dominated by "a devilish indifference" towards "all things having to do with art or metaphysics", focusing instead on eroticism.[234] The guest of a pastor, the scholar ponders sexual adventures with his host's wife, servant girl, and finally with his daughter Isabel. Persuading the pastor's adolescent son to run away from home, becoming the sexual initiator of a twelve-year-old girl and the lover of a much older woman, the character also attempts to seduce Isabel. Although she falls in love, the young woman does not give in to his pressures, but eventually allows herself to be abused and impregnated by another character, letting the object of her affection know that she had thought of him all along.[235]

One of Eliade's best-known works, the novel *Maitreyi*, dwells on Eliade's own experience, comprising camouflaged details of his relationships with Surendranath Dasgupta and Dasgupta's daughter Maitreyi Devi. The main character, Allan, is an Englishman who visits the Indian engineer Narendra Sen and courts his daughter, herself known as Maitreyi. The narrative is again built on "notebooks" to which Allan adds his comments. This technique Călinescu describes as "boring", and its result "cynical".[235]

Allan himself stands alongside Eliade's male characters, whose focus is on action, sensation and experience—his chaste contacts with Maitreyi are encouraged by Sen, who hopes for a marriage which is nonetheless abhorred by his would-be European son-in-law.[235] Instead, Allan is fascinated to discover Maitreyi's Oriental version of Platonic love, marked by spiritual attachment more than by physical contact.[236] However, their affair soon after turns physical, and she decides to attach herself to Allan as one would to a husband, in what is an informal and intimate wedding ceremony (which sees her vowing her love and invoking an earth goddess as the seal of union).[231] Upon discovering this, Narendra Sen becomes enraged, rejecting their guest and keeping Maitreyi in confinement. As a result, his daughter decides to have intercourse with a lowly stranger, becoming pregnant in the hope that her parents would consequently allow her to marry her lover. However, the story also casts doubt on her earlier actions, reflecting rumors that Maitreyi was not a virgin at the time she and Allan first met, which also seems to expose her father as a hypocrite.[231]

George Călinescu objected to the narrative, arguing that both the physical affair and the father's rage seemed artificial, while commenting that Eliade placing doubt on his Indian characters' honesty had turned the plot into a piece of "ethnological humor".[231] Noting that the work developed on a classical theme of miscegenation, which recalled the prose of François-René de Chateaubriand and Pierre Loti,[235] the critic proposed that its main merit was in introducing the exotic novel to local literature.[231]

Mircea Eliade's other early works include *Şantier* ("Building Site"), a part-novel, part-diary account of his Indian sojourn. George Călinescu objected to its "monotony", and, noting that it featured a set of "intelligent observations", criticized the "banality of its ideological conversations."[231] *Şantier* was also noted for its portrayal of drug addiction and intoxication with opium, both of which could have referred to Eliade's actual travel experience.[65]

Portraits of a generation

In his earliest novel, titled *Novel of the Nearsighted Adolescent* and written in the first person, Eliade depicts his experience through high school.[7] It is proof of the influence exercised on him by the literature of Giovanni Papini, and in particular by Papini's story *Un uomo finito*.[7] Each of its chapters reads like an independent novella, and, in all, the work experiments with the limits traced between novel and diary.[7] Literary critic Eugen Simion called it "the most valuable" among Eliade's earliest literary attempts, but noted that, being "ambitious", the book had failed to achieve "an aesthetically satisfactory format".[7] According to Simion, the innovative intent of the *Novel...* was provided by its technique, by its goal of providing authenticity in depicting experiences, and by its insight into adolescent psychology.[7] The novel notably shows its narrator practicing self-flagellation.[7]

Eliade's 1934 novel *Întoarcerea din rai* ("Return from Paradise") centers on Pavel Anicet, a young man who seeks knowledge through what Călinescu defined as "sexual excess".[231] His search leaves him with a reduced sensitivity: right after being confronted with his father's death, Anicet breaks out in tears only after sitting through an entire dinner.[231] The other characters, standing for Eliade's generation, all seek knowledge through violence or retreat from the world—nonetheless, unlike Anicet, they ultimately fail at imposing rigors upon themselves.[231] Pavel himself eventually abandons his belief in sex as a means for enlightenment, and commits suicide in hopes of reaching the level of primordial unity. The solution, George Călinescu noted, mirrored the strange murder in Gide's *Lafcadio's Adventures*.[231] Eliade himself indicated that the book dealt with the "loss of the beatitude, illusions, and optimism that had dominated the first twenty years of 'Greater Romania'."[237] Robert Ellwood connected the work to Eliade's recurring sense of loss in respect to the "atmosphere of euphoria and faith" of his adolescence.[198] Călinescu criticizes *Întoarcerea din rai*, describing its dialog sequences as "awkward", its narrative as "void", and its artistic interest as "non-existent", proposing that the reader could however find it relevant as the "document of a mentality".[231]

The lengthy novel *Huliganii* ("The Hooligans") is intended as the fresco of a family, and, through it, that of an entire generation. The book's main protagonist, Petru Anicet, is a composer who places value in experiments; other characters include Dragu, who considers "a hooligan's experience" as "the only fertile debut into life", and the totalitarian Alexandru Pleşa, who is on the search for "the heroic life" by enlisting youth in "perfect regiments, equally intoxicated by a collective myth."[238][239] Călinescu thought that the young male characters all owed inspiration to Fyodor Dostoevsky's Rodion Romanovich Raskolnikov (*see Crime and Punishment*).[230] Anicet, who partly shares Pleşa's vision for a collective experiment, is also prone to sexual adventures, and seduces the women of the Lecca family (who have hired him as a piano teacher).[230] Romanian-born novelist Norman Manea called Anicet's experiment: "the paraded defiance of bourgeois conventions, in which venereal disease and lubricity dwell together."[238] In one episode of the book, Anicet convinces Anişoara Lecca to gratuitously steal from her parents—an outrage which leads her mother to moral decay and, eventually, to suicide.[230] George Călinescu criticized the book for inconsistencies and "excesses in Dostoyevskianism", but noted that the Lecca family portrayal was "suggestive", and that the dramatic scenes were written with "a remarkable poetic calm."[230]

The novel *Nuntă în cer* depicts the correspondence between two male friends, an artist and a common man, who complain to each other about their failures in love: the former complains about a lover who wanted his children when he did not, while the other recalls being abandoned by a woman who, despite his intentions, did not want to become pregnant by him. Eliade lets the reader understand that they are in fact talking about the same woman.[232]

Fantasy literature

Mircea Eliade's earliest works, most of which were published at later stages, belong to the fantasy genre. One of the first such literary exercises to be printed, the 1921 *Cum am găsit piatra filosofală*, showed its adolescent author's interest in themes that he was to explore throughout his career, in particular esotericism and alchemy.[7] Written in the first person, it depicts an experiment which, for a moment, seems to be the discovery of the philosophers' stone.[7] These early writings also include two sketches for novels: *Minunata călătorie a celor cinci cărăbuşi în ţara furnicilor roşii* ("The Wonderful Journey of the Five Beetles into the Land of the Red Ants") and *Memoriile unui soldat de plumb* ("The Memoirs of a Lead Soldier").[7] In the former, a company of beetle spies is sent among the red ants—their travel offers a setting for satirical commentary.[7] Eliade himself explained that *Memoriile unui soldat de plumb* was an ambitious project, designed as a fresco to include the birth of the Universe, abiogenesis, human evolution, and the entire world history.[7]

Eliade's fantasy novel *Domnişoara Christina*, was, on its own, the topic of a scandal.[230] The novel deals with the fate of an eccentric family, the Moscus, who are haunted by the ghost of a murdered young woman, known as Christina. The apparition shares characteristics with vampires and with *strigoi*: she is believed to be drinking the blood of cattle and that of a young family member.[230] The young man Egor becomes the object of Christina's desire, and is shown to have intercourse with her.[230] Noting that the plot and setting reminded one of horror fiction works by the German author Hanns Heinz Ewers, and defending *Domnişoara Christina* in front of harsher criticism, Călinescu nonetheless argued that the "international environment" in which it took place was "upsetting".[230] He also depicted the plot as focused on "major impurity", summarizing the story's references to necrophilia, menstrual fetish and ephebophilia.[230]

Eliade's short story *Şarpele* ("The Snake") was described by George Călinescu as "hermetic".[230] While on a trip to the forest, several persons witness a feat of magic performed by the male character Andronic, who summons a snake from the bottom of a river and places it on an island. At the end of the story, Andronic and the female character Dorina are found on the island, naked and locked in a sensual embrace.[230] Călinescu saw the piece as an allusion to Gnosticism, to the Kabbalah, and to Babylonian mythology, while linking the snake to the Greek mythological figure and major serpent symbol Ophion.[230] He was however dissatisfied with this introduction of iconic images, describing it as "languishing".[232]

The short story *Un om mare* ("A Big Man"), which Eliade authored during his stay in Portugal, shows a common person, the engineer Cucoanes, who grows steadily and uncontrollably, reaching immense proportions and ultimately disappearing into the wilderness of the Bucegi Mountains.[240] Eliade himself referenced the story and Aldous Huxley's experiments in the same section of his private notes, a matter which allowed Matei Călinescu to propose that *Un om mare* was a direct product of its author's experience with drugs.[65] The same commentator, who deemed *Un om mare* "perhaps Eliade's most memorable short story", connected it with the *uriaşi* characters present in Romanian folklore.[240]

Other writings

Eliade's reinterpreted the Greek mythological figure Iphigeneia in his eponymous 1941 play. Here, the maiden falls in love with Achilles, and accepts to be sacrificed on the pyre as a means to ensure both her lover's happiness (as predicted by an oracle) and her father Agamemnon's victory in the Trojan War.[241] Discussing the association Iphigenia's character makes between love and death, Romanian theater critic Radu Albala noted that it was a possible echo of *Meşterul Manole* legend, in which a builder of the Curtea de Argeş Monastery has to sacrifice his wife in exchange for permission to complete work.[241] In contrast with early renditions of the myth by authors such as Euripides and Jean Racine, Eliade's version ends with the sacrifice being carried out in full.[241]

In addition to his fiction, the exiled Eliade authored several volumes of memoirs and diaries and travel writings. They were published sporadically, and covered various stages of his life. One of the earliest such pieces was *India*, grouping accounts of the travels he made through the Indian subcontinent.[64] Writing for the Spanish journal *La Vanguardia*, commentator Sergio Vila-Sanjuán described the first volume of Eliade's *Autobiography* (covering the years 1907 to 1937) as "a great book", while noting that the other main volume was "more conventional and insincere."[6] In Vila-Sanjuán's view, the texts reveal Mircea Eliade himself as "a Dostoyevskyian character", as well as "an accomplished person, a Goethian figure".[6]

A work that drew particular interest was his *Jurnal portughez* ("Portuguese Diary"), completed during his stay in Lisbon and published only after its author's death. A portion of it dealing with his stay in Romania is believed to have been lost.[5] The travels to Spain, partly recorded in *Jurnal portughez*, also led to a separate volume, *Jurnal cordobez* ("Cordoban Diary"), which Eliade compiled from various independent notebooks.[64] *Jurnal portughez* shows Eliade coping with clinical depression and political crisis, and has been described by Andrei Oişteanu as "an overwhelming [read], through the immense suffering it exhales."[65] Literary historian Paul Cernat argued that part of the volume is "a masterpiece of its time", while concluding that some 700 pages were passable for the "among others" section of Eliade's bibliography.[26] Noting that the book featured parts where Eliade spoke of himself in eulogistic terms, notably comparing himself favorably to Goethe and Romania's national poet Mihai Eminescu, Cernat accused the writer of "egolatry", and deduced that Eliade was "ready to step over dead bodies for the sake of his spiritual 'mission' ".[26] The same passages led philosopher and journalist Cătălin Avramescu to argue that Eliade's behavior was evidence of "megalomania".[58]

Eliade also wrote various essays of literary criticism. In his youth, alongside his study on Julius Evola, he published essays which introduced the Romanian public to representatives of modern Spanish literature and philosophy, among them Adolfo Bonilla San Martín, Miguel de Unamuno, José Ortega y Gasset, Eugeni d'Ors, Vicente Blasco Ibáñez and Marcelino Menéndez y Pelayo.[64] He also wrote an essay on the works of James Joyce, connecting it with his own theories on the eternal return ("[Joyce's literature is] saturated with nostalgia for the myth of the eternal repetition"), and deeming Joyce himself an anti-historicist "archaic" figure among the modernists.[242] In the 1930s, Eliade edited the collected works of Romanian historian Bogdan Petriceicu Hasdeu.[7]

Controversy: antisemitism and links with the Iron Guard

Early statements

The early years in Eliade's public career show him to have been highly tolerant of Jews in general, and of the Jewish minority in Romania in particular. His early condemnation of Nazi antisemitic policies was accompanied by his caution and moderation in regard to Nae Ionescu's various anti-Jewish attacks.[30][243]

Late in the 1930s, Mihail Sebastian was marginalized by Romania's antisemitic policies, and came to reflect on his Romanian friend's association with the far right. The subsequent ideological break between him and Eliade has been compared by writer Gabriela Adameşteanu with that between Jean-Paul Sartre and Albert Camus.[238] In his *Journal*, published long after his 1945 death, Sebastian claimed that Eliade's actions during the 1930s show him to be an antisemite. According to Sebastian, Eliade had been friendly to him until the start of his political commitments, after which he severed all ties.[30][244] Before their friendship came apart, however, Sebastian claimed that he took notes on their conversations (which he later published) during which Eliade was supposed to have expressed antisemitic views. According to Sebastian, Eliade said in 1939:

> The Poles' resistance in Warsaw is a Jewish resistance. Only yids are capable of the blackmail of putting women and children in the front line, to take advantage of the Germans' sense of scruple. The Germans have no interest in the destruction of Romania. Only a pro-German government can save us.... What is happening on the frontier with Bukovina is a scandal, because new waves of Jews are flooding into the country. Rather than a Romania again invaded by kikes, it would be better to have a German protectorate.[245]

The friendship between Eliade and Sebastian drastically declined during the war: the latter writer, fearing for his security during the pro-Nazi Ion Antonescu regime (*see Romania during World War II*), hoped that Eliade, by then a diplomat, could intervene in his favor; however, upon his brief return to Romania, Eliade did not see or approach Sebastian.[6][30]

Later, Mircea Eliade expressed his regret at not having had the chance to redeem his friendship with Sebastian before the latter was killed in a car accident.[26][62] Paul Cernat notes that Eliade's statement includes an admission that he "counted on [Sebastian's] support, in order to get back into Romanian life and culture", and proposes that Eliade may have expected his friend to vouch for him in front of hostile authorities.[26] Some of Sebastian's late recordings in his diary show that their author was reflecting with nostalgia on his relationship with Eliade, and that he deplored the outcome.[6][30]

Eliade provided two distinct explanations for not having met with Sebastian: one was related to his claim of being followed around by the Gestapo, and the other, expressed in his diaries, was that the shame of representing a regime that humiliated Jews had made him avoid facing his former friend.[30] Another take on the matter was advanced in 1972 by the Israeli magazine *Toladot*, who claimed that, as an official representative, Eliade was aware of Antonescu's agreement to implement the Final Solution in Romania and of how this could affect Sebastian (*see Holocaust in Romania*).[30] In addition, rumors were sparked that Sebastian and Nina Mareş had a physical relationship, one which could have contributed to the clash between the two literary figures.[6]

Beyond his involvement with a movement known for its antisemitism, Eliade did not usually comment on Jewish issues. However, an article titled *Piloţii orbi* ("The Blind Pilots"), contributed to the journal *Vremea* in 1936, showed that he supported at least some Iron Guard accusations against the Jewish community:

> Since the war [that is, World War I], Jews have occupied the villages of Maramureş and Bukovina, and gained the absolute majority in the towns and cities in Bessarabia.[246] [...] It would be absurd to expect Jews to resign themselves in order to become a minority with certain rights and very many duties—after they have tasted the honey of power and conquered as many command positions as they have. Jews are currently fighting with all forces to maintain their positions, expecting a future offensive—and, as far as I am concerned, I understand their fight and admire their vitality, tenacity, genius.[247]

One year later, a text, accompanied by his picture, was featured as answer to an inquiry by the Iron Guard's *Buna Vestire* about the reasons he had for supporting the movement. A short section of it summarizes an anti-Jewish attitude:

> Can the Romanian nation end its life in the saddest decay witnessed by history, undermined by misery and syphilis, conquered by Jews and torn to pieces by foreigners, demoralized, betrayed, sold for a few million lei?[30][248]

According to the literary critic Z. Ornea, in the 1980s Eliade denied authorship of the text. He explained the use of his signature, his picture, and the picture's caption, as having been applied by the magazine's editor, Mihail Polihroniade, to a piece the latter had written after having failed to obtain Eliade's contribution; he also claimed that, given his respect for Polihroniade, he had not wished to publicize this matter previously.[249]

Polemics and exile

Dumitru G. Danielopol, a fellow diplomat present in London during Eliade's stay in the city, later stated that the latter had identified himself as "a guiding light of [the Iron Guard] movement" and victim of Carol II's repression.[52] In October 1940, as the National Legionary State came into existence, the British Foreign Office blacklisted Mircea Eliade, alongside other five Romanians, due to his Iron Guard connections and suspicions that he was prepared to spy in favor of Nazi Germany.[75] According to various sources, while in Portugal, the diplomat was also preparing to disseminate propaganda in favor of the Iron Guard.[52] In *Jurnal portughez*, Eliade defines himself as "a Legionary",[6][26] and speaks of his own "Legionary climax" as a stage he had gone through during the early 1940s.[26][30]

The depolitisation of Eliade after the start of his diplomatic career was also mistrusted by his former close friend Eugène Ionesco, who indicated that, upon the close of World War II, Eliade's personal beliefs as communicated to his friends amounted to "all is over now that Communism has won".[250] This forms part of Ionesco's severe and succinct review of the careers of Legionary-inspired intellectuals, many of them his friends and former friends, in a letter he sent to Tudor Vianu.[52][251] In 1946, Ionesco indicated to Petru Comarnescu that he did not want to see either Eliade or Cioran, and that he considered the two of them "Legionaries for ever"—adding "we are hyenas to one another".[252]

Eliade's former friend, the communist Belu Zilber, who was attending the Paris Conference in 1946, refused to see Eliade, arguing that, as an Iron Guard affiliate, the latter had "denounced left-wingers", and contrasting him with Cioran ("They are both Legionaries, but [Cioran] is honest").[253] Three years later, Eliade's political activities were brought into discussion as he was getting ready to publish a translation of his *Techniques du Yoga* with the left-leaning Italian company *Giulio Einaudi Editore*—the denunciation was probably orchestrated by Romanian officials.[254]

In August 1954, when Horia Sima, who led the Iron Guard during its exile, was rejected by a faction inside the movement, Mircea Eliade's name was included on a list of persons who supported the latter—although this may have happened without his consent.[254] According to exiled dissident and novelist Dumitru Țepeneag, around that date, Eliade expressed his sympathy for Iron Guard members in general, whom he viewed as "courageous".[255] However, according to Robert Ellwood, the Eliade he met in the 1960s was entirely apolitical, remained aloof from "the passionate politics of that era in the United States", and "[r]eportedly [...] never read newspapers"[256] (an assessment shared by Sorin Alexandrescu).[5] Eliade's student Ioan Petru Culianu noted that journalists had come to refer to the Romanian scholar as "the great recluse".[8] Despite Eliade's withdrawal from radical politics, Ellwood indicates, he still remained concerned with Romania's welfare. He saw himself and other exiled Romanian intellectuals as members of a circle who worked to "maintain the culture of a free Romania and, above all, to publish texts that had become unpublishable in Romania itself".[257]

Beginning in 1969, Eliade's past became the subject of public debate in Israel. At the time, historian Gershom Scholem asked Eliade to explain his attitudes, which the latter did using vague terms.[30][52][258] As a result of this exchange, Scholem declared his dissatisfaction, and argued that Israel could not extend a welcome to the Romanian academic.[52] During the final years of Mircea Eliade's life, his disciple Culianu exposed and publicly criticized his 1930s pro-Iron Guard activities; relations between the two soured as a result.[259] Eliade's other Romanian disciple, Andrei Oişteanu, noted that, in the years following Eliade's death, conversations with various people who had known the scholar had made Culianu less certain of his earlier stances, and had led him to declare: "Mr. Eliade was never antisemitic, a member of the Iron Guard, or pro-Nazi. But, in any case, I am led to believe that he was closer to the Iron Guard than I would have liked to believe."[260]

At an early stage of his polemic with Culianu, Mircea Eliade complained in writing that "it is not possible to write an objective history" of the Iron Guard and its leader Corneliu Zelea Codreanu.[261] Arguing that people "would only accept apologetics [...] or executions", he contended: "After Buchenwald and Auschwitz, even honest people cannot afford being objective".[261]

Posterity

Alongside the arguments introduced by Daniel Dubuisson, criticism of Mircea Eliade's political involvement with antisemitism and fascism came from Adriana Berger, Leon Volovici, Alexandra Laignel-Lavastine, Florin Țurcanu and others, who have attempted to trace Eliade's antisemitism throughout his work and through his associations with contemporary antisemites, such as the Italian fascist occultist Julius Evola. Volovici, for example, is critical of Eliade not only because of his support for the Iron Guard, but also for spreading antisemitism and anti-Masonry in 1930s Romania.[262] In 1991, exiled novelist Norman Manea published an essay firmly condemning Eliade's attachment to the Iron Guard.[6]

Other scholars, like Bryan S. Rennie, have claimed that there is, to date, no evidence of Eliade's membership, active services rendered, or of any real involvement with any fascist or totalitarian movements or membership organizations, nor that there is any evidence of his continued support for nationalist ideals after their inherently violent nature was revealed. They further assert that there is no imprint of overt political beliefs in Eliade's scholarship, and also claim that Eliade's critics are following political agendas.[19][263] Romanian scholar Mircea Handoca, editor of Eliade's writings, argues that the controversy surrounding Eliade was encouraged by a group of exiled writers, of whom Manea was a main representative, and believes that Eliade's association with the Guard was a conjectural one, determined by the young author's Christian values and conservative stance, as well as by his belief that a Legionary Romania could mirror Portugal's *Estado Novo*.[6] Handoca opined that Eliade changed his stance after discovering that the Legionaries had turned violent, and argued that there was no evidence of Eliade's actual affiliation with the Iron Guard as a political movement.[6] Additionally, Joaquín Garrigós, who translated Eliade's works into Spanish, claimed that none of Eliade's texts he ever encountered show him to be an antisemite.[6] Mircea Eliade's nephew and commentator Sorin Alexandrescu himself proposed that Eliade's politics were essentially conservative and patriotic, in part motivated by a fear of the Soviet Union which he shared with many other young intellectuals.[6] Based on Mircea Eliade's admiration for Gandhi, various other authors assess that Eliade remained committed to nonviolence.[6]

Robert Ellwood also places Eliade's involvement with the Iron Guard in relation to scholar's conservatism, and connects this aspect of Eliade's life with both his nostalgia and his study of primal societies. According to Ellwood, the part of Eliade that felt attracted to the "freedom of new beginnings suggested by primal myths" is the same part that felt attracted to the Guard, with its almost mythological notion of a new beginning through a "national resurrection".[264] On a more basic level, Ellwood describes Eliade as a "instinctively spiritual" person who saw the Iron Guard as a spiritual movement.[265] In Ellwood's view, Eliade was aware that the "golden age" of antiquity was no longer accessible to secular man, that it could be recalled but not re-established. Thus, a "more accessible" object for nostalgia was a "secondary silver age within the last few hundred years"—the Kingdom of Romania's 19th century cultural renaissance.[266] To the young Eliade, the Iron Guard seemed like a path for returning to the silver age of Romania's glory, being a movement "dedicated to the cultural and national renewal of the Romanian people by appeal to their spiritual roots".[256] Ellwood describes the young Eliade as someone "capable of being fired up by mythological archetypes and with no awareness of the evil that was to be unleashed".[267]

Because of Eliade's withdrawal from politics, and also because the later Eliade's religiosity was very personal and idiosyncratic,[224] Ellwood believes the later Eliade probably would have rejected the "corporate sacred" of the Iron Guard.[224] According to Ellwood, the later Eliade had the same desire for a Romanian "resurrection" that had motivated the early Eliade to support the Iron Guard, but he now channeled it apolitically through his efforts to "maintain the culture of a free Romania" abroad.[268] In one of his writings, Eliade says, "Against the terror of History there are only two possibilities of defense: action or contemplation."[269] According to Ellwood, the young Eliade took the former option, trying to reform the world through action, whereas the older Eliade tried to resist the terror of history intellectually.[198]

Eliade's own version of events, presenting his involvement in far right politics as marginal, was judged to contain several inaccuracies and unverifiable claims.[52][270] For instance, Eliade depicted his arrest as having been solely caused by his friendship with Nae Ionescu.[271] On another occasion, answering Gershom Scholem's query, he is known to have explicitly denied ever having contributed to *Buna Vestire*.[52] According to Sorin Antohi, "Eliade died without ever clearly expressing regret for his Iron Guard sympathies".[272] Z. Ornea noted that, in a short section of his *Autobiography* where he discusses the *Einaudi* incident, Eliade speaks of "my imprudent acts and errors committed in youth", as "a series of malentendus that would follow me all my life."[273] Ornea commented that this was the only instance where the Romanian academic spoke of his political involvement with a dose of self-criticism, and contrasted the statement with Eliade's usual refusal to discuss his stances "pertinently".[254] Reviewing the arguments brought in support of Eliade, Sergio Vila-Sanjuán concluded: "Nevertheless, Eliade's pro-Legionary columns endure in the newspaper libraries, he never showed his regret for this connection [with the Iron Guard] and always, right up to his final writings, he invoked the figure of his teacher Nae Ionescu."[6]

In his *Felix Culpa*, Manea directly accused Eliade of having embellished his memoirs in order to minimize an embarrassing past.[6] A secondary debate surrounding Eliade's alleged unwillingness to dissociate with the Guard took place after *Jurnalul portughez* saw print. Sorin Alexandrescu expressed a belief that notes in the diary show Eliade's "break with his far right past".[5] Cătălin Avramescu defined this conclusion as "whitewashing", and, answering to Alexandrescu's claim that his uncle's support for the Guard was always superficial, argued that *Jurnal portughez* and other writings of the time showed Eliade's disenchantment with the Legionaries' Christian stance in tandem with his growing sympathy for Nazism and its pagan messages.[58] Paul Cernat, who stressed that it was the only one of Eliade's autobiographical works not to have been reworked by its author, concluded that the book documented Eliade's own efforts to "camouflage" his political sympathies without rejecting them altogether.[26]

Oişteanu argued that, in old age, Eliade moved away from his earlier stances and even came to sympathize with the non-Marxist Left and the hippie youth movement.[72][78] He noted that Eliade initially felt apprehensive about the consequences of hippie activism, but that the interests they shared, as well as their advocacy of communalism and free love had made him argue that hippies were "a quasi-religious movement" that was "rediscovering the sacrality of Life".[274] Andrei Oişteanu, who proposed that Eliade's critics were divided into a "maximalist" and a "minimalist" camp (trying to, respectively, enhance or shadow the impact Legionary ideas had on Eliade), argued in favor of moderation, and indicated that Eliade's fascism needed to be correlated to the political choices of his generation.[258]

Political symbolism in Eliade's fiction

Various critics have traced links between Eliade's fiction works and his political views, or Romanian politics in general. Early on, George Călinescu argued that the totalitarian model outlined in *Huliganii* was: "An allusion to certain bygone political movements [...], sublimated in the ever so abstruse philosophy of death as a path to knowledge."[230] By contrast, *Întoarcerea din rai* partly focuses on a failed communist rebellion, which enlists the participation of its main characters.[231]

Iphigenia 's story of self-sacrifice, turned voluntary in Eliade's version, was taken by various commentators, beginning with Mihail Sebastian, as a favorable allusion to the Iron Guard's beliefs on commitment and death, as well as to the bloody outcome of the 1941 Legionary Rebellion.[30] Ten years after its premiere, the play was reprinted by Legionary refugees in Argentina: on the occasion, the text was reviewed for publishing by Eliade himself.[30] Reading *Iphigenia* was what partly sparked Culianu's investigation of his mentor's early political affiliations.[30]

A special debate was sparked by *Un om mare*. Culianu viewed it as a direct reference to Corneliu Zelea Codreanu and his rise in popularity, an interpretation partly based on the similarity between, on one hand, two monikers ascribed to the Legionary leader (by, respectively, his adversaries and his followers), and, on the other, the main character's name (*Cucoanes*).[240] Matei Călinescu did not reject Culianu's version, but argued that, on its own, the piece was beyond political interpretations.[240] Commenting on this dialog, literary historian and essayist Mircea Iorgulescu objected to the original verdict, indicating his belief that there was no historical evidence to substantiate Culianu's point of view.[240]

Alongside Eliade's main works, his attempted novel of youth, *Minunata călătorie a celor cinci cărăbuşi in ţara furnicilor roşii*, which depicts a population of red ants living in a totalitarian society and forming bands to harass the beetles, was seen as a potential allusion to the Soviet Union and to communism.[7] Despite Eliade's ultimate reception in Communist Romania, this writing could not be published during the period, after censors singled out fragments which they saw as especially problematic.[7]

Cultural legacy

Tributes

An endowed chair in the History of Religions at the University of Chicago Divinity School was named after Eliade in recognition of his wide contribution to the research on this subject; the current (and first incumbent) holder of this chair is Wendy Doniger.

To evaluate the legacy of Eliade and Joachim Wach within the discipline of the history of religions, the University of Chicago chose 2006 (the intermediate year between the 50th anniversary of Wach's death and the 100th anniversary of Eliade's birth), to hold a two-day conference in order to reflect upon their academic contributions and their political lives in their social and historical contexts, as well as the relationship between their works and their lives.[70]

Eliade's portrait on a Moldovan stamp

In 1990, after the Romanian Revolution, Eliade was elected posthumously to the Romanian Academy. In Romania, Mircea Eliade's legacy in the field of the history of religions is mirrored by the journal *Archaeus* (founded 1997, and affiliated with the University of Bucharest Faculty of History). The 6th European Association for the Study of Religion and International Association for the History of Religions Special Conference on *Religious History of Europe and Asia* took place from September 20 to September 23, 2006, in Bucharest. An important section of the Congress was dedicated to the memory of Mircea Eliade, whose legacy in the field of history of religions was scrutinized by various scholars, some of whom were his direct students at the University of Chicago.[275]

As Antohi noted, Eliade, Emil Cioran and Constantin Noica "represent in Romanian culture ultimate expressions of excellence, [Eliade and Cioran] being regarded as proof that Romania's interwar culture (and, by extension, Romanian culture as a whole) was able to reach the ultimate levels of depth, sophistication and creativity."[272] A Romanian Television 1 poll carried out in 2006 nominated Mircea Eliade as the 7th Greatest Romanian in history; his case was argued by the writer Dragoş Bucurenci (*see 100 greatest Romanians*). His name was given to a boulevard in the northern Bucharest area of Primăverii, to a street in Cluj-Napoca, and to high schools in Bucharest, Sighişoara, and Reşiţa. The Eliades' house on Melodiei Street was torn down during the communist regime, and an apartment block was raised in its place; his second residence, on Dacia Boulevard, features a memorial plaque in his honor.[6]

Eliade's image in contemporary culture also has political implications. Historian Irina Livezeanu proposed that the respect he enjoys in Romania is matched by that of other "nationalist thinkers and politicians" who "have reentered the contemporary scene largely as heroes of a pre- and anticommunist past", including Nae Ionescu and Cioran, but also Ion Antonescu and Nichifor Crainic.[276] In parallel, according to Oişteanu (who relied his assessment on Eliade's own personal notes), Eliade's interest in the American hippie community was reciprocated by members of the latter, some of whom reportedly viewed Eliade as "a guru".[72]

Portrait on the Alley of Classics, Chişinău

Eliade has also been hailed as an inspiration by German representatives of the *Neue Rechte*, claiming legacy from the Conservative Revolutionary movement (among them is the controversial magazine *Junge Freiheit* and the essayist Karlheinz Weißmann).[277] In 2007, Florin Ţurcanu's biographical volume on Eliade was issued in a German translation by the Antaios publishing house, which is mouthpiece for the *Neue Rechte*.[277] The edition was not reviewed by the mainstream German press.[277] Other sections of the European far right also claim Eliade as an inspiration, and consider his contacts with the Iron Guard to be a merit—among their representatives are the Italian neofascist Claudio Mutti and Romanian groups who trace their origin to the Legionary Movement.[258]

Portrayals, filmography and dramatizations

Early on, Mircea Eliade's novels were the subject of satire: before the two of them became friends, Nicolae Steinhardt, using the pen name *Antisthius*, authored and published parodies of them.[12] Maitreyi Devi, who strongly objected to Eliade's account of their encounter and relationship, wrote her own novel as a reply to his *Maitreyi*; written in Bengali, it was titled *Na Hanyate* (translated into English as "It Does Not Die").[20] Several authors, including Ioan Petru Culianu, have drawn a parallel between Eugène Ionesco's Absurdist play of 1959, *Rhinoceros*, which depicts the population of a small town falling victim to a mass metamorphosis, and the impact fascism had on Ionesco's closest friends (Eliade included).[278]

In 2000, Saul Bellow published his controversial *Ravelstein* novel. Having for its setting the University of Chicago, it had among its characters Radu Grielescu, who was identified by several critics as Eliade. The latter's portrayal, accomplished through statements made by the eponymous character, is polemical: Grielescu, who is identified as a disciple of Nae Ionescu, took part in the Bucharest Pogrom, and is in Chicago as a refugee scholar, searching for the friendship of a Jewish colleague as a means to rehabilitate himself.[279] In 2005, the Romanian literary critic and translator Antoaneta Ralian, who was an acquaintance of Bellow's, argued that much of the negative portrayal was owed to a personal choice Bellow made (after having divorced from Alexandra Bagdasar, his Romanian wife and Eliade disciple).[280] She also mentioned that, during a 1979 interview, Bellow had expressed admiration for Eliade.[280]

The 1988 film *The Bengali Night*, directed by Nicolas Klotz and based upon the French translation of *Maitreyi*, stars British actor Hugh Grant as Allan, the European character based on Eliade, while Supriya Pathak is Gayatri, a character based on Maitreyi Devi (who had refused to be mentioned by name).[20] The film, considered "pornographic" by Hindu activists, was only shown once in India.[20] In addition to *The Bengali Night*, films based on, or referring to, his works, include: *Mircea Eliade et la redécouverte du Sacré* (1987), part of the television series

Architecture et Géographie sacrée, by Paul Barbă Neagră; *Domnişoara Christina* (1996), by Viorel Sergovici; *Eu Adam* (1996), by Dan Piţa; *Youth Without Youth* (2007), by Francis Ford Coppola.

Eliade's *Iphigenia* was again included in theater programs during the late years of the Nicolae Ceauşescu regime: in January 1982, a new version, directed by Ion Cojar, premiered at the National Theater Bucharest, starring Mircea Albulescu, Tania Filip and Adrian Pintea in some of the main roles.[241] Dramatizations based on his work include *La Ţigănci*, which has been the basis for two theater adaptations: *Cazul Gavrilescu* ("The Gavrilescu Case"), directed by Gelu Colceag and hosted by the Nottara Theater,[281] and an eponymous play by director Alexandru Hausvater, first staged by the Odeon Theater in 2003 (starring, among others, Adriana Trandafir, Florin Zamfirescu, and Carmen Tănase).[282] In March 2007, on Eliade's 100th birthday, the Romanian Radio Broadcasting Company hosted the *Mircea Eliade Week*, during which radio drama adaptations of several works were broadcast.[283] In September of that year, director and dramatist Cezarina Udrescu staged a multimedia performance based on a number of works Mircea Eliade wrote during his stay in Portugal; titled *Apocalipsa după Mircea Eliade* ("The Apocalypse According to Mircea Eliade"), and shown as part of a Romanian Radio cultural campaign, it starred Ion Caramitru, Oana Pellea and Răzvan Vasilescu.[284] *Domnişoara Christina* has been the subject of two operas: the first, carrying the same Romanian title, was authored by Romanian composer Şerban Nichifor and premiered in 1981 at the Romanian Radio;[285] the second, titled *La señorita Cristina*, was written by Spanish composer Luis de Pablo and premiered in 2000 at the Teatro Real in Madrid.[64]

Notes

[1] Wendy Doniger, "Foreword to the 2004 Edition", Eliade, *Shamanism*, p.xiii
[2] *Biografie*, in Handoca
[3] Silviu Mihai, "A doua viaţă a lui Mircea Eliade" ("Mircea Eliade's Second Life") (http://www.cotidianul.ro/index.php?id=3920& art=8997&diraut=123&cHash=ae6af0be58), in *Cotidianul*, February 6, 2006; retrieved July 31, 2007 (Romanian)
[4] Călinescu, p.956
[5] Simona Chiţan, "Nostalgia după România" ("Nostalgia for Romania"), interview with Sorin Alexandrescu, in *Evenimentul Zilei*, June 24, 2006
[6] Sergio Vila-Sanjuán, "Paseo por el Bucarest de Mircea Eliade" ("Passing through Mircea Eliade's Bucharest") (http://www.lavanguardia. es/lv24h/20070530/51355796343.html), in *La Vanguardia*, May 30, 2007 (Spanish); retrieved January 16, 2008
[7] Ion Hadârcă, "Mircea Eliade la începuturi" ("Mircea Eliade at His Beginnings") (http://www.sud-est.md/numere/20070428/article_3/), in *Revista Sud-Est*, 1/2007; retrieved January 21, 2008 (Romanian)
[8] Ioan P. Culianu, "Mahaparanirvana", in *El Hilo de Ariadna* (http://www.elhilodeariadna.org/index.asp), Vol. II
[9] Ellwood, p.98–99
[10] Eliade, *Autobiography*, in Ellwood, p.98–99
[11] Ellwood, p.5
[12] Steinhardt, in Handoca
[13] Veronica Marinescu, " 'Am luat din întâmplarile vieţii tot ce este mai frumos', spune cercetatorul operei brâncuşiene" (" 'I Took the Best Out of Life's Occurrences', Says Researcher of Brancusi's Work") (http://www.curierulnational.ro/Specializat/2004-03-13/â A m + luat+ din+intamplarile+vietii+tot+ce+este+mai+frumosâ,+spune+cercetatorul+operei+brancusiene), interview with Barbu Brezianu, in *Curierul Naţional*, March 13, 2004; retrieved February 22, 2008 (Romanian)
[14] Maria Vlădescu, "100 de ani de cercetaşi" ("100 Years of Scouting"), in *Evenimentul Zilei*, August 2, 2007
[15] Constantin Roman, *Continental Drift: Colliding Continents, Converging Cultures*, CRC Press, Institute of Physics Publishing, Bristol and Philadelphia, 2000, p.60 ISBN 0-7503-0686-6
[16] Călinescu, p.954, 955; Nastasă, p.76
[17] Nastasă, p.237
[18] McGuire, p.150; Nastasă, p.237
[19] Kelley L. Ross, *Mircea Eliade* (http://www.friesian.com/eliade.htm), on friesian.com (http://www.friesian.com/); retrieved July 16, 2007
[20] Ginu Kamani, "A Terrible Hurt: The Untold Story behind the Publishing of Maitreyi Devi" (http://www.press.uchicago.edu/Misc/ Chicago/143651.html), at the University of Chicago Press website; retrieved July 16, 2007
[21] *Biografie*, in Handoca; Nastasă, p.237
[22] Albert Ribas, "Mircea Eliade, historiador de las religiones" ("Mircea Eliade, Historian of Religions"), in *El Ciervo. Revista de pensamiento y cultura*, Año 49, Núm. 588 (Marzo 2000), p.35–38
[23] Eliade, in Nastasă, p.238
[24] McGuire, p.150
[25] Nastasă, p.442; Ornea, p.452
[26] Paul Cernat, "Jurnalul unui om mare" ("The Diary of A Big Man") (http://www.observatorcultural.ro/informatiiarticol. phtml?xid=16282&print=true), in *Observator Cultural*, Nr. 338, September 2006; retrieved January 23, 2008 (Romanian)
[27] Şora, in Handoca
[28] Ornea, p.150–151, 153
[29] Ornea, p.174–175
[30] Andrei Oişteanu, "Mihail Sebastian şi Mircea Eliade: cronica unei prietenii accidentate" ("Mihail Sebastian and Mircea Eliade: the Chronicle of an Abrupt Friendship)" (http://www.revista22.ro/html/index.php?nr=2007-12-05&art=4157), in *22*, Nr. 926, December 2007; retrieved January 18, 2008 (Romanian)
[31] Eliade, 1934, in Ornea, p.408; see also Ellwood, p.85
[32] Eliade, 1934, in Ornea, p.408–409
[33] Eliade, 1936, in Ornea, p.410
[34] Eliade, 1933, in Ornea, p.167
[35] Ornea, Chapter IV
[36] Stelian Tănase, "Belu Zilber", Part II (http://www.revista22.ro/html/index.php?art=569&nr=2003-08-18), in *22*, Nr. 701, August 2003; retrieved October 4, 2007 (Romanian)

[37] Paul Cernat, "Eliade în cheie ezoterică" ("Eliade in Esoterical Key") (http://www.observatorcultural.ro/informatiiarticol. phtml?xid=8679&print=true), review of Marcel Tolcea, *Eliade, ezotericul* ("Eliade, the Esoteric"), in *Observator Cultural*, Nr. 175, July 2003; retrieved July 16, 2007 (**Romanian**)

[38] Paul Cernat, "Recuperarea lui Ionathan X. Uranus" ("The Recuperation of Ionathan X. Uranus") (http://www.observatorcultural.ro/ informatiiarticol.phtml?xid=14626), in *Observator Cultural*, Nr. 299, December 2005; retrieved November 22, 2007 (**Romanian**)

[39] Eliade, 1933, in Ornea, p.32

[40] Eliade, 1936, in Ornea, p.32

[41] Eliade, 1937, in Ornea, p.53

[42] Eliade, 1927, in Ornea, p.147

[43] Eliade, 1935, in Ornea, p.128

[44] Eliade, 1934, in Ornea, p.136

[45] Eliade, 1933, in Ornea, p.178, 186

[46] Ornea, p.445–455

[47] Nastasă, p.525–526

[48] Nastasă, p.86; Ornea, p.452–453; Şora, in Handoca

[49] Ornea, p.453

[50] Eliade, 1937, in Ornea, p.203

[51] Ornea, p.202–206

[52] Ovidiu Şimonca, "Mircea Eliade şi 'căderea în lume'" ("Mircea Eliade and 'the Descent into the World'") (http://www.observatorcultural. ro/informatiiarticol.phtml?xid=14834), review of Florin Ţurcanu, *Mircea Eliade. Le prisonnier de l'histoire* ("Mircea Eliade. The Prisoner of History"), in *Observator Cultural*, Nr. 305, January–February 2006; retrieved July 16, 2007 (**Romanian**)

[53] Ornea, p.180

[54] Ornea, p.207

[55] Ornea, p.208–209

[56] Ornea, p.209

[57] *Biografie*, in Handoca; Nastasă, p.442

[58] Cătălin Avramescu, "Citim una, înţelegem alta" ("We Read One Thing and Understand Another") (http://www.dilemaveche.ro/index. php?nr=135&cmd=articol&id=3508), in *Dilema Veche*, Vol. III, August 2006; retrieved January 28, 2008 (**Romanian**)

[59] Michael Löwy, Review of Daniel Dubuisson, *Impostures et pseudo-science. L'œuvre de Mircea Eliade* (http://assr.revues.org/ document3128.html), in *Archives de Science Sociale et Religion* (http://assr.revues.org/), 132 (2005) (**French**); retrieved January 22, 2008

[60] Eliade, *Salazar*, in "Eliade despre Salazar" ("Eliade on Salazar"), *Evenimentul Zilei*, October 13, 2002

[61] Ellwood, p.90

[62] Eliade, in Handoca

[63] Nastasă, p.442–443

[64] Joaquín Garrigós, "Pasiunea lui Mircea Eliade pentru Spania" ("Mircea Eliade's Passion for Spain") (http://www.dilemaveche.ro/index. php?nr=191&cmd=articol&id=6740), in *Dilema Veche*, Vol. IV, October 2007; retrieved January 21, 2008 (**Romanian**)

[65] Andrei Oişteanu, "Mircea Eliade, de la opium la amfetamine" ("Mircea Eliade, from Opium to Amphetamines") (http://www.revista22. ro/html/index.php?nr=2007-05-11&art=3719), in *22*, Nr. 896, May 2007; retrieved January 17, 2008 (**Romanian**)

[66] Mihai Sorin Rădulescu, "Cotteştii: familia soţiei lui Mircea Eliade" ("The Cottescus: the Family of Mircea Eliade's Wife") (http://www.zf. ro/articol_87328/cottestii__familia_sotiei_lui_mircea_eliade.html), in *Ziarul Financiar*, June 30, 2006; retrieved January 22, 2008 (**Romanian**)

[67] Dan Gulea, "O perspectivă sintetică" ("A Syncretic Perspective") (http://www.observatorcultural.ro/informatiiarticol.phtml?xid=12070), in *Observator Cultural*, Nr. 242, October 2004; retrieved October 4, 2007 (**Romanian**)

[68] McGuire, p.150–151

[69] McGuire, p.151

[70] Conference on *Hermeneutics in History: Mircea Eliade, Joachim Wach, and the Science of Religions* (http://marty-center.uchicago.edu/ conferences/wach_eliade/about.shtml), at the University of Chicago Martin Marty Center. Institute for the Advanced Study of Religion (http://marty-center.uchicago.edu/); retrieved July 29, 2007

[71] McGuire, p.151–152

[72] Oişteanu, "Mircea Eliade şi mişcarea hippie"

[73] *România Liberă, passim* September–October 1944, in Frunză, p.251

[74] Vladimir Tismăneanu, *Stalinism pentru eternitate* (Romanian translation of *Stalinism for All Seasons*), Polirom, Iaşi, 2005, p.187, 337. ISBN 973-681-899-3

[75] Alexandru Popescu, "Scriitorii şi spionajul" ("Writers and Spying") (http://www.zf.ro/articol_109162/ alexandru_popescu__ix___scriitorii_si_spionajul.html), in *Ziarul Financiar*, January 26, 2007; retrieved November 8, 2007 (**Romanian**)

[76] Frunză, p.448–449

[77] Eliade, 1970, in Paul Cernat, "Îmblânzitorul României Socialiste. De la Bîrca la Chicago şi înapoi" ("The Tamer of Socialist Romania. From Bîrca to Chicago and Back"), part of Paul Cernat, Ion Manolescu, Angelo Mitchievici, Ioan Stanomir, *Explorări în comunismul românesc* ("Forays into Romanian Communism"), Polirom, Iaşi, 2004, p.346

[78] Cristian Teodorescu, "Eliade şi Culianu prin ocheanul lui Oişteanu" ("Eliade and Culianu through Oişteanu's Lens") (http://cotidianul.ro/ index.php?id=11526&art=30480&cHash=19a3e7c987), in *Cotidianul*, June 14, 2007; retrieved November 7, 2007 (**Romanian**)

[79] Doniger's foreword to Eliade's *Shamanism* (Princeton University Press edition, 1972, p.xii)

[80] Dumézil, "Introducere", in Eliade, *Tratat de istorie a religiilor: Introducere* ("Religious History Treatise" – *Patterns in Comparative Religion*), Humanitas, Bucharest, 1992

[81] Ellwood, p.99

[82] Ellwood, p.104

[83] Eliade, *Patterns in Comparative Religion*, p.1

[84] Eliade, *The Myth of the Eternal Return*, p.5

[85] Eliade, *The Sacred and the Profane*, p.20–22; *Shamanism*, p. xiii

[86] Eliade, *The Sacred and the Profane*, p.22

[87] Eliade, *The Sacred and the Profane*, p.21

[88] Eliade, *The Sacred and the Profane*, p.20

[89] Eliade, *Myths, Dreams and Mysteries*, p.23

[90] Eliade, *Myth and Reality*, p.6

[91] Eliade, *Myth and Reality*, p.15

[92] Eliade, *Myth and Reality*, p.34
[93] Eliade, *Myths, Dreams and Mysteries*, p.44
[94] Eliade, *The Sacred and the Profane*, p.68–69
[95] Leeming, "Archetypes"
[96] Eliade, *Myth and Reality, p.47–49*
[97] Eliade, *The Myth of the Eternal Return*, Chapter 4; *Myths, Dreams and Mysteries*, p.231–245
[98] In *Patterns in Comparative Religion* (p.419), Eliade gives a section about the *coincidentia oppositorum* the title "Coincidentia Oppositorum—THE MYTHICAL PATTERN". Beane and Doty chose to retain this title when excerpting this section in *Myths, Rites, Symbols* (p. 449).
[99] Eliade, *Myths, Rites, Symbols*, p. 449
[100] Eliade, *Myths, Rites, Symbols*, p. 450
[101] Eliade, *Myths, Rites, Symbols*, p. 439
[102] Eliade, *Myths, Rites, Symbols*, p. 440
[103] Eliade, *Myth and Reality*, p.169
[104] Eliade, *Myth and Reality*, p. 64–65, 169
[105] Eliade, *The Myth of the Eternal Return*, p.124
[106] Eliade, *A History of Religious Ideas*, vol. 1, p. 302
[107] Eliade, *A History of Religious Ideas*, vol. 1, p. 356
[108] Eliade, *The Sacred and the Profane*, p.109
[109] Eliade, *Myths, Rites, Symbols*, Volume 2, p.312–14
[110] Eliade, *The Sacred and the Profane*, p. 21
[111] Eliade, *Shamanism*, p.259–260
[112] Eliade, *The Sacred and the Profane*, p.32–36
[113] Eliade, *The Sacred and the Profane*, p.40, 42
[114] Eliade, *Images and Symbols*, p.44
[115] Eliade, *The Sacred and the Profane*, p.43
[116] Eliade, *Images and Symbols*, p.39
[117] Eliade, *The Sacred and the Profane*, p.29
[118] Eliade, *Images and Symbols*, pp. 39–40; Eliade, *The Sacred and the Profane*, p.30
[119] Eliade, "The Quest for the 'Origins' of Religion", p.157, 161
[120] Eliade, *Myth and Reality*, p.93; *Patterns in Comparative Religion*, p.38–40, 54–58
[121] Eliade, "The Quest for the 'Origins' of Religion", p.161
[122] Eliade, *Patterns in Comparative Religion*, p.38, 54; *Myths, Dreams and Mysteries*, p.176
[123] Eliade, *Patterns in Comparative Religion*, p.38
[124] Eliade, "The Quest for the 'Origins' of Religion", p.162; see also Eliade, *Patterns in Comparative Religion*, p.54–58
[125] Eliade, *Myths, Dreams and Mysteries*, p. 176
[126] *Myths, Dreams and Mysteries*, p. 176–77
[127] Eliade, *Patterns in Comparative Religion*, p.54–55
[128] Eliade, *Myths, Dreams and Mysteries*, p.138
[129] See Eliade, *Patterns in Comparative Religion*, p.54–56
[130] Eliade, *Myths, Dreams and Mysteries*, p.134–36; *The Myth of the Eternal Return*, p.97
[131] Eliade, *Myth and Reality*, p.93–94
[132] Eliade, *Myths, Dreams and Mysteries*, p.134
[133] Eliade, *Myths, Dreams and Mysteries*, p.66
[134] *Shamanism*, p. 3–4
[135] Eliade, *Shamanism*, p.4
[136] Eliade, *Shamanism*, p.6, 8–9
[137] See, for example, *Myths, Dreams and Mysteries*, pp.82–83
[138] Eliade, *Shamanism*, p.43
[139] Eliade, *Shamanism*, p.63
[140] Eliade, *Myths, Dreams and Mysteries*, p.84
[141] Eliade, *Myths, Dreams and Mysteries*, p.102
[142] Eliade, *Myths, Dreams and Mysteries*, p.63
[143] Eliade, *Myths, Dreams and Mysteries*, p.64
[144] Călinescu, p.954
[145] Călinescu, p.955
[146] Eliade, in Călinescu, p.954
[147] Ionescu, in Călinescu, p.953, 954
[148] Ellwood, p.110–11
[149] For example, according to Wendy Doniger (Doniger, "Foreword to the 2004 Edition", Eliade, *Shamanism*, p.xv), Eliade has been accused "of being a crypto-theologian"; however, Doniger argues that Eliade is better characterized as "an open hierogian". Likewise, Robert Ellwood (Ellwood, p.111) denies that Eliade practiced "covert theology".
[150] Douglas Allen, *Myth and Religion in Mircea Eliade*, Routledge, London, 2002, p.45–46; Adrian Marino, *L'Herméneutique de Mircea Eliade*, Éditions Gallimard, Paris, 1981, p.60
[151] Eliade, *Images and Symbols*, p.32
[152] Eliade, *Images and Symbols*, p. 32
[153] Eliade, *Images and Symbols*, p.33
[154] Eliade, *Images and Symbols*, p.17
[155] Eliade, *Images and Symbols*, p.16–17
[156] Eliade, *The Myth of the Eternal Return*, p.34
[157] Eliade, in Dadosky, p.105
[158] Dadosky, p.105
[159] Dadosky, p.106
[160] Segal, in Dadosky, p.105–106
[161] Eliade, *The Sacred and the Profane*, p.202
[162] *The Sacred and the Profane*, p.202

[163] Eliade, *The Sacred and the Profane*, p.203
[164] Eliade, *Myth and Reality*, p.12; see also Eliade, *Myth and Reality*, p.20, 145.
[165] Eliade, *The Sacred and the Profane*, p.204
[166] Eliade, *The Sacred and the Profane*, p.205
[167] Eliade, *The Sacred and the Profane*, p.205; *Myth and Reality*, p.191
[168] Eliade, *The Sacred and the Profane*, p.205; see also Eliade, *Myth and Reality*, p.192
[169] Eliade, "The Quest for the 'Origins' of Religion", p.158
[170] Eliade, "The Quest for the 'Origins' of Religion", p.160
[171] Eliade, *Myths, Dreams, and Mysteries* 1960, p.25–26, in Ellwood, p.91–92
[172] Eliade, *Myths, Dreams, and Mysteries* 1960, p.25–26, in Ellwood, p.92
[173] Eliade, *Myth and Reality*, p. 192
[174] Eliade, *Myth and Reality*, p.193
[175] Eliade, *The Myth of the Eternal Return*, p.151
[176] Eliade, *The Myth of the Eternal Return*, p.152
[177] Eliade, *Myths, Dreams, and Mysteries*, p.240–241
[178] Eliade, *Myths, Dreams, and Mysteries*, p. 241
[179] Eliade, *Myths, Dreams, and Mysteries*, p.242
[180] Eliade, *Myths, Dreams, and Mysteries*, p.243
[181] Eliade, *Myths, Dreams, and Mysteries*, p.243–244
[182] Eliade, *Myths, Dreams, and Mysteries*, p.244
[183] Eliade, *Myths, Dreams, and Mysteries*, p.245
[184] Eliade, *Myth and Reality*, p. 65
[185] Eliade, *Myths, Dreams, and Mysteries*, p.153
[186] Eliade, *Images and Symbols*, p.170
[187] Jesi, p.66–67
[188] Jesi, p.66–70
[189] Eliade, *The Myth of the Eternal Return*, p.162
[190] Ellwood, p.6
[191] Ellwood, p.9
[192] Ellwood, p.15
[193] Ellwood, p.2
[194] Ellwood, p.19
[195] Ellwood, p.1
[196] Ellwood, p.99, 117
[197] Eliade, quoted by Virgil Ierunca, *The Literary Work of Mircea Eliade*, in Ellwood, p.117
[198] Ellwood, p.101
[199] Ellwood, p.97
[200] Ellwood, p.102
[201] Ellwood, p.103
[202] Douglas Allen, "Eliade and History", in *Journal of Religion*, 52:2 (1988), p.545
[203] Kirk, *Myth...*, footnote, p.255
[204] Kirk, *The Nature of Greek Myths*, p.64–66
[205] Kirk, *The Nature of Greek Myths*, p.66
[206] Wendy Doniger, "Foreword to the 2004 Edition", Eliade, *Shamanism*, p. xii
[207] Wendy Doniger, "Foreword to the 2004 Edition", Eliade, *Shamanism*, p. xiii
[208] Mac Linscott Ricketts, "Review of *Religion on Trial: Mircea Eliade and His Critics* by Guilford Dudley III", in *Journal of the American Academy of Religion*, Vol. 46, No. 3 (September 1978), p.400–402
[209] Gregory D. Alles, "Review of *Changing Religious Worlds: The Meaning and End of Mircea Eliade* by Brian Rennie", in *Journal of the American Academy of Religion*, Vol. 71, p.466–469 (Alles' italics)
[210] Alice Kehoe, *Shamans and Religion: An Anthropological Exploration in Critical Thinking*, Waveland Press, London, 2000, *passim*. ISBN 1-57766-162-1
[211] Kees W. Bolle, *The Freedom of Man in Myth*, Vanderbilt University Press, Nashville, 1968, p.14. ISBN 0-8265-1248-8
[212] Inden, in Morny Joy, "Irigaray's Eastern Expedition", Chapter 4 of Morny Joy, Kathleen O'Grady, Judith L. Poxon, *Religion in French Feminist Thought: Critical Perspectives*, Routledge, London, 2003, p.63. ISBN 0-415-21536-6
[213] Griffin, *passim*
[214] Eliade, *Fragments d'un Journal 11, 1970–1978*, Éditions Gallimard, Paris, 1981, p.194
[215] Griffin, p.173; Douglas R. Holmes, *Integral Europe: Fast-Capitalism, Multiculturalism, Neofascism*, Princeton University Press, Princeton, 2000, p.78
[216] Lucian Boia, *Istorie şi mit în conştiinţa românească*, Humanitas, Bucharest, 1997 (tr. *History and Myth in Romanian Consciousness*, Central European University Press, Budapest, 2001), p.152
[217] Eliade, "Zalmoxis, The Vanishing God", in *Slavic Review*, Vol. 33, No. 4 (December 1974), p.807–809
[218] Antohi, preface to Liiceanu, p.xx
[219] Ellwood, p.xiii–xiv
[220] Ellwood, p.13
[221] Ellwood, p.119
[222] Ellwood, p.118
[223] Ellwood, p.119–20
[224] Ellwood, p.120
[225] Ellwood, p.111
[226] Ellwood, p.x
[227] Călinescu, p.963
[228] Călinescu, p.843
[229] Călinescu, p.967
[230] Călinescu, p.959
[231] Călinescu, p.958
[232] Călinescu, p.960

[233] Carmen Muşat, "Despre fantastica alcătuire a realului" ("On the Fantastic Shape of Reality") (http://www.observatorcultural.ro/informatiiarticol.phtml?xid=4693&print=true), in *Observator Cultural*, Nr. 131, August–September 2002; retrieved January 17, 2008**(Romanian)**

[234] Eliade, in Călinescu, p.956

[235] Călinescu, p.957

[236] Călinescu, p.957–958

[237] Eliade, in Ellwood, p.101

[238] Gabriela Adameşteanu, "Cum suportă individul şocurile Istoriei. Dialog cu Norman Manea" ("How the Individual Bears the Shocks of History. A Dialog with Norman Manea") (http://www.observatorcultural.ro/informatiiarticol.phtml?xid=14797), in *Observator Cultural*, Nr. 304, January 2006; retrieved January 16, 2008 **(Romanian)**

[239] Eliade, in Călinescu, p.958–959

[240] Mircea Iorgulescu, "*L'Affaire*, după Matei" (*L'Affaire*, according to Matei"), Part II (http://www.revista22.ro/html/index.php?art=99&nr=2002-05-20), in *22*, Nr. 636, May 2002; retrieved January 17, 2008 **(Romanian)**

[241] Radu Albala, "Teatrul Naţional din Bucureşti. *Ifigenia* de Mircea Eliade" ("National Theater Bucharest. *Ifigenia* by Mircea Eliade"), in *Teatru* (http://www.cimec.ro/Teatre/revista/1982/1982_feb.htm), Vol. XXVII, Nr. 2, February 1982 – text facsimile (http://www.cimec.ro/Teatre/revista/1982/Nr.2.anul.XXVII.februarie.1982/imagepages/16755.1982.02.pag040-pag041.html) republished by the Institute for Cultural Memory (http://www.cimec.ro/e_default.htm); retrieved January 19, 2008 **(Romanian)**

[242] Eliade, in Robert Spoo, *James Joyce and the Language of History: Dedalus's Nightmare*, Oxford University Press, New York, Oxford, 1994, p.158. ISBN 0-19-508749-6

[243] Ornea, p.408–409, 412

[244] Sebastian, *passim*

[245] Sebastian, p. 238

[246] It was popular prejudice in the late 1930s to claim that Ukrainian Jews in the Soviet Union had obtained Romanian citizenship illegally after crossing the border into Maramureş and Bukovina. In 1938, this accusation served as an excuse for the Octavian Goga-A. C. Cuza government to suspend and review all Jewish citizenship guaranteed after 1923, rendering it very difficult to regain (Ornea, p.391). Eliade's mention of Bessarabia probably refers to an earlier period, being his interpretation of a pre-Greater Romania process.

[247] Eliade, 1936, in Ornea, p.412–413; partially in the *Final Report*, p.49

[248] Eliade, 1937, in Ornea, p.413; in the *Final Report*, p.49

[249] Ornea, p.206; Ornea is skeptical of these explanations, given the long period of time spent before Eliade gave them, and especially the fact that the article itself, despite the haste in which it must have been written, has remarkably detailed references to many articles written by Eliade in various papers over a period of time.

[250] Ionesco, 1945, in Ornea, p.184

[251] Ornea, p.184–185

[252] Ionesco, 1946, in Ornea, p.211

[253] Stelian Tănase, "Belu Zilber" (III) (http://www.revista22.ro/html/index.php?art=575&nr=2003-08-25), in *22*, Nr.702, August 2003; retrieved October 4, 2007 **(Romanian)**

[254] Ornea, p.210

[255] Constantin Coroiu, "Un român la Paris" (http://www.evenimentul.ro/articol/un-roman-la-paris-0.html), in *Evenimentul*, August 31, 2006; retrieved October 4, 2007 **(Romanian)**

[256] Ellwood, p.83

[257] Eliade, *Ordeal by Labyrinth*, in Ellwood, p.115

[258] Oişteanu, "Angajamentul..."

[259] Sorin Antohi, "Exploring the Legacy of Ioan Petru Culianu" (http://www.iwm.at/index.php?option=com_content&task=view&id=306&Itemid=478), in the *Institut für die Wissenschaften vom Menschen Post* (http://www.iwm.at/index.php?option=com_content&task=view&id=109&Itemid=231), Newsletter 72, Spring 2001; retrieved July 16, 2007; Ted Anton, "The Killing of Professor Culianu" (http://linguafranca.mirror.theinfo.org/9209/culianu.html), in *Lingua Franca*, Volume 2, No. 6, September/October 1992; retrieved July 29, 2007; Oişteanu, "Angajamentul..."

[260] Culianu, in Oişteanu, "Angajamentul..."

[261] Eliade, in Ellwood, p.91; in Oişteanu, "Angajamentul..."

[262] Leon Volovici, *Nationalist Ideology and Antisemitism: The Case of Romanian Intellectuals in the 1930s*, Pergamon Press, Oxford, 1991, p.104–105, 110–111, 120–126, 134

[263] Bryan S. Rennie, *Reconstructing Eliade: Making Sense of Religion*, State University of New York Press, Albany, 1996, p.149–177. ISBN 0-7914-2763-3

[264] Ellwood, p.100–101

[265] Ellwood, p.86

[266] Ellwood, p.xiv

[267] Ellwood, p.91

[268] Ellwood, p.115

[269] Eliade, *The Forbidden Forest*, in Ellwood, p.101

[270] Ornea, p.202, 208–211, 239–240

[271] Ornea, p.202, 209

[272] Antohi, preface to Liiceanu, p.xxiii

[273] Eliade, in Ornea, p.210

[274] Eliade, in Oişteanu, "Mircea Eliade şi mişcarea hippie"

[275] *The Sixth EASR and IAHR Special Conference* (http://web.archive.org/web/20061011070115/http://www.rahr.ro/RAHR/Conference2006/index.htm); retrieved July 29, 2007

[276] Irina Livezeanu, *Cultural Politics in Greater Romania: Regionalism, Nation Building and Ethnic Struggle, 1918-1930*, Cornell University Press, New York City, 1995, p.x. ISBN 0-8014-8688-2

[277] "Biografia lui Mircea Eliade la o editură germană radicală de dreapta" ("Mircea Eliade's Biography at a Right-Wing Radical German Publishing House") (http://www.altitudini.ro/articles.php?ai=1399), in *Altitudini* (http://www.altitudini.ro/), Nr. 17, July 2007; retrieved November 8, 2007 **(Romanian)**

[278] Oişteanu, "Angajamentul..."; Ornea, p.19, 181

[279] Mircea Iorgulescu, "Portretul artistului ca delincvent politic" ("The Portrait of the Artist as a Political Offender"), Part I (http://www.revista22.ro/html/index.php?nr=2002-05-27&art=103), in *22*, Nr.637, May 2002; retrieved July 16, 2007 **(Romanian)**

[280] Antoaneta Ralian, interviewed on the occasion of Saul Bellow's death (http://www.hotnews.ro/articol_19388-A-incetat-din-viata-laureatul-Premiului-Nobel-Saul-Bellow.htm), BBC Romania, April 7, 2005 (hosted by hotnews.ro);

retrieved July 16, 2007 **(Romanian)**

[281] Irina-Margareta Nistor, "Un cuplu creator de teatru − Gelu şi Roxana Colceag" ("A Theater Producing Couple − Gelu and Roxana Colceag") (http://agenda.liternet.ro/articol/5148/Irina-Margareta-Nistor/Un-cuplu-creator-de-teatru---Gelu-si-Roxana-Colceag.html), September 2001, at the LiterNet publishing house (http://agenda.liternet.ro/); retrieved January 18, 2008 **(Romanian)**

[282] "La ţigănci... cu Popescu" (To the Gypsy Girls... with Popescu") (http://www.adevarul.ro/index.php?section=articole&screen=index&id=39710&duminica=1), in Adevărul, May 31, 2003; retrieved December 4, 2007 **(Romanian)**

[283] "Săptămâna Mircea Eliade la Radio România" ("The Mircea Eliade Week on Radio Romania") (http://agenda.liternet.ro/articol/3964/Comunicat-de-presa/Saptamana-Mircea-Eliade-la-Radio-Romania.html) (2007 press communique) **(Romanian)**, at the LiterNet publishing house (http://agenda.liternet.ro/); retrieved December 4, 2007

[284] "Scrieri de Eliade şi Vişniec, în cadrul festivalului Enescu" ("Texts by Eliade and Vişniec, as Part of the Enescu Festival") (http://www.gandul.info/arte/scrieri-eliade-visniec-cadrul-festivalului-enescu.html?3940;909322), in Gândul, September 12, 2007; retrieved December 4, 2007 **(Romanian)**

[285] Săptămâna Internaţională a Muzicii Noi. Ediţia a 14-a − 23−30 Mai 2004. Detalii festival ("The International New Music Week. 14th Edition − May 23−30, 2004. Festival Details" (http://www.cimec.ro/Muzica/evenimadd/simn2004/ZiuaIV.htm) **(Romanian)**, at the Institute for Cultural Memory (http://www.cimec.ro/e_default.htm); retrieved February 18, 2008

References

- Mircea Eliade:
  - A History of Religious Ideas, Vol. 1 (trans. Willard R. Trask), University of Chicago Press, Chicago, 1978
  - Images and Symbols: Studies in Religious Symbolism (trans. Philip Mairet), Princeton University Press, Princeton, 1991
  - Myth and Reality (trans. Willard R. Trask), Harper & Row, New York, 1963
  - Myths, Dreams and Mysteries (trans. Philip Mairet), Harper & Row, New York, 1967
  - Myths, Rites, Symbols: A Mircea Eliade Reader, Vol. 2, Ed. Wendell C. Beane and William G. Doty, Harper Colophon, New York, 1976
  - Patterns in Comparative Religion, Sheed & Ward, New York, 1958
  - Shamanism: Archaic Techniques of Ecstasy, Princeton University Press, Princeton, 2004
  - The Myth of the Eternal Return: Cosmos and History (trans. Willard R. Trask), Princeton University Press, Princeton, 1971
  - "The Quest for the 'Origins' of Religion", in History of Religions 4.1 (1964), p. 154−169
  - The Sacred and the Profane: The Nature of Religion (trans. Willard R. Trask), Harper Torchbooks, New York, 1961
  - Yoga: Immortality and Freedom (trans. Willard R. Trask), Princeton University Press, Princeton, 2009
- Final Report (http://www.inshr-ew.ro/pdf/Final_Report.pdf) of the International Commission on the Holocaust in Romania, Polirom, Iaşi, 2004. ISBN 973-681-989-2; retrieved October 8, 2007
- Sorin Antohi, "Commuting to Castalia: Noica's 'School', Culture and Power in Communist Romania", preface to Gabriel Liiceanu, The Păltiniş Diary: A Paideic Model in Humanist Culture, Central European University Press, Budapest, 2000, p.vii−xxiv. ISBN 963-9116-89-0
- George Călinescu, Istoria literaturii române de la origini până în prezent ("The History of Romanian Literature from Its Origins to Present Times"), Editura Minerva, Bucharest, 1986
- John Daniel Dadosky, The Structure of Religious Knowing: Encountering the Sacred in Eliade and Lonergan, State University of New York Press, Albany, 2004
- Robert Ellwood, The Politics of Myth: A Study of C. G. Jung, Mircea Eliade, and Joseph Campbell, State University of New York Press, Albany, 1999
- Victor Frunză, Istoria stalinismului în România ("The History of Stalinism in Romania"), Humanitas, Bucharest, 1990
- Roger Griffin, The Nature of Fascism, Routledge, London, 1993
- Mircea Handoca, Convorbiri cu şi despre Mircea Eliade ("Conversations with and about Mircea Eliade") (http://autori.humanitas.ro/eliade/despre.php) on Autori ("Published Authors") (http://autori.humanitas.ro) page of the Humanitas publishing house **(Romanian)**
- Furio Jesi, Mito, Mondadori, Milan, 1980
- G. S. Kirk,
  - Myth: Its Meaning and Functions in Ancient and Other Cultures, University of California Press, Berkeley, 1973
  - The Nature of Greek Myths, Penguin Books, Harmondsworth, 1974
- William McGuire, Bollingen: An Adventure in Collecting the Past, Princeton University Press, Princeton, 1982. ISBN 0-691-01885-5
- Lucian Nastasă, "Suveranii" universităţilor româneşti ("The 'Sovereigns' of Romanian Universities"), Editura Limes, Cluj-Napoca, 2007 (available online (http://www.history-cluj.ro/Istorie/cercet/Nastasa/SuveraniiUniversitatilorI.pdf) at the Romanian Academy's George Bariţ Institute of History (http://www.history-cluj.ro/))
- Andrei Oişteanu,

- "Angajamentul politic al lui Mircea Eliade" ("Mircea Eliade's Political Affiliation") (http://www.revista22.ro/html/index.php?art=3610&nr=2007-04-06), in *22*, Nr. 891, March–April 2007; retrieved November 15, 2007; retrieved January 17, 2008 (Romanian)
- "Mircea Eliade şi mişcarea hippie" ("Mircea Eliade and the Hippie Movement") (http://www.dilemaveche.ro/index.php?nr=120&cmd=articol&id=615), in *Dilema Veche*, Vol. III, May 2006; retrieved November 7, 2007 (Romanian)
- Z. Ornea, *Anii treizeci. Extrema dreaptă românească* ("The 1930s: The Romanian Far Right"), Editura Fundaţiei Culturale Române, Bucharest, 1995
- Mihail Sebastian, *Journal, 1935–1944: The Fascist Years*, Ivan R. Dee, Chicago, 2000. ISBN 1-56663-326-5
- David Leeming. "Archetypes". *The Oxford Companion to World Mythology*. Oxford University Press, 2004. *Oxford Reference Online*. Oxford University Press. UC—Irvine. 30 May 2011 <http://www.oxfordreference.com/views/ENTRY.html?subview=Main&entry=t208.e126>

Further reading

English

- Carrasco, David and Law, Jane Marie (eds.). 1985. *Waiting for the Dawn*. Boulder: Westview Press.
- Dudley, Guilford. 1977. *Religion on Trial: Mircea Eliade & His Critics*. Philadelphia: Temple University Press.
- Idinopulos, Thomas A., Yonan, Edward A. (eds.) 1994. *Religion and Reductionism: Essays on Eliade, Segal, and the Challenge of the Social Sciences for the Study of Religion*, Leiden: Brill Publishers. ISBN 90-04-06788-4
- McCutcheon, Russell T. 1997. *Manufacturing Religion: The Discourse on Sui Generis Religion and the Politics of Nostalgia*. New York: Oxford University Press.
- Olson, Carl. 1992. *The Theology and Philosophy of Eliade: A Search for the Centre*. New York: St Martins Press.
- Pals, Daniel L. 1996. *Seven Theories of Religion*. USA: Oxford University Press. ISBN 0-19-508725-9
- Rennie, Bryan S. 1996. *Reconstructing Eliade: Making Sense of Religion*. Albany: State University of New York Press.
- Rennie, Bryan S. (ed.). 2001. *Changing Religious Worlds: The Meaning and End of Mircea Eliade*. Albany: State University of New York Press.
- Rennie, Bryan S. 2007. *The International Eliade*. Albany: State University of New York Press. ISBN 0-7914-7087-3
- Simion, Eugen. 2001. *Mircea Eliade: A Spirit of Amplitude*. Boulder: East European Monographs.
- Strenski, Ivan. 1987. *Four Theories of Myth in Twentieth-Century History: Cassirer, Eliade, Levi Strauss and Malinowski*. Iowa City: University of Iowa Press.
- Wasserstrom, Steven M. 1999. *Religion after Religion: Gershom Scholem, Mircea Eliade, and Henry Corbin at Eranos*. Princeton: Princeton University Press
- Wedemeyer, Christian; Doniger, Wendy. (eds.). 2010. *Hermeneutics, Politics, and the History of Religions: The Contested Legacies of Joachim Wach and Mircea Eliade*. Oxford etc.: Oxford University Press

Other languages

- Alexandrescu, Sorin. 2007. *Mircea Eliade, dinspre Portugalia*. Bucharest: Humanitas. ISBN 973-50-1220-0
- Băicuş, Iulian, 2009, *Mircea Eliade. Literator şi mitodolog. În căutarea Centrului pierdut*. Bucharest: Editura Universităţii Bucureşti
- Călinescu, Matei. 2002. *Despre Ioan P. Culianu şi Mircea Eliade. Amintiri, lecturi, reflecţii*. Iaşi: Polirom. ISBN 973-681-064-X
- Culianu, Ioan Petru. 1978. *Mircea Eliade*. Assisi: Cittadella Editrice; 2008 Roma: Settimo Sigillo.
- De Martino, Marcello. 2008. *Mircea Eliade esoterico*. Roma: Settimo Sigillo.
- Dubuisson, Daniel. 2005. *Impostures et pseudo-science. L'œvre de Mircea Eliade*. Villeneuve d'Ascq: Presses Universitaires du Septentrion
- Gorshunova, Olga. 2008. *Terra Incognita of Ioan Culianu*, in *Ètnografičeskoe obozrenie*. N° 6, pp. 94–110. ISSN : 0869-5415.(Russian).
- Laignel-Lavastine, Alexandra. 2002. *Cioran, Eliade, Ionesco — L'oubli du fascisme*. Paris: Presses Universitaires de France-Perspectives critiques.
- Oişteanu, Andrei. 2007. *Religie, politică şi mit. Texte despre Mircea Eliade şi Ioan Petru Culianu*. Iaşi: Polirom.
- Posada, Mihai. 2006. *Opera publicistică a lui Mircea Eliade*. Bucharest: Editura Criterion. ISBN 978-973-8982-14-7
- Ruşti, Doina. 1997. *Dicţionar de simboluri din opera lui Mircea Eliade*. Bucharest: Editura Coresi
- Tacou, Constantin (ed.). 1977. *Cahier Eliade*. Paris: L'Herne.
- Tolcea, Marcel. 2002. *Eliade, ezotericul*. Timişoara: Editura Mirton.

- Ţurcanu, Florin. 2003. *Mircea Eliade. Le prisonnier de l'histoire*. Paris: Editions La Découverte.

External links

- Biography of Mircea Eliade (http://www.westminster.edu/staff/brennie/eliade/mebio.htm)
- Books and Writers: Mircea Eliade (http://www.kirjasto.sci.fi/eliade.htm)
- Mircea Eliade, *From Primitives to Zen* (http://www.mircea-eliade.com/from-primitives-to-zen/index.html)
- List of Terms Used in Mircea Eliade's *The Sacred and The Profane* (http://www.friesian.com/vocab.htm)
- Bryan S. Rennie on Mircea Eliade (http://www.scils.rutgers.edu/~mjoseph/rennie.html)
- Joseph G. Muthuraj, *The Significance of Mircea Eliade for Christian Theology* (http://www.religion-online. org/showarticle.asp?title=1901)
- Mircea Eliade presentation on the "100 Greatest Romanians" site (http://www.mariromani.ro/personaj. php?id=147) (Romanian)
- *Archaeus* magazine (http://www.rahr.ro/) (Romanian)
- Claudia Guggenbühl, *Mircea Eliade and Surendranath Dasgupta. The History Of Their Encounter* (http:// archiv.ub.uni-heidelberg.de/savifadok/volltexte/2008/149/pdf/Guggenbuehl_Eliade_DasGupta_Gesamt2. pdf)

Article Sources and Contributors

Rudolf Otto *Source*: http://en.wikipedia.org/w/index.php?oldid=455388029 *Contributors*: 11614soup, Adam sk, Adrian.benko, Alan347, Andres, Blainster, Bobo192, Celeritas, Clossius, D6, Felixfelis, Flo98, Fredrik, Gregbard, Heesung, Hikui87, IanFJ, Irishguy, JaGa, Janeofellenave, John Carter, Johnpacklambert, Justforthesakeofargument, Karl-Henner, Lkitrossky, Lucidish, Matthew Fennell, Mel Etitis, MilitaryTarget, Modeha, Monegasque, Moonriddengirl, Mu, Mz, Norhelt, Olessi, Pastordavid, Philipalmond, Pigman, Radicalsubversiv, RedWolf, Rjwilmsi, Roberto Cruz, Sluzzelin, Smack, Stephensuleeman, Tassedethe, Tomisti, Upsunday, Vandy, WeniWidiWiki, Yeatesy, Zenohockey, 32 anonymous edits

Religion *Source*: http://en.wikipedia.org/w/index.php?oldid=463082250 *Contributors*: (aeropagitica), -=CHAINSAW GRINGO=-, -Ril-, 100DashSix, 12.110.81.xxx, 128.12.156.xxx, 144.118.193.xxx, 165.155.128.xxx, 165.155.160.xxx, 16@r, 195.188.96.xxx, 198.54.202.xxx, 1pezguy, 1shields1, 1tephania, 203.25.148.xxx, 207.173.25.xxx, 209.161.68.xxx, 209.20.135.xxx, 213.253.39.xxx, 2ct7, 4RM0, 78.26, 8r13n, 94.132, 999, A ntv, A purple wikiuser, A. Ben-Shema, A.Nath, A340-313X, AA, ABF, ADM, AJR, AJourney, Aaarrrggh, Aaron Brenneman, Abah21, Abdull, Abdullais4u, Abid6814, Academic Challenger, Acetic Acid, Acs4b, Adamrce, Adashiel, Adriansrfr, Adriatikus, Aeonoris, Aetheling, Afterwriting, Agathman, Ahoerstemeier, Aidfarh, Ajraddatz, Akasseb, Aksi great, Alan Liefting, AlbertEdwards, AlbertJacherHolyProphet, Alex S, AlexPlank, Alexandroid, Alexbeard, Alexsau1991, All Is One, Alphador, Altenmann, Alterego, Amakuru, Amalthea, Ambassadoraftab, Ambi saba, Ambystom01, Amcaja, AmesG, AmiDaniel, Amitst, Anacapa, Andrevan, Andrew Lancaster, AndrewC, Andrewa, Andrewjuren, Andrewpmk, Andries, Andycjp, Angel2000, Angela, Angelo De La Paz, Anger22, Angoodkind, Anomenat, AnonEus, AnonMoos, Antandrus, Anthonyhcole, Antonrojo, Anupam, Apol0gies, Apox, Aranymalinko, Arcan, Archer7, Argon233, Ariele, Ariesmillenian, Arjun01, Arjun024, Arvindn, Ashley Y, Ashwinr, Askewmind, Assyria 90, Atemperman, Athanasius28, Atheuz, Athkalani, Atif.t2, AuburnPilot, Aude, Auric, Autonova, Avenged Evanfold, AvicAWB, Avicennasis, AxelBoldt, Az1568, Aza001300, B, B. Fairbairn, B2rtch, B9 hummingbird hovering, BD2412, BMF81, BWD, Babalobi, Badbilltucker, BahaiGuy, Balthazarduju, Barbara Shack, Baronnet, Barootazoo, Bartrules2003, Bbatsell, Bccomm, Bcorr, Bdean1963, Bearnfæder, Begoon, Beland, Belg4mit, Belovedfreak, Ben Zealley, Ben j min, BenBaker, Benjaminleebrackman, Benne, Beria, Beta.s2ph, Betterer87, Bfinn, Bhadani, Bhig3, Bibliobum4vr, BigEyedFish, Bigbluefish, Bignoter, Binksternet, Bk22, Blagoslovi, Blah2000, Blainster, Blcarson, Blenderhead, BlueSoxSWJ, Bluegecko, Bluemask, Bmicomp, Bobblewik, Bobo192, Bobrayner, Bogdangiusca, Bogey97, Boing! said Zebedee, Boothy443, Booyabazooka, Borisblue, Borislav, Bortschussvon, Boxed, Bradeos Graphon, Branddobbe, Brandonmonahan, Brettz9, Brian the Editor, Brian0918, BrianHoltz, BrightBlackHeaven, Brion VIBBER, Britcom, BritishWatcher, Brockert, Brokensanity27, Bryanjox, Buddhist72802, Bulmabriefs144, Burden50, Byelf2007, C6541, CANUTELOOL, CIS, COMPFUNK2, Cactus.man, Caesura, Calaschysm, Caleb13Prince, Cameron Bruce, Cameron hayter1990, Can't sleep, clown will eat me, Canadian-Bacon, Canderson7, Caper13, Carla Pehlke, Carlaude, Carrionluggage, Casito, Casper2k3, Catherineyronwode, Catman1210, Cazort, CecilWard, Celerityfm, Centrx, CesarB, Cgb8176, Chadders, Chamdarae, Charles Matthews, Charlesdarwin, CharlotteWebb, Chaser, Chinasaur, Chinju, Choesarian, Chris 73, Chris Roy, Chris Strolia-Davis, Chris the speller, ChrisGlew, Chrisjj, Christiaan, Christian List, Christian Skeptic, ChristianEdwardGruber, Christofurio, Christophore, Chsbcgs, Chuck Smith, Chun-hian, Cimon Avaro, Cirt, Citicat, Cj67, Clasqm, Clayoquot, Clngre, CloudNine, Clout, Clq, Clutch, Cocoaguy, Coder Dan, CommonsDelinker, Concept14, Conscious, Conversion script, Coppertwig, Cornerbock, Corrie.engelbrecht, Cosmic Latte, Cowbud2006, Cpicon92, Cpuwhiz11, Craigkbryant, Crazycomputers, Crazytales, Croganhore, Cruckshank2, Crusadeonilliteracy, Crypticmyth, Csbodine, Csernica, Cubbyguy123, Cunado19, Curious1i, Curps, Cybercobra, Cymru.lass, DARTH SIDIOUS 2, DHN, DJ Clayworth, DO'Neil, DRosenbach, DVD R W, DaGizza, DabBearsRule, Dabugas, Dacium, Dakinijones, Dalai lama ding dong, Damnreds, Dan D. Ric, Dan100, DanielCD, DanielDemaret, Danlevy100, Danthekarateman2, Dantheman531, DarkFalls, Darklilac, Dave Runger, Dave Taylor, Dave souza, Dave6, Davenbelle, David Hockey, David-Sarah Hopwood, David.Monniaux, DavidL (usurped), Davidhamer, Davinciscode, Dbabbitt, Dbachmann, Dbarber59, Dbtfz, Dchmelik, Dcljr, Ddadmin, Deathhell77, Deep Purple Dreams, Deepak, Deeptrivia, Delirium, Delirium of disorder, Delldot, Demerzel, Dennis Brown, DennyColt, Derangedtaco, Descendall, Diablo65, Diannaa, Didactohedron, DigitalHoodoo, Digitalme, Dina, Dino, Dionyseus, Discospinster, Disdero, DivineAlpha, Djcastel, Dmerrill, Dmg46664, Doc Tropics, Docu, Dodo bird, Doldrums, Dominio, Donjanssen, Dooky, Dorkules, DouglasGreen, Dougmurray27, Dougweller, Dr bab, Dr.enh, Dragfyre, Dralansun, Dreadstar, Drieakko, Drmaik, Drmies, Dtremenak, Ducain, Duracell, Durin, ESkog, Eaefremov, EamonnPKeane, Eardrop, East718, Eboily, Ecb29, EdGl, Edcolins, Editor2020, Edward321, Edwardando, Eequor, Eercc, Efutter, Ekhalom, El C, Elfguy, ElinorD, Eliyak, Elizabethrhodes, Elonka, Eluchil, Elvenscout742, Embitter, Emc2, Emiellaiendiay, Emoticon, EnderHegemony, Enigma546, Enormousdude, Entropy1963, Eob, Eraserhead1, Erik9, ErikHaugen, Erkacrank, Ermeyers, Esarac, Eu.stefan, Eubulides, Euchiasmus, EuroTom, Euyyn, Evercat, Everyking, Everything Inane, Evil saltine, FF2010, Fairandbalanced, Falcorian, Famguy231, Fanghong, Faus, FayssalF, FeloniousMonk, Ferdinand Pienaar, Fergie-, Ffaker, Fiona, FireBrandon, Flatterworld, Flauto Dolce, Flibjib8, Flo98, Florian Blaschke, Foobaz, Fottry55i6, Fractain, Fram, Fred Bauder, FreplySpang, FrummerThanThou, Frymaster, Fubar Obfusco, Fui in terra aliena, Fullstop, Funandtrvl, Furby100, Future Perfect at Sunrise, FutureNJGov, Fuzheado, Fuzzform, Fvw, Fyver528, FyzixFighter, GMT, GOER, Gaius Cornelius, GalaazV, Gam3r626, GameKeeper, Garrett Albright, Gary D, GayanRS, Geneb1955, Geogeogeo, Georgemein, Getaway, Ghelae, Giasha, Gilliam, Gimmetrow, Glen, Glenn, GnatsFriend, GoOdCoNtEnT, Godardesque, Goethean, Gogo Dodo, Gogoboy2293, Golbez, Goldenwinds, Goluboi pider, GourangaUK, Govontario, Gracefool, Gracenotes, GraemeL, Grafen, Graham87, GrahamN, Green Giant, Greenday21, GreetingsEarthling, GregAsche, Gregbard, Gregcaletta, Grinders, Grunt, Gryffindorap, Gsociology, Gtrmp, Guaka, Guanaco, Gurch, Guy Peters, Guy rules, Guðsþegn, Gwernol, H2g2bob, HJ Mitchell, HVH, Hadal, Hadj, Haemo, Hagedis, Haipa Doragon, HaireDunya, Haisch, Hajhouse, HalfShadow, Hardyplants, Harisingh, Harkenbane, Hashar, Haunti, Hazard-SJ, Headbomb, Helilesi, Helios solaris, Hellmonkey42, Hephaestos, Heqs, Hermione1980, Heron, Herunar, Hi Kestrel 420, Hires an editor, HistoricalPisces, Hitneosh, Hmains, Hojimachong, Holocene, Holy Ganga, Homestarmy, Hopelin, Hoshiryo, Hugoreis, Husond, Hut 8.5, Høst, I like spooging, ID, IZAK, Iamunknown, Ian.thomson, Ian13, Ig0774, Igiffin, Ihcoyc, Ikh, Ilovehouse, Imagine Reason, Impetuss, ImpuMozhi, Indian Chronicles, Indiealtphreak, Ineffable3000, InfoSect CultWatch Europe, Infrogmation, Inge-Lyubov, Introgressive, InverseHypercube, Irishpunktom, Islamaah, Isosping, IstvanWolf, Itisalive, Iwanttoeditthissh, Ixfd64, J Lorraine, J04n, JFDenault, JNW, JRM, JRR Trollkien, JaGa, Jacek Kendysz, Jacek Z. Poland, Jack Holbrook, Jackiestud, Jackohare, Jacobolus, Jacoplane, Jagged 85, Jamdonut, Jameselmo, Jan Tik, Jandalhandler, Janus Shadowsong, Javewu, Jbabrams2, Jdemarcos, Jeandré du Toit, Jecar, Jedidan747, Jeff3000, JeffW, Jeffhoy, JeremyA, Jersyko, Jfdwolff, Jgritz, Jguk 2, Jh51681, Jiang, Jiddisch, Jim Douglas, JimWae, Jimboish, Jimothytrotter, Jjmckool, Jni, Jnlwriter, Joe Jarvis, Joey Roe, John Price, John Stattic, John.Henry.Phelan, JohnBlackburne, JohnOwens, JohnWittle, Johndemers, Johnleemk, Johnstone, Johnthescavenger, Jon Awbrey, Jonashart, Jonathunder, Jonkerz, Joseph Solis in Australia, Josephcunningham, Jossi, Jtkiefer, Ju66l3r, Julian Morrison, Juliusе15, Junaidasm, Jusdafax, Justinfr, Jwestbrook, Jwissick, K, K-UNIT, KVDP, Kafray, Kafziel, KailzAcidTrip, Karafias, Kate, KazakhPol, Kedamono, Keilana, KellyCoinGuy, Kenyon, Kered77, Kerron20, Kevin B12, KevinTernes, Kevinjwright, Kevyn, Keyrok, Keysvolume, Kf4bdy, Khaosworks, Khazar, King kong92, King of Hearts, Kintetsubuffalo, Kinu, Kirobos, Kissonthis, Kitfoxxe, Kkawohl, Kkkdc, Kmccoy, Knotwork, KnowledgeOfSelf, Koakhtzvigad, Koavf, Kody123789, Korosuke, Korovioff, Koyaanis Qatsi, Kozuch, Krithin, Krystals, Kshitij, Kukkurovaca, Kung fu fuck, Kungfuadam, Kupos, Kuru, Kvaks, Kwamikagami, Kylu, L Kensington, LA2, LAXBESTIE, LDHan, Lacrimosus, Lagoyu, Lajsikonik, LambaJan, Lambiam, Langdell, Lantrix, Larry Sanger, Laurinavicius, Laurips, Laxbeastie, Le Anh-Huy, Le Blue Dude, Leafhopper, Led Zeppelin Rules, Leevanjackson, Leflyman, LegCircus, LeighvsOptimvsMaximvs, Leinad-Z, Leo.mtz, Leon1948, Leonard Falke, LethalReflex, Lewys, Liftarn, Lightmouse, Lil ginge, LilHelpa, Lilevilbrian, Link72649, LinoPop, Lionhead99, Little sawyer, LittleOldMe, Llloydfrancer, Lobsterkins, Londers, LordSimonofShropshire, Lordkazan, Lorynote, Lucas606, Ludovical, Luna Santin, M gol, M.Imran, M.e, MARussellPESE, MECU, MER-C, MONGO, MSJapan, Mackensen, Madhu kesarkar, Madmedea, Magioladitis, Magister Mathematicae, Mahaabaala, Maheshkumaryadav, Mailer diablo, Mairi, Majorly, Malcolm, Mamalujo, Mani1, Manop, Manthano, Mapetite526, MarSch, Marcoranuzzi, Marcos, Mark, MarkMcClelland, Markmichaelh, Markus Schmaus, Marnanel, MarsRover, Marshall46, Marudubshinki, Mary Calm, Master Jay, Mathukutty, MattTM, Matthew Stannard, MatthewDBA, Mattt296, Matuenih, Maurice Carbonaro, Maurreen, Mav, Max David, Mayooranathan, Mccready, Megan1967, Meieimatai, Mel Etitis, Melamed, Melpomenon, Merovingian, MerricMaker, Meshal Obeidallah, Metamagician3000, Mew Xacata, Mfzb04, Mgiganteus1, Mhking, Michael A. White, Michael Hardy, Michael Hodgson, Midnightblueowl, Mihoshi, Mikael Häggström, Mike Rosoft, Mike Young, Mike0001, Miles, Mindbodyfitness, Mindspillage, Minna Sora no Shita, Misaw, MishaPan, Misou, Misza13, Mix Bouda-Lycaon, Mjw65, Mkmcconn, Mlessard, Mmmdonutt, Mmu56, Mmyotis, Mo0, Mocu, MoederDao, Monado, Monkeykiss, Mooseofshadows, Morgaledth, Mort42, Mpondopondo, Mpradeep, Mqduck, Mr Adequate, Mr Stephen, Mr roces, Mr100percent, Mr5020, MrFish, Msleeman, Mtoussieh, Mtribe, Muhaidib, Multiman, Mumble45, Munci, Muntuwandi, Murftown, Muriel Gottrop, Mushroom, Musical Linguist, Mwanner, Mwborwmb, Mxn, Myran4000, Myth Buster, N-k, N-true, NMChico24, Nadavspi, Naddy, Nahald, Nakon, Nanshu, Naphtali, Naryathegreat, Nashhinton, Nat Krause, Natalie Erin, Navidazizi, NawlinWiki, Nayvik, Nazir Kafray, Neapoli, Nectarflowed, Neelix, Neotribal42, NerdyNSK, Netesq, Neutralhomer, Neutrality, NewEnglandYankee, Nick Number, Nigelj, Nihiltres, Nikai, Nikodemos, NimbleTurtle, Nimesh0775, Ninjagecko, Nirvana2013, Nishith Prabhakar, Niteowlneils, Nived 90, Njskimmer, Nk, Nlarch1, No Guru, NoIdeaNick, NoSeptember, Noahlaws, Northumbrian, Notheruser, Nsmerrill, Nullproductions, Numbo3, OFortuna, OGoncho, OLP1999, Obhave, Ocaasi, Okasha, OlEnglish, OleMaster, Olhogordo, Oliver Pereira, Olivier, Olorin28, Omicronpersei8, Omvegan, One-dimensional Tangent, OneGuy, Onias, Oolong, Optakeover, Optichan, Orcar967, Orion11M87, Ortolan88, Ost316, Ostiarius, Otashiro, Ouijalover, Outdaback, OwenX, Owl, P0lyglut, PRODUCER, Pablo-flores, Page Up, Paine Ellsworth, Paleorthid, Pallu, PandarenLord, Paradiso, Pariah, Paridigm, Parudox, PatrickDunfordNZ, Patstuart, Paul 012, Paul Raj, PaulHammond, Pax:Vobiscum, Pdn, Pearle, Pedant, Pegga, PelleSmith, PenguinCookies, PericlesofAthens, Peruvianllama, Peter the Great, Peter.M.D., Pethan, Petter Strandmark, Pgk, Phanerozoic, Pharos, Phatius McBluff, PhilSchabus, Philadelphia 2009, Philip J. Rayment, Philosopher, Pho3nix-, Pholio44, Photonikonman, PiCo, PierreAbbat, Pigman, Planescape, Plastikspork, Pne, Pollinator, Pookel, Pookster11, Poor Yorick, Porqin, Poulton, Power2084, Ppaterson, Ppntori, Practice, Pranathi, Pretty Good Satan, Profoss, Prolog, Prophet121, Prowikipedians, Pseudo-Richard, PsyMar, Psyche, Ptrwatson418, Puffin, Puja 13, Purpleturple, Pvosta, Pwhitwor, Pérez, Quadell, QuantumEleven, Queenb 666, Quintessent, Qxz, R'n'B, RDF, RED13, RG2, RHStockman, RJII, RK, RRRAD, RSpeeter, RaCha'ar, Rachelcutie, Radar1100, RadioKirk, Rafy, Raj2004, Ral315, Ram einstein, Ram-Man, Ramayan, Ramthbo, Randerson 3535, Raphael26, Rasillon, Rattatui, Raven Mew, Raven Stahlnecker, Ravi Verma, Rawling, Rdsmith4, Realm of Shadows, Reaperx90, RedWolf, Reddi, Rednblu, Reiddp, Reinoutr, Reinyday, Rejax, Remong, Renata, Rev. Michael S. Margolin, RevRagnarok, Revoarkagiri, RexNL, Rho, Rholton, Rich Farmbrough, Richard Keatinge, RichardF, Rick Norwood, Rickyrab, Rintrah, RitaBijlsma, Rjensen, Rjstott, Rmhermen, Rnapier, Roachie, RobNutt, Robert Daoust, Robert P. O'Shea, Robkellas, RockMaestro, Rohan1, Roland Deschain, Roland Longbow, Ronbo76, Rosencrantz1, Rothorpe, Roy Brumback, RoyBoy, Royalguard11, Rreagan007, Rrenner, Rsfontenot, Rtvl73, Ruptor, Rursus, RyanParis, Ryulong, S rafiee, S. Randall, S1080041, SJP, SROSET, ST47, SWAdair, Sabs2112, Sacramentis, Salt Yeung, Sam Hocevar, Sam Li, Sam Spade, Samdacruel, Sandbreak, Sango123, Sannse, Sardanaphalus, Sasuke Sarutobi, Satanael, Scepia, Schizmatic, Schuetzm, Schwnj, Scott Burley, ScottMcTony, Scriberius, Sdorrance, Seb az86556, Seeleschneider, Selket, Sendrin, Sengkang, Senori, Sentinel, Seren-dipper, Seric2, Sevilledade, Shadow josh360, Shafiq.ahmed, Shakajo, Shambalala, Shan Jayran, Shanel, Shanoman, Shantavira, Shashamula, Shawnc, ShelfSkewed, Shell Kinney, Shenme, ShiftFn, Shii, Shirulashem, Shoaler, Shrivenzale, Shsilver, Shub iitkgp, Shuipzv3, Sibom, Sietse Snel, SigPig, Silly rabbit, Silver Maple, Silverhelm, SimonP, Simonkoldyk, Sinas, Sir Escher, Sir Nicholas de Mimsy-Porpington, Sir Paul, Sjc, Sk8 b 11, Skribb, Skulipwns, Skysmith, Skywalker, SlowJog, Slrubenstein, Smee, Smeira, Smkolins, Snafflekid, Snake712, Sneltrekker, Snigne, Snowboardpunk, Sodicadl, Sohailstyle, Soleado, Soman, Someguy1221, Someone65,

Somerset219, Son Goku, Sooner Dave, Soporaeternus, Soulpatch, Soundofmusicals, SouthernNights, Speedy la cucaracha, Spirituality, Splash, SqueakBox, Srm07, Srtxg, Sseiter, St33lbird, Starfunker226, Stbalbach, SteinbDJ, Stephen Gilbert, Stephenb, Stereotek, Sterio, Stevertigo, Stewartadcock, Stormie, Str1977, Straw Cat, Striver, Studge, Subidei, Sunborn, Sunil g t, Sunnybondsinghjalwehra, Sunray, Sunshine4921, Superheadman, Supertask, Supertouch, Svick, Svig, Sycthos, Sylvangu2000, Synedri, SyntaxError55, Syvanen, T-1, T. Anthony, TBRoberts, THE friendlyfriend, TPK, TShilo12, TTwist, Tangotango, Tannin, Tapuu, Tawker, Tbhotch, Teammandog, TechnoFou, Tedius Zanarukando, Teh prophet, Teknorath, Tenmei, Texture, Thalesdotnet, The Anome, The Epopt, The Human Trumpet Solo, The Moose, The Rev of Bru, The Thing That Should Not Be, The Transhumanist, The Transhumanist (AWB), The man who had some fun, TheGreenEditor, TheKMan, ThePointblank, Therock1oo, Thesteve4242, Thisisyourwayout, Thomasmeeks, Thucydides411, Thursiya, Tiddly Tom, Tide rolls, TimShell, Timberframe, Timir2, Timo Honkasalo, Tmopkisn, Tobby72, Todfox, Toetoetoetoe, Tom X. Tobin, Tom harrison, Tomertomer, Tomlillis, Tommy2010, Tomsega, Tony Sidaway, TonyClarke, Tosayit, Tpbradbury, Trabucogold, Trafford09, Traroth, Trasman, Trc, Tregoweth, Trevor H., Trevor MacInnis, Trewbuk, Trigaranus, Trob030490, True Pagan Warrior, Tryptofish, Tsuzuki26, Tuna027, TurabianNights, Turfslaw, Tuspm, Tuxide, Twinsday, Tydaj, Tznkai, Ubarfay, Ultramartin, Ultraphil, Undead Herle King, Undead warrior, Ungtss, UnicornTapestry, Universal Hero, Universe inside, Unknownworld, Unreal7, Unused0029, Upfront, Usedbook, Usmausma, VJ Emsi, Vaikunda Raja, Valley2city, Van der Hoorn, Vanished User 0001, Vary, Vbrobert01, Vegaswikian, Venu62, Vibiesh, Vice regent, Vinay Varma, Violetriga, Vkvora2001, Volition, Vssun, WBardwin, WJBscribe, Wakuran, Walter O'Dim, Wandering Star, Wapondaponda, Warfieldian, Warofdreams, Wavelength, Wayne Hardman, Wayward, Wdflake, We used to sit, Weedwacker01, Weeman12342, Werrlg, Wesley, Wesley cool12, West Brom 4ever, West-side, Wetman, Weyes, Wezman1221, WholemealBaphomet, Wi-king, Wiki alf, Wikidas, Wikijac, Wikiklrsc, Wikilibrarian, Wikinv, WikipedianMarlith, Wikiposter0123, William Avery, Wingspeed, Winner 42, Wisco, Wisconsinner, Wknight94, Wmahan, Wolfdog, Wolfkeeper, Woohookitty, Wookipedian, World1world, WpZurp, Wrathjtr, Wrc wolfbrother, Wshun, Wtfdude, XJamRastafire, Xavier March, Xcvz, Xinyu, Xkingoftheworldx, Xosa, Xp54321, Yahel Guhan, Yahweh destroyer, Yamamoto Ichiro, Yanivg, Yaw pakhtoon, Yelyos, YizhaqbenAvraham, Yoninah, ZAROVE, Zain engineer, Zara1709, Zardiel, Zazaban, Zd12, Zeichman, Zenberg, Zhelja, Zigger, Zjem01, Zoe, Zoney, Zsinj, Zundark, Zzyzx11, ΙωάννηςΚαραμήτρος, ИРобман, ماني, افشا عقيل, , 1878 anonymous edits

Numinous *Source*: http://en.wikipedia.org/w/index.php?oldid=463333412 *Contributors*: Aluban, AnonMoos, Avidemux, Barbara Shack, Blainster, Can't sleep, clown will eat me, Cgingold, Ciphergoth, DBaba, DVD R W, Darth Panda, Dawright12, Deflective, Denelson83, Dreadstar, Drumguy8800, ELApro, Editor2020, Ex penumbrae, Filll, Fred114, Fuzzform, Hallows AG, J04n, Jayjg, Knightrunner, Knotwork, Kwamikagami, Leastfixedpoint, Leibniz, Likeavirginia, Lucyintheskywithdada, Mamgeorge, Mazwiki, MerryXIV, Metzae, Michael Hardy, Noosphere, Obsidian Soul, OlEnglish, OttoMäkelä, Patrickcm, Paul A, Practicingathiest, Rrmsjp, Sdpodmore, Sean William, Selket, Skomorokh, Smithfarm, Starmax777, Stephenb, Thr4wn, Twipley, Tydaj, Wareh, Warrior777, Woohookitty, Wordwebber, Zenohockey, ΑΩ, 89 anonymous edits

Peine *Source*: http://en.wikipedia.org/w/index.php?oldid=435151812 *Contributors*: Ahoerstemeier, Amandave814, BYF, CarolGray, Crux, DShamen, Darwinek, Egthegreat, Extrala, Felix Folio Secundus, Gmaxwell, Hmains, Huge69m, Inter, Jared Preston, Jza84, Magister Mathematicae, Markussep, Mion, Ospalh, Quarl, SDC, Soulviver, Staffelde, The real Marcoman, Unyoyega, Upsunday, Wisg, 11 anonymous edits

University of Marburg *Source*: http://en.wikipedia.org/w/index.php?oldid=461589406 *Contributors*: Aatomic1, Akkolon, Axt, Bduke, Brewcrewer, Catapult, Choster, Clossius, Coffeinfreak, D6, Daderot, DanMS, Doco, Doug Coldwell, Edmund1989, Gabodon, Goldfritha, Greenshed, Gun Powder Ma, Gzornenplatz, Hmains, Hnr, Hugo999, Ian Pitchford, Isenki, Jlittlet, Jllm06, John, Jonas Mur, Jpbrenna, Justus Nussbaum, Kaihsu, Leutha, Magadan, Magafuzula, Mets501, Milton Stanley, Mytwocents, Olessi, Omegastar, Ot, P.M. Kernkamp, Phe, Pi lambda, Président, QueenAdelaide, Reading glasses, Reitboeck, RoDeWo, Skitnik, Sky, Steamturn, StefanW-en, Stephensuleeman, Tassedethe, Terot, Uppland, VorpalBlade, Welsh, Wikiborg, Woohookitty, Xhyljen, Zemlod, Zoicon5, 114 anonymous edits

Theology *Source*: http://en.wikipedia.org/w/index.php?oldid=462597629 *Contributors*: *drew, -), 165.230.240.xxx, 16@r, 1700-talet, 207.93.56.xxx, A.J.A., Aaronkmthomas, AbsolutDan, Adam sk, Aetheling, Afaprof01, Alan Liefting, Alan347, Alansohn, Alastair Haines, Albatross2147, AlimanRuna, Altenmann, Anakin101, Andres, Andrewa, Andris, AndySimpson, Andycjp, Angr, Animationsun, Anna Lincoln, Antaeus Feldspar, Anya sm, Apfaq, Aphaia, Arado, Arb, Aristides, Arpit100, AugPi, Aviados, Aymatth2, B9 hummingbird hovering, BD2412, Baastuul, Babajobu, Babub, Banno, Bart133, Bcjordan, Beao, Becky81894, Ben Ben, Ben-Zin, Bensaccount, Bieberisgaylol, Biofase, Biruitorul, Blue Tie, Bobblehead, Bobo192, Bogdangiusca, Boing! said Zebedee, Bongwarrior, Bradeos Graphon, Bryan Derksen, C.hunter, CROCKERormeau, CWatchman, CalJW, Canihaveacookie, Capricorn42, Careless hx, CarlosPatiño, Carmichael, Carolynparrishfan, Ccraccnam, Ceyockey, ChaseCameron, CheeseDreams, Chipsandfish, Christian Left, Christian List, Cielbleu, Ciphergoth, Circeus, ClamDip, Clemmy, Cmdrjameson, ComIntern, Conversion script, Crowsnest, Csernica, D-Katana, DJ Clayworth, Da baum, Dali, DanMS, DanielCD, David aukerman, David l johns, DavidMacD, Davidkinnen, Dbrodbeck, December12AC, Der Spion, Devilraysfan06, Devourer09, Diana LeCrois, Didactohedron, DionysiusThrax, Discospinster, Donreed, Dougweller, Dr.K., Drboisclair, Drmies, Dtremenak, Dvsk8t3r, ESkog, EastTN, Editor2020, Editor8888, Egmontaz, Egoinos, Eiler7, Ekrub-ntyh, El C, Eleassar777, Elvire, Equendil, Everyking, Excirial, F1i2n3t4a5n6, Fagittt, Fan-1967, Fastfission, Feureau, Filastin, Firefly322, FisherQueen, FitzColinGerald, Flex, Fondfire, Frank Thomas, Galoubet, Gary King, Garzo, Gdarin, Geekgal, Geoffcampos, GertsiJuanzaitaste, Gianfranco, Giler, Gilkobrin, Glenn, GoingBatty, Gracenotes, Graham87, Gregbard, Gtrott73, Guy Peters, Guðsþegn, HG, Hail True Body, Hdt83, HermaniscusVII, History2007, Hoskinsjohn08, Icecradle, Ihcoyc, Iridescent, Iwantbatteries, Ixfd64, J.delanoy, JGoldman9, JLaTondre, JRR Trollkien, JackSparrow Ninja, Jackiestud, Jacobe14, Jacquerie27, Jagged 85, Jason 315, Jasperdoomen, Jauhienij, Jayarathina, Jersyko, Jezzabr, Jiddisch, Jimic be, Jimothytrotter, Jmc, Jncraton, JoanneB, Joegriff4, Joey5555, John, Johncapistrano, Johnthebuddhist, Jojalozzo, Jojit fb, Jonathunder, JonoPSA, Josh Parris, Jossi, Jsablow, Jshalom1, Juan Ponderas, Julian Mendez, Jusjih, KHM03, Kane5187, Kaveh, Kdbuffalo, Kehrbykid, Keilana, Kevin Rector, Kickyandfun, Kinu, Kkawohl, Koavf, Koyaanis Qatsi, Kpearce, KrakatoaKatie, Kubra, KyHilarious, Kznf, L Trezise, LaMenta3, Lambiam, Larris56, Larry_Sanger, LeBofSportif, Lenthe, Leolaursen, Lewis Theology, Liftarn, Lightmouse, Lindert, Lir, Ljpgoodwin, Logologist, Lothar76, LoveMonkey, Luk, Lukeisham, Lumos3, LutP, M.O.X, M3taphysical, MPS, MacGyverMagic, Macedonian, Mackan79, Madukan, Magicalsaumy, Magister Mathematicae, Mahigton, Mani1, Manjiboy, Marc Venot, Martynas Patasius, Mav, Mdiamante, Meegs, Mel Etitis, Mentifisto, MerricMaker, Michael Hardy, Mike Rosoft, Mindcontrol100, Mira Gambolputty, MishaPan, Mkmcconn, Mladifilozof, Mohanjodaro21, Monedula, Moriori, Mpondopondo, Mpsena, Mr5020, Msin10, MuffledThud, Myanw, NaiPiak, NameIsRon, Nbierma, Netesq, Netoholic, Nino Gonzales, Nirvana2013, Northamerica1000, Nposs, Nuno Tavares, Nurg, Nuview, Nyenyec, Odie5533, Ohnoitsjamie, Oliver Pereira, Olivier, One Salient Oversight, Oxonian2006, Paisan30, PamD, Passw0rd, Paul August, Paul foord, Pearle, Per Ardua, Peter Damian, Philly Dickinson, Pigman, Plug ye, Poached Turkey, Pontificalibus, Powelldinho, PreacherDoc1, Psb777, Ptolemy Caesarion, Quangbao, R'n'B, RJaguar3, RK, RSpeed23, Rainada, Randolph, RandomCritic, Ranveig, Rednblu, Rekleov, Remi0o, Rholton, Richard001, Rinald, Rinconsoleao, Rjwilmsi, Rnb, Rob2418, Roccondil, Rodhullandemu, Roland Longbow, Ronhenzel, RyanParis, Ryulong, SWAdair, Schmerguls, Schmiteye, Schocketlt, Sdorrance, Seeleschneider, Selket, Shalom Yechiel, Shoeofdeath, Siddhant.verma2, Signalhead, Simetrical, Sjharte, SkyWalker, Skywalker, Slackbuie, Smalljim, Snow1215, SpeedyGonsales, Spellcast, Srnec, Sshafran, StAnselm, Stalin IV, Stephensuleeman, Sterrettc, Stevertigo, Susvolans, TBRoberts, Tassedethe, Tbook, Teetotaler, TeleComNasSprVen, Tezcat, Thanatos666, The Thing That Should Not Be, The Transhumanist, TheRanger, Theoist, Theologian42, Theonemesis, Thingg, Timotheus Canens, Timwi, Tkynerd, Tony Sidaway, Torontonian1, Totalthinker, Traxs7, Trc, Trekkie4christ, Troche1104, TurabianNights, Tyrol5, Unyounyo, Urschel, Utcursch, Vague Rant, Vanisheduser12345, Vaquero100, Vassyana, Venu62, Verbal, Vinophil, Violetriga, Vladislaus Draculea, Vojvodaen, VolatileChemical, Vsmith, Warchdr7906a, WarthogDemon, Wavelength, Waynenoogen, Webbbbbbber, Wesley, WestonWyse, Wetman, WikHead, WikipedianMarlith, Wimt, Wjjefferies, Woohookitty, Wphow, XJamRastafire, Xompanthy, Yakudza, Yk Yk Yk, Youssefsan, Zabdiel, Zaf159, Zak2u786, Zeichman, Zvn, Александър, 503 anonymous edits

Mysticism *Source*: http://en.wikipedia.org/w/index.php?oldid=458998051 *Contributors*: 1shaman, 213.153.175.xxx, 30daysinAK, 64.12.105.xxx, 8oclockmovement, 999, A. Ben-Shema, AC2000, Aaroamal, Abracadab, AdelaMae, Alansohn, Aleister Wilson, Alexisniche, All Is One, Allenjwsc, Amalas, Ambkj123, Amcbride, Anapraxic, Andonic, Andy Baker, Andy Marchbanks, Andycjp, Antandrus, Apeman, Arado, Arb, Arenarax, Aristophanes68, Arthur B, AstroHurricane001, Atulkulki, Axaladl, B9 hummingbird hovering, BD2412, Bailo26, BananaFiend, Bassbonerocks, BastardoTheGreat, Bcorr, BeckyBeck, Benny the wayfarer, Bigwyrm, Billegge, Blainster, Blaze1974, Bmju, Bobo192, Bradeos Graphon, BrandonCsSanders, Bridesmill, BrightBlackHeaven, Bunnyhop11, CALR, Cacahuate, Cacala17, Caterinato, Charles Matthews, Chiswick Chap, ChrisCork, Cincybluffa, ClaudeMuncey, Clifflandis, Conversion script, Cool3, Cpiral, Csfun1, Cybercobra, DAVIDY, DBaba, DLPanther, DSGruss, Da baum, Dakinijones, Dan1138, Danny, Danny lost, David Plum, Dbachmann, Deli nk, Denispir, DerHexer, Dgreenbergz, Dinurcenter, Djnjwd, Doctorilluminatus, Dougofborg, Dragenfly, Dragice, Dragonnas, DreamGuy, Drhipp, Drift chambers, Drpaluga, ELinguist, ERcheck, Earthdenizen, Eclecticology, Editor2020, Edward, Eequor, Ekabhishek, Ekhalom, El C, Eleassar, EliTaz, Elwin-bennington, Ency456, Eumolpo, Evenmadderjon, Evercat, FAThomssen, FT2, FWadel, Fan-1967, Favonian, Forteanajones, Fourdee, Frater5, Fredrik, Friday, Froderik, FuelWagon, Future Perfect at Sunrise, Fuzzypeg, Gabrielsimon, Gadfium, Gaius Cornelius, GalaazV, GameKeeper, Gary D, Gavin Kettis!, Gdallaire, Gdzierlenga, Geokerk, Get2therage, Gilliam, Go for it!, Goethean, GourangaUK, Graham87, Greenie2600, Gregbard, H0riz0n, Hadal, Happy138, Harisingh, Havermayer, Headlikeawhole, Heah, Hectorian, Hede2000, Heidimo, Hele 7, Helpsome, Hiyya54, Hjuk, Holy Ganga, Hoof Hearted, Hrafn, IZAK, Ian Pitchford, Ig0774, Igiffin, Imma, ImmortalYawn, Infinity0, Iosef, Iridescent, IronChris, Isatay, Ixfd64, J. Van Meter, J.delanoy, J04n, JFQ, JStewart, JaGa, Jacobolus, James Arthur Reed, Jared Preston, Jayjg, Jayrav, Jds, Jeraphine Gryphon, Jfurr1981, Jgrantduff, Jjshapiro, JoeMystical, John, John Z, John courtneidge, Johnuniq, Jojit fb, Jonathanbethel, Jonel, Joseph Solis in Australia, Joshuareagan, Josiah Rowe, Jossi, Joy, Jrh98409, Juggins, Julia Rossi, Jwrosenzweig, Kaldar, Kalki, Kariteh, Kelly Martin, Kent Witham, Kered77, Kevin Rector, Kf4bdy, Kh7, Kintetsubuffalo, Kippson, Kirtanman, Kkawohl, Kngwa83, Koavf, Kokoriko, Konstantinos, Kostisl, Kozuch, Kripkenstein, Kristinemcole, Kungfuadam, Kzollman, Lama Ding Dong, Langdell, Larry laptop, Laurence Boyce, Lcarscad, Lectert, Leewonbum, Leftsideend, Leonjbrm, Lestrade, Libratune, Liftarn, Lighthead, LilHelpa, Logan0703, Loosestring, Lostsocks, Lotje, LoveMonkey, Lsousek, Lucky 6.9, Ludwigs2, Lumos3, Luna Santin, M.hayek, MOBY, Madmedea, Mak Thorpe, Makeswell, Malcolmxl5, Mandarax, Mani1, Marcgblainey, Mark Christensen, Maroux, MartinHarper, Mateuszica, Maurice Carbonaro, Mav, Maximus Rex, Mboverload, McGeddon, Mel Etitis, Metanoid, Michael Hardy, MichaelTinkler, Michaelchecht, Micione, Midnite Critic, Miguel de Servet, Mild Bill Hiccup, Mitsube, Mjerskey, Modernist, MolBioMan, MouseRancher, Myklove, Myrddin Masery, MysticReaders, Mystiq0, Mytchill, N.B. Miller, NancyBrownMiller, Naqshabandi, Narayani, Nasnema, Nathanael Bar-Aur L., Naval Scene, Nazroon, Nehrams2020, Neonic333, Neophile, Neutrality, Nhelferty, Nirvana2013, Nishkid64, Nixeagle, Nobody60, Norwikian, Novangelis, Nposs, Nullist, Ogambear, Ogo, Ogress, Ojl, OlEnglish, Ophion, Optim, PPdd, PSY7, PWhittle, Pacific PanDeist, Paddel, Palica, Paradiso, Pasha Abd, Patrickwooldridge, Pedant17, Perennial, Perrybrad1, Peter G Werner, PhiloNysh, Phoenixthebird, Piano non troppo, Pietzsche, Pigman, PinchasC, Pmanderson, Pollinosisss, Potashnik, Presearch, Priyanath, Psican, Psuliin, Punanimal, Queenmomcat, Questmaster, R'n'B, RDF, RJASE1, RJII, Raj2004, Ramashray, Randerson 3535, Raphael26, RedHillian, RedWolf, RexNL, Rgamble, Rich Farmbrough, Rivertorch, Rjwilmsi,

Rmbtm p, RodC, Romaioi, Rosenknospe, Rrburke, Rursus, Sam Li, Sam Spade, San de Berg, Satori, Scarecroe, Seano1, Setu, SgtSchumann, Sharnak, Sheiknazim2, Shirulashem, Shotwell, Sikander.alis, Silly rabbit, Simon D M, SimonP, Skysmith, Smkolins, Sobaka, Solace098, Soma77, Sopher99, Sopholatre, Soulpatch, Stangbat, Static Universe, Steel, StevenTCramer, Stevenwagner, Stevertigo, Stewartadcock, Suddha, Sunray, Superbeatles, Superm401, Sylartk, TUF-KAT, Tarotcards, Tedder, Tenofour, Texture, The kicker, TheGunslinger, Thedanturner, Themfromspace, Theun k, Thirdgatebaptist, Tide rolls, Tillmangirl72, Tjpob, Tom Morris, Tommytocker, Traben, Trainra, Trapolator, Trc, Trelawnie, Trismegistus33, Truthspreader, Twisturbed Tachyon, Uncle G, Universal1300, VBGFscJUn3, Vanwhistler, Vaquero100, VedicScience, VirginiaLou, Voiceofspirit, Vortexengineer, Vsmith, WadeSimMiser, Wednesday Next, Wesley, WikiDao, Wisco, Wmahan, Wolf Ashkenazi, Woohookitty, Wordwebber, Wrp103, Wwwdlhow27, Xchri5o8x, YorkBW, ZZyXx, Zachorious, Zambaccian, Zelse81, Zigger, ZuluPapa5, Александър, ‫تسیلم‬, 700 anonymous edits

Paul Tillich *Source*: http://en.wikipedia.org/w/index.php?oldid=462713972 *Contributors*: ACEOREVIVED, Aletheia, Alma Pater, Ambrosius007, Anastrophe, Andres, Angoodkind, Antonio Lopez, Arsisp, BSveen, Balloonman, Bcorr, Bearian, Blainster, BobK, Bobo192, Bolinator, Bubba hotep, Canis Lupus, Charles Matthews, ChrisCork, Christopher Kraus, Clossius, Curps, D6, DNewhall, DTOx, Dadofsam, Delirium, Epiphyllumlover, Erauch, EstherLois, ExistentialBliss, Fanofnaruto2, Favonian, Fclingerman, Furor Teutonicus, Gamorgan10, Garybishop, Gcarlisle, Gleiberg, Gobonobo, Goethean, Good Olfactory, Gordonofcartoon, Gpscholar, Gregbard, GregorBrand, Gui le Roi, HeartofaDog, Here2fixCategorizations, Hmains, Hoops gza, Instinct, J JMesserly, J S Ayer, JEN9841, Jeppi, JimFarm, Jlrobertson, Jlundell, Jmc, John Milton XIV, Johnpacklambert, Jonalexdeval, Joshcarstensen, Jpboogle, KHM03, Karl Dickman, Kencf0618, Kered77, Kgrad, Kircherrecht, Koavf, LarryBH, LaszloWalrus, Lynxmb, Madmedea, Mais oui!, Michael Gäbler, Mind meal, Mistico, Monegasque, Musickna, N05even07, NantucketNoon, Norm mit, Olessi, Omnipaedista, POBOX319, Pariah23, Pastordavid, Pastorwayne, Peter1c, Philonus, Pigman, Poor Yorick, Prumpf, Pteron, Radicalsubversiv, Rainada, Randolph, Remanning, Retired username, Rev. Ressl, Rjwilmsi, SDC, Saul Tillich, Scarian, Sceptic Watcher, Schinleber, Ser Amantio di Nicolao, Shanes, Shiki2, Smdo, Sohollywood, Sokrat3000, Stephensuleeman, Steve2011, Tergum violinae, Threeafterthree, Tra, Trrenaud, Txomin, UC Bill, Ulf Heinsohn, Ulric1313, Vathek, Vera from upstairs, Vojvodaen, Vuvar1, Waggers, Waynechuck, WickerGuy, Wikix, Woohookitty, Wulf Isebrand, Zenohockey, 171 anonymous edits

Mircea Eliade *Source*: http://en.wikipedia.org/w/index.php?oldid=462558313 *Contributors*: ***Ria777, AdiJapan, Aircea, Alexander Gieg, Ali'i, Andreea8848, Andries, Antidote, Asimsky, Atlantia, Attilios, AxelBoldt, Azotlichid, BD2412, BMF81, Bbsrock, Bebina, Biruitorul, Blainster, Bogdangiusca, Bonaparte, Boris Barowski, CJLL Wright, Camisa10, Catherineyronwode, Cberlet, Centrx, Chalst, Charles Matthews, Chris the speller, Chzz, Cimon Avaro, Classicfilms, Cmdrjameson, Cool Hand Luke, CryptoDerk, Crzrussian, Csörföly D, Cthane, Curero, D6, DBaba, DGJM, Dahn, Dalderdj, Daniel Mahu, Danny lost, Docnixon, Donjanssen, Doug4, Download, Dpotop, Dsp13, Dudewheresmywallet, Duja, Ekrenor, EngineRoom9, Ephilei, Euchiasmus, Ex caelo, Felixfelis, Flori2009, Frankie816, Fredrik, Furkhaocean, Gabbe, Gadget850, Gaius Cornelius, Gamaliel, Giordaano, Gkiely, Goldenrowley, Good Olfactory, Grenavitar, H0riz0n, Hoimo, Hornplease, Hugo.arg, ITSENJOYABLE, Illythr, Inter, J.delanoy, Jan Van Biervliet, Jeanenawhitney, Jhobson1, Jmabel, John1, Johnor, Jossi, Jpers36, Kalki, Kevinalewis, Khoikhoi, Kintetsubuffalo, Kithira, Koavf, Kubra, Kwamikagami, LordGulliverofGalben, Lucian Dantes, Lucidish, Majorly, Mberaka, Medmoth, Mellery, Michael Devore, Michael Hardy, Mimihitam, Mircead, Moldoveanul, Monegasque, Mpolo, Netage, Nihiltres, Nishidani, Npeters22, Parkwells, Patrick0Moran, PelleSmith, Peter IBM, Peterak, Phatius McBluff, Physchim62, Pigman, Piotrus, Poor Yorick, Practice, Qsaw, Quadell, Radgeek, Radh, Ragib, Razvan NEAGOE, RepublicanJacobite, Ricky81682, Rjensen, Rjwilmsi, RomânescEsteLatin, Ross Rhodes, RubyQ, Savitardevi, Serbannichifor, Seth Ilys, Sherpa, Shirt58, SlackerMom, Smdo, Smmerril, Ssd, Stalepie, Stevertigo, TOO, The Thing That Should Not Be, Thumperward, Timor Stultorum, Timur Stultorum, Tom Lougheed, Tsubasa no shiroi, Turgidson, UCSCRC, Ultratomio, VegaDark, Viriditas, Vojvodaen, Vzbs34, Warshy, Welsh, Whitehorse1, Wighson, Wiki-uk, William M. Connolley, Woohookitty, Writtenright, Yanks-rule, Yaseen.Kader, Yworo, Z10x, Zserghei, ‫ירעל ירייהנזאראט‬, Ό οίστρος, 218 anonymous edits

Image Sources, Licenses and Contributors

Image:RudolfOtto.jpg *Source*: http://en.wikipedia.org/w/index.php?title=File:RudolfOtto.jpg *License*: Public Domain *Contributors*: Contemporary photograph

File:Religious syms.svg *Source*: http://en.wikipedia.org/w/index.php?title=File:Religious_syms.svg *License*: Public Domain *Contributors*: User:Rursus

File:Prevailing world religions map.png *Source*: http://en.wikipedia.org/w/index.php?title=File:Prevailing_world_religions_map.png *License*: GNU Free Documentation License *Contributors*: Original uploader was LilTeK21 at en.wikipedia

File:Molnár Ábrahám kiköltözése 1850.jpg *Source*: http://en.wikipedia.org/w/index.php?title=File:Molnár_Ábrahám_kiköltözése_1850.jpg *License*: Public Domain *Contributors*: Csanády, Pe-Jo, Skipjack, 1 anonymous edits

Image:Kaaba mirror edit jj.jpg *Source*: http://en.wikipedia.org/w/index.php?title=File:Kaaba_mirror_edit_jj.jpg *License*: unknown *Contributors*: edited by jjron

File:Rama, Lakshman and Sita at the Kalaram Temple, Nashik..jpg *Source*: http://en.wikipedia.org/w/index.php?title=File:Rama,_Lakshman_and_Sita_at_the_Kalaram_Temple,_Nashik..jpg *License*: Creative Commons Attribution-Sharealike 2.5 *Contributors*: Ekabhishek at en.wikipedia

File:Maneckji Sett Agiary entrance.jpg *Source*: http://en.wikipedia.org/w/index.php?title=File:Maneckji_Sett_Agiary_entrance.jpg *License*: Creative Commons Attribution-Sharealike 2.0 *Contributors*: Pablo Ares Gastesi

File:Chinese temple incence burner.jpg *Source*: http://en.wikipedia.org/w/index.php?title=File:Chinese_temple_incence_burner.jpg *License*: GNU Free Documentation License *Contributors*: Chun-hian, Miuki, Nyo, Olivier2, Xenophon, Yaohua2000, 1 anonymous edits

File:Sepulveda Unitarian Universalist Society Sanctuary.PNG *Source*: http://en.wikipedia.org/w/index.php?title=File:Sepulveda_Unitarian_Universalist_Society_Sanctuary.PNG *License*: unknown *Contributors*: Office of Historic Resources, City of Los Angeles

File:Holika Dahan, Kathamandu, Nepal.jpg *Source*: http://en.wikipedia.org/w/index.php?title=File:Holika_Dahan,_Kathamandu,_Nepal.jpg *License*: Creative Commons Attribution 2.0 *Contributors*: http://www.flickr.com/photos/wonker/

Image:Urarina shaman B Dean.jpg *Source*: http://en.wikipedia.org/w/index.php?title=File:Urarina_shaman_B_Dean.jpg *License*: Creative Commons Attribution-ShareAlike 3.0 Unported *Contributors*: Andersmusician, Bridesmill, Davius, Javierme, Jonkerz, Mattes, Themightyquill, Uyvsdi, Vonvon, 5 anonymous edits

Image:SiegeofAntioch.jpeg *Source*: http://en.wikipedia.org/w/index.php?title=File:SiegeofAntioch.jpeg *License*: Public Domain *Contributors*: engraving by Jean Colombe from Sébastien Mamerot's Les Passages d'Outremer.

Image:Huxisanxiaotu.jpg *Source*: http://en.wikipedia.org/w/index.php?title=File:Huxisanxiaotu.jpg *License*: Public Domain *Contributors*: Dominic Z., HéctorTabaré, Miuki, PericlesofAthens, 3 anonymous edits

File:Loudspeaker.svg *Source*: http://en.wikipedia.org/w/index.php?title=File:Loudspeaker.svg *License*: Public Domain *Contributors*: Bayo, Gmaxwell, Husky, Iamunknown, Mirithing, Myself488, Nethac DIU, Omegatron, Rocket000, The Evil IP address, Wouterhagens, 18 anonymous edits

Image:Image-Peineammarkt 2005.JPG *Source*: http://en.wikipedia.org/w/index.php?title=File:Image-Peineammarkt_2005.JPG *License*: Public Domain *Contributors*: Huge69m

File:Wappen Stadt Peine.jpg *Source*: http://en.wikipedia.org/w/index.php?title=File:Wappen_Stadt_Peine.jpg *License*: Public Domain *Contributors*: Crux, Magul, Rauenstein, 2 anonymous edits

file:Germany location map.svg *Source*: http://en.wikipedia.org/w/index.php?title=File:Germany_location_map.svg *License*: Creative Commons Attribution-Sharealike 3.0 *Contributors*: NordNordWest

File:Red_pog.svg *Source*: http://en.wikipedia.org/w/index.php?title=File:Red_pog.svg *License*: Public Domain *Contributors*: Anomie

File:Peine altes Rathaus.jpg *Source*: http://en.wikipedia.org/w/index.php?title=File:Peine_altes_Rathaus.jpg *License*: Creative Commons Attribution-Sharealike 2.5 *Contributors*: Benutzer:Crux

File:Image-Peineburgpark 2005.JPG *Source*: http://en.wikipedia.org/w/index.php?title=File:Image-Peineburgpark_2005.JPG *License*: Public Domain *Contributors*: Huge69m

File:Peine Jakobi-Kirche.jpg *Source*: http://en.wikipedia.org/w/index.php?title=File:Peine_Jakobi-Kirche.jpg *License*: Creative Commons Attribution-Sharealike 2.5 *Contributors*: Benutzer:Crux

File:Peine Töpfers Mühle.jpg *Source*: http://en.wikipedia.org/w/index.php?title=File:Peine_Töpfers_Mühle.jpg *License*: Creative Commons Attribution-Sharealike 2.5 *Contributors*: Benutzer:Crux

File:Peine Stahlwerk.jpg *Source*: http://en.wikipedia.org/w/index.php?title=File:Peine_Stahlwerk.jpg *License*: Creative Commons Attribution-Sharealike 2.5 *Contributors*: Benutzer:Crux

File:Peine Wasserturm.jpg *Source*: http://en.wikipedia.org/w/index.php?title=File:Peine_Wasserturm.jpg *License*: Creative Commons Attribution-Sharealike 3.0,2.5,2.0,1.0 *Contributors*: Sebman81

File:Bahnhof Peine.JPG *Source*: http://en.wikipedia.org/w/index.php?title=File:Bahnhof_Peine.JPG *License*: Creative Commons Attribution-Sharealike 3.0,2.5,2.0,1.0 *Contributors*: Sebman81

File:Siegel_uni-marburg.png *Source*: http://en.wikipedia.org/w/index.php?title=File:Siegel_uni-marburg.png *License*: Public Domain *Contributors*: BrightRaven, Cwbm (commons), EugeneZelenko, Gurkenpeter, PsY.cHo

Image:Uni Marburg 01.jpg *Source*: http://en.wikipedia.org/w/index.php?title=File:Uni_Marburg_01.jpg *License*: Creative Commons Attribution-Sharealike 2.5 *Contributors*: Ies, Neodyne, Suguri F

Image:Uni Marburg 05.jpg *Source*: http://en.wikipedia.org/w/index.php?title=File:Uni_Marburg_05.jpg *License*: Creative Commons Attribution-Sharealike 2.5 *Contributors*: AndreasPraefcke, Neodyne, Suguri F

File:AlbertusMagnus.jpg *Source*: http://en.wikipedia.org/w/index.php?title=File:AlbertusMagnus.jpg *License*: Public Domain *Contributors*: Bahatur, DenghiùComm, G.dallorto, GDK, Gabor, Ies, Leinad-Z, Siebrand, Svencb

File:NAMA Relief Eleusis Persephone.jpg *Source*: http://en.wikipedia.org/w/index.php?title=File:NAMA_Relief_Eleusis_Persephone.jpg *License*: Creative Commons Attribution-ShareAlike 3.0 Unported *Contributors*: User:Marsyas

File:Allsehendes Auge am Tor des Aachener Dom.JPG *Source*: http://en.wikipedia.org/w/index.php?title=File:Allsehendes_Auge_am_Tor_des_Aachener_Dom.JPG *License*: Creative Commons Attribution-ShareAlike 3.0 Unported *Contributors*: 663highland, AnonMoos, Trexer, Wikig

File:Peter Paul Rubens 166.jpg *Source*: http://en.wikipedia.org/w/index.php?title=File:Peter_Paul_Rubens_166.jpg *License*: Public Domain *Contributors*: Kokodyl, Mattes, Pierpao, Vincent Steenberg

File:templeofrosycross.png *Source*: http://en.wikipedia.org/w/index.php?title=File:Templeofrosycross.png *License*: Public Domain *Contributors*: Axon, Campani, Dbenzhuser, Mattes, Wst, 1 anonymous edits

File:Buddha der Liebe.jpg *Source*: http://en.wikipedia.org/w/index.php?title=File:Buddha_der_Liebe.jpg *License*: Creative Commons Attribution 3.0 *Contributors*: Nobody60

Image:Paul Johannes Tillich's gravestone in the Paul Tillich Park, New Harmony, Indiana.jpg *Source*: http://en.wikipedia.org/w/index.php?title=File:Paul_Johannes_Tillich's_gravestone_in_the_Paul_Tillich_Park,_New_Harmony,_Indiana.jpg *License*: Public Domain *Contributors*: Michael Gaebler

File:Bust of Paul Johannes Tillich (daylight).JPG *Source*: http://en.wikipedia.org/w/index.php?title=File:Bust_of_Paul_Johannes_Tillich_(daylight).JPG *License*: GNU Free Documentation License *Contributors*: Richard Keeling

File:Casa lui Eliade.jpg *Source*: http://en.wikipedia.org/w/index.php?title=File:Casa_lui_Eliade.jpg *License*: Public Domain *Contributors*: AndreiOM

File:Mosesshoesspeculum.jpeg *Source*: http://en.wikipedia.org/w/index.php?title=File:Mosesshoesspeculum.jpeg *License*: Public Domain *Contributors*: Dahn, Ecphora, Shakko

File:Meister von Torcello 001.jpg *Source*: http://en.wikipedia.org/w/index.php?title=File:Meister_von_Torcello_001.jpg *License*: Public Domain *Contributors*: AndreasPraefcke, David Angel, G.dallorto, Gveret Tered, Lalupa, Man vyi, Shakko, Wst, Xenophon, 2 anonymous edits

File:AM 738 4to Yggdrasill.png *Source*: http://en.wikipedia.org/w/index.php?title=File:AM_738_4to_Yggdrasill.png *License*: Public Domain *Contributors*: ALE!, Bloodofox, Dsmdgold, EugeneZelenko, Gryffindor, Holt, Jorunn, S.babylonica, Sigo, VIGNERON, Wolfmann, Wst, Überraschungsbilder

File:Ru200107280198.jpg *Source*: http://en.wikipedia.org/w/index.php?title=File:Ru200107280198.jpg *License*: Creative Commons Attribution 2.0 *Contributors*: Dr. Andreas Hugentobler

License

Creative Commons Attribution-ShareAlike 3.0 Unported - Deed

This is a human-readable summary of the Creative Commons Attribution ShareAlike 3.0 Unported License (http://en.wikipedia.org/wiki/Wikipedia:Text_of_Creative_Commons_Attribution-ShareAlike_3.0_Unported_License)
You are free:

- **to Share**—to copy, distribute and transmit the work, and
- **to Remix**—to adapt the work

Under the following conditions:

- **Attribution**—You must attribute the work in the manner specified by the author or licensor (but not in any way that suggests that they endorse you or your use of the work.)
- **Share Alike**—If you alter, transform, or build upon this work, you may distribute the resulting work only under the same, similar or a compatible license.

With the understanding that:

- **Waiver**—Any of the above conditions can be waived if you get permission from the copyright holder.
- **Other Rights**—In no way are any of the following rights affected by the license:
  - your fair dealing or fair use rights;
  - the author's moral rights; and
  - rights other persons may have either in the work itself or in how the work is used, such as publicity or privacy rights.
- **Notice**—For any reuse or distribution, you must make clear to others the license terms of this work. The best way to do that is with a link to http://creativecommons.org/licenses/by-sa/3.0/

GNU Free Documentation License

As of July 15, 2009 Wikipedia has moved to a dual-licensing system that supersedes the previous GFDL only licensing. In short, this means that text licensed under the GFDL can no longer be imported to Wikipedia. Additionally, text contributed after that date can not be exported under the GFDL license. See Wikipedia:Licensing update for further information.

Version 1.3, 3 November 2008 Copyright (C) 2000, 2001, 2002, 2007, 2008 Free Software Foundation, Inc. <http://fsf.org/>
Everyone is permitted to copy and distribute verbatim copies of this license document, but changing it is not allowed.

0. PREAMBLE

The purpose of this License is to make a manual, textbook, or other functional and useful document "free" in the sense of freedom: to assure everyone the effective freedom to copy and redistribute it, with or without modifying it, either commercially or noncommercially. Secondarily, this License preserves for the author and publisher a way to get credit for their work, while not being considered responsible for modifications made by others.
This License is a kind of "copyleft", which means that derivative works of the document must themselves be free in the same sense. It complements the GNU General Public License, which is a copyleft license designed for free software.
We have designed this License in order to use it for manuals for free software, because free software needs free documentation: a free program should come with manuals providing the same freedoms that the software does. But this License is not limited to software manuals; it can be used for any textual work, regardless of subject matter or whether it is published as a printed book. We recommend this License principally for works whose purpose is instruction or reference.

1. APPLICABILITY AND DEFINITIONS

This License applies to any manual or other work, in any medium, that contains a notice placed by the copyright holder saying it can be distributed under the terms of this License. Such a notice grants a world-wide, royalty-free license, unlimited in duration, to use that work under the conditions stated herein. The "Document", below, refers to any such manual or work. Any member of the public is a licensee, and is addressed as "you". You accept the license if you copy, modify or distribute the work in a way requiring permission under copyright law.
A "Modified Version" of the Document means any work containing the Document or a portion of it, either copied verbatim, or with modifications and/or translated into another language.
A "Secondary Section" is a named appendix or a front-matter section of the Document that deals exclusively with the relationship of the publishers or authors of the Document to the Document's overall subject (or to related matters) and contains nothing that could fall directly within that overall subject. (Thus, if the Document is in part a textbook of mathematics, a Secondary Section may not explain any mathematics.) The relationship could be a matter of historical connection with the subject or with related matters, or of legal, commercial, philosophical, ethical or political position regarding them.
The "Invariant Sections" are certain Secondary Sections whose titles are designated, as being those of Invariant Sections, in the notice that says that the Document is released under this License. If a section does not fit the above definition of Secondary then it is not allowed to be designated as Invariant. The Document may contain zero Invariant Sections. If the Document does not identify any Invariant Sections then there are none.
The "Cover Texts" are certain short passages of text that are listed, as Front-Cover Texts or Back-Cover Texts, in the notice that says that the Document is released under this License. A Front-Cover Text may be at most 5 words, and a Back-Cover Text may be at most 25 words.
A "Transparent" copy of the Document means a machine-readable copy, represented in a format whose specification is available to the general public, that is suitable for revising the document straightforwardly with generic text editors or (for images composed of pixels) generic paint programs or (for drawings) some widely available drawing editor, and that is suitable for input to text formatters or for automatic translation to a variety of formats suitable for input to text formatters. A copy made in an otherwise Transparent file format whose markup, or absence of markup, has been arranged to thwart or discourage subsequent modification by readers is not Transparent. An image format is not Transparent if used for any substantial amount of text. A copy that is not "Transparent" is called "Opaque".
Examples of suitable formats for Transparent copies include plain ASCII without markup, Texinfo input format, LaTeX input format, SGML or XML using a publicly available DTD, and standard-conforming simple HTML, PostScript or PDF designed for human modification. Examples of transparent image formats include PNG, XCF and JPG. Opaque formats include proprietary formats that can be read and edited only by proprietary word processors, SGML or XML for which the DTD and/or processing tools are not generally available, and the machine-generated HTML, PostScript or PDF produced by some word processors for output purposes only.
The "Title Page" means, for a printed book, the title page itself, plus such following pages as are needed to hold, legibly, the material this License requires to appear in the title page. For works in formats which do not have any title page as such, "Title Page" means the text near the most prominent appearance of the work's title, preceding the beginning of the body of the text.
The "publisher" means any person or entity that distributes copies of the Document to the public.
A section "Entitled XYZ" means a named subunit of the Document whose title either is precisely XYZ or contains XYZ in parentheses following text that translates XYZ in another language. (Here XYZ stands for a specific section name mentioned below, such as "Acknowledgements", "Dedications", "Endorsements", or "History".) To "Preserve the Title" of such a section when you modify the Document means that it remains a section "Entitled XYZ" according to this definition.
The Document may include Warranty Disclaimers next to the notice which states that this License applies to the Document. These Warranty Disclaimers are considered to be included by reference in this License, but only as regards disclaiming warranties: any other implication that these Warranty Disclaimers may have is void and has no effect on the meaning of this License.

2. VERBATIM COPYING

You may copy and distribute the Document in any medium, either commercially or noncommercially, provided that this License, the copyright notices, and the license notice saying this License applies to the Document are reproduced in all copies, and that you add no other conditions whatsoever to those of this License. You may not use technical measures to obstruct or control the reading or further copying of the copies you make or distribute. However, you may accept compensation in exchange for copies. If you distribute a large enough number of copies you must also follow the conditions in section 3.
You may also lend copies, under the same conditions stated above, and you may publicly display copies.

3. COPYING IN QUANTITY

If you publish printed copies (or copies in media that commonly have printed covers) of the Document, numbering more than 100, and the Document's license notice requires Cover Texts, you must enclose the copies in covers that carry, clearly and legibly, all these Cover Texts: Front-Cover Texts on the front cover, and Back-Cover Texts on the back cover. Both covers must also clearly and legibly identify you as the publisher of these copies. The front cover must present the full title with all words of the title equally prominent and visible. You may add other material on the covers in addition. Copying with changes limited to the covers, as long as they preserve the title of the Document and satisfy these conditions, can be treated as verbatim copying in other respects.
If the required texts for either cover are too voluminous to fit legibly, you should put the first ones listed (as many as fit reasonably) on the actual cover, and continue the rest onto adjacent pages.
If you publish or distribute Opaque copies of the Document numbering more than 100, you must either include a machine-readable Transparent copy along with each Opaque copy, or state in or with each Opaque copy a computer-network location from which the general network-using public has access to download using public-standard network protocols a complete Transparent copy of the Document, free of added material. If you use the latter option, you must take reasonably prudent steps, when you begin distribution of Opaque copies in quantity, to ensure that this Transparent copy will remain thus accessible at the stated location until at least one year after the last time you distribute an Opaque copy (directly or through your agents or retailers) of that edition to the public.
It is requested, but not required, that you contact the authors of the Document well before redistributing any large number of copies, to give them a chance to provide you with an updated version of the Document.

4. MODIFICATIONS

You may copy and distribute a Modified Version of the Document under the conditions of sections 2 and 3 above, provided that you release the Modified Version under precisely this License, with the Modified Version filling the role of the Document, thus licensing distribution and modification of the Modified Version to whoever possesses a copy of it. In addition, you must do these things in the Modified Version:

A. Use in the Title Page (and on the covers, if any) a title distinct from that of the Document, and from those of previous versions (which should, if there were any, be listed in the History section of the Document). You may use the same title as a previous version if the original publisher of that version gives permission.
B. List on the Title Page, as authors, one or more persons or entities responsible for authorship of the modifications in the Modified Version, together with at least five of the principal authors of the Document (all of its principal authors, if it has fewer than five), unless they release you from this requirement.
C. State on the Title page the name of the publisher of the Modified Version, as the publisher.
D. Preserve all the copyright notices of the Document.
E. Add an appropriate copyright notice for your modifications adjacent to the other copyright notices.
F. Include, immediately after the copyright notices, a license notice giving the public permission to use the Modified Version under the terms of this License, in the form shown in the Addendum below.
G. Preserve in that license notice the full lists of Invariant Sections and required Cover Texts given in the Document's license notice.
H. Include an unaltered copy of this License.
I. Preserve the section Entitled "History", Preserve its Title, and add to it an item stating at least the title, year, new authors, and publisher of the Modified Version as given on the Title Page. If there is no section Entitled "History" in the Document, create one stating the title, year, authors, and publisher of the Document as given on its Title Page, then add an item describing the Modified Version as stated in the previous sentence.
J. Preserve the network location, if any, given in the Document for public access to a Transparent copy of the Document, and likewise the network locations given in the Document for previous versions it was based on. These may be placed in the "History" section. You may omit a network location for a work that was published at least four years before the Document itself, or if the original publisher of the version it refers to gives permission.
K. For any section Entitled "Acknowledgements" or "Dedications", Preserve the Title of the section, and preserve in the section all the substance and tone of each of the contributor acknowledgements and/or dedications given therein.
L. Preserve all the Invariant Sections of the Document, unaltered in their text and in their titles. Section numbers or the equivalent are not considered part of the section titles.
M. Delete any section Entitled "Endorsements". Such a section may not be included in the Modified version.
N. Do not retitle any existing section to be Entitled "Endorsements" or to conflict in title with any Invariant Section.
O. Preserve any Warranty Disclaimers.

If the Modified Version includes new front-matter sections or appendices that qualify as Secondary Sections and contain no material copied from the Document, you may at your option designate some or all of these sections as invariant. To do this, add their titles to the list of Invariant Sections in the Modified Version's license notice. These titles must be distinct from any other section titles.
You may add a section Entitled "Endorsements", provided it contains nothing but endorsements of your Modified Version by various parties—for example, statements of peer review or that the text has been approved by an organization as the authoritative definition of a standard.
You may add a passage of up to five words as a Front-Cover Text, and a passage of up to 25 words as a Back-Cover Text, to the end of the list of Cover Texts in the Modified Version. Only one passage of Front-Cover Text and one of Back-Cover Text may be added by (or through arrangements made by) any one entity. If the Document already includes a cover text for the same cover, previously added by you or by arrangement made by the same entity you are acting on behalf of, you may not add another; but you may replace the old one, on explicit permission from the previous publisher that added the old one.
The author(s) and publisher(s) of the Document do not by this License give permission to use their names for publicity for or to assert or imply endorsement of any Modified Version.

5. COMBINING DOCUMENTS

You may combine the Document with other documents released under this License, under the terms defined in section 4 above for modified versions, provided that you include in the combination all of the Invariant Sections of all of the original documents, unmodified, and list them all as Invariant Sections of your combined work in its license notice, and that you preserve all their Warranty Disclaimers.
The combined work need only contain one copy of this License, and multiple identical Invariant Sections may be replaced with a single copy. If there are multiple Invariant Sections with the same name but different contents, make the title of each such section unique by adding at the end of it, in parentheses, the name of the original author or publisher of that section if known, or else a unique number. Make the same adjustment to the section titles in the list of Invariant Sections in the license notice of the combined work.
In the combination, you must combine any sections Entitled "History" in the various original documents, forming one section Entitled "History"; likewise combine any sections Entitled "Acknowledgements", and any sections Entitled "Dedications". You must delete all sections Entitled "Endorsements".

6. COLLECTIONS OF DOCUMENTS

You may make a collection consisting of the Document and other documents released under this License, and replace the individual copies of this License in the various documents with a single copy that is included in the collection, provided that you follow the rules of this License for verbatim copying of each of the documents in all other respects.
You may extract a single document from such a collection, and distribute it individually under this License, provided you insert a copy of this License into the extracted document, and follow this License in all other respects regarding verbatim copying of that document.

7. AGGREGATION WITH INDEPENDENT WORKS

A compilation of the Document or its derivatives with other separate and independent documents or works, in or on a volume of a storage or distribution medium, is called an "aggregate" if the copyright resulting from the compilation is not used to limit the legal rights of the compilation's users beyond what the individual works permit. When the Document is included in an aggregate, this License does not apply to the other works in the aggregate which are not themselves derivative works of the Document.

If the Cover Text requirement of section 3 is applicable to these copies of the Document, then if the Document is less than one half of the entire aggregate, the Document's Cover Texts may be placed on covers that bracket the Document within the aggregate, or the electronic equivalent of covers if the Document is in electronic form. Otherwise they must appear on printed covers that bracket the whole aggregate.

8. TRANSLATION

Translation is considered a kind of modification, so you may distribute translations of the Document under the terms of section 4. Replacing Invariant Sections with translations requires special permission from their copyright holders, but you may include translations of some or all Invariant Sections in addition to the original versions of these Invariant Sections. You may include a translation of this License, and all the license notices in the Document, and any Warranty Disclaimers, provided that you also include the original English version of this License and the original versions of those notices and disclaimers. In case of a disagreement between the translation and the original version of this License or a notice or disclaimer, the original version will prevail.

If a section in the Document is Entitled "Acknowledgements", "Dedications", or "History", the requirement (section 4) to Preserve its Title (section 1) will typically require changing the actual title.

9. TERMINATION

You may not copy, modify, sublicense, or distribute the Document except as expressly provided under this License. Any attempt otherwise to copy, modify, sublicense, or distribute it is void, and will automatically terminate your rights under this License.

However, if you cease all violation of this License, then your license from a particular copyright holder is reinstated (a) provisionally, unless and until the copyright holder explicitly and finally terminates your license, and (b) permanently, if the copyright holder fails to notify you of the violation by some reasonable means prior to 60 days after the cessation.

Moreover, your license from a particular copyright holder is reinstated permanently if the copyright holder notifies you of the violation by some reasonable means, this is the first time you have received notice of violation of this License (for any work) from that copyright holder, and you cure the violation prior to 30 days after your receipt of the notice.

Termination of your rights under this section does not terminate the licenses of parties who have received copies or rights from you under this License. If your rights have been terminated and not permanently reinstated, receipt of a copy of some or all of the same material does not give you any rights to use it.

10. FUTURE REVISIONS OF THIS LICENSE

The Free Software Foundation may publish new, revised versions of the GNU Free Documentation License from time to time. Such new versions will be similar in spirit to the present version, but may differ in detail to address new problems or concerns. See http://www.gnu.org/copyleft/.

Each version of the License is given a distinguishing version number. If the Document specifies that a particular numbered version of this License "or any later version" applies to it, you have the option of following the terms and conditions either of that specified version or of any later version that has been published (not as a draft) by the Free Software Foundation. If the Document does not specify a version number of this License, you may choose any version ever published (not as a draft) by the Free Software Foundation. If the Document specifies that a proxy can decide which future versions of this License can be used, that proxy's public statement of acceptance of a version permanently authorizes you to choose that version for the Document.

11. RELICENSING

"Massive Multiauthor Collaboration Site" (or "MMC Site") means any World Wide Web server that publishes copyrightable works and also provides prominent facilities for anybody to edit those works. A public wiki that anybody can edit is an example of such a server. A "Massive Multiauthor Collaboration" (or "MMC") contained in the site means any set of copyrightable works thus published on the MMC site.

"CC-BY-SA" means the Creative Commons Attribution-Share Alike 3.0 license published by Creative Commons Corporation, a not-for-profit corporation with a principal place of business in San Francisco, California, as well as future copyleft versions of that license published by that same organization.

"Incorporate" means to publish or republish a Document, in whole or in part, as part of another Document.

An MMC is "eligible for relicensing" if it is licensed under this License, and if all works that were first published under this License somewhere other than this MMC, and subsequently incorporated in whole or in part into the MMC, (1) had no cover texts or invariant sections, and (2) were thus incorporated prior to November 1, 2008.

The operator of an MMC Site may republish an MMC contained in the site under CC-BY-SA on the same site at any time before August 1, 2009, provided the MMC is eligible for relicensing.

How to use this License for your documents

To use this License in a document you have written, include a copy of the License in the document and put the following copyright and license notices just after the title page:

> Copyright (c) YEAR YOUR NAME.
>
> Permission is granted to copy, distribute and/or modify this document
>
> under the terms of the GNU Free Documentation License, Version 1.3
>
> or any later version published by the Free Software Foundation;
>
> with no Invariant Sections, no Front-Cover Texts, and no Back-Cover Texts.
>
> A copy of the license is included in the section entitled "GNU
>
> Free Documentation License".

If you have Invariant Sections, Front-Cover Texts and Back-Cover Texts, replace the "with...Texts." line with this:

> with the Invariant Sections being LIST THEIR TITLES, with the
>
> Front-Cover Texts being LIST, and with the Back-Cover Texts being LIST.

If you have Invariant Sections without Cover Texts, or some other combination of the three, merge those two alternatives to suit the situation.

If your document contains nontrivial examples of program code, we recommend releasing these examples in parallel under your choice of free software license, such as the GNU General Public License, to permit their use in free software.

Creative Commons Attribution-ShareAlike 3.0 Unported License

License

THE WORK (AS DEFINED BELOW) IS PROVIDED UNDER THE TERMS OF THIS CREATIVE COMMONS PUBLIC LICENSE («CCPL» OR «LICENSE»). THE WORK IS PROTECTED BY COPYRIGHT AND/OR OTHER APPLICABLE LAW. ANY USE OF THE WORK OTHER THAN AS AUTHORIZED UNDER THIS LICENSE OR COPYRIGHT LAW IS PROHIBITED.

BY EXERCISING ANY RIGHTS TO THE WORK PROVIDED HERE, YOU ACCEPT AND AGREE TO BE BOUND BY THE TERMS OF THIS LICENSE. TO THE EXTENT THIS LICENSE MAY BE CONSIDERED TO BE A CONTRACT, THE LICENSOR GRANTS YOU THE RIGHTS CONTAINED HERE IN CONSIDERATION OF YOUR ACCEPTANCE OF SUCH TERMS AND CONDITIONS.

1. Definitions

"Adaptation" means a work based upon the Work, or upon the Work and other pre-existing works, such as a translation, adaptation, derivative work, arrangement of music or other alterations of a literary or artistic work, or phonogram or performance and includes cinematographic adaptations or any other form in which the Work may be recast, transformed, or adapted including in any form recognizably derived from the original, except that a work that constitutes a Collection will not be considered an Adaptation for the purpose of this License. For the avoidance of doubt, where the Work is a musical work, performance or phonogram, the synchronization of the Work in timed-relation with a moving image ("synching") will be considered an Adaptation for the purpose of this License.

"Collection" means a collection of literary or artistic works, such as encyclopedias and anthologies, or performances, phonograms or broadcasts, or other works or subject matter other than works listed in Section 1(f) below, which, by reason of the selection and arrangement of their contents, constitute intellectual creations, in which the Work is included in its entirety in unmodified form along with one or more other contributions, each constituting separate and independent works in themselves, which together are assembled into a collective whole. A work that constitutes a Collection will not be considered an Adaptation (as defined below) for the purposes of this License.

"Creative Commons Compatible License" means a license that is listed at http://creativecommons.org/compatiblelicenses that has been approved by Creative Commons as being essentially equivalent to this License, including, at a minimum, because that license: (i) contains terms that have the same purpose, meaning and effect as the License Elements of this License; and, (ii) explicitly permits the relicensing of adaptations of works made available under that license under this License or a Creative Commons jurisdiction license with the same License Elements as this License.

"Distribute" means to make available to the public the original and copies of the Work or Adaptation, as appropriate, through sale or other transfer of ownership.

"License Elements" means the following high-level license attributes as selected by Licensor and indicated in the title of this License: Attribution, ShareAlike.

"Licensor" means the individual, individuals, entity or entities that offer(s) the Work under the terms of this License.

"Original Author" means, in the case of a literary or artistic work, the individual, individuals, entity or entities who created the Work or if no individual or entity can be identified, the publisher; and in addition (i) in the case of a performance the actors, singers, musicians, dancers, and other persons who act, sing, deliver, declaim, play in, interpret or otherwise perform literary or artistic works or expressions of folklore; (ii) in the case of a phonogram the producer being the person or legal entity who first fixes the sounds of a performance or other sounds; and, (iii) in the case of broadcasts, the organization that transmits the broadcast.

"Work" means the literary and/or artistic work offered under the terms of this License including without limitation any production in the literary, scientific and artistic domain, whatever may be the mode or form of its expression including digital form, such as a book, pamphlet and other writing; a lecture, address, sermon or other work of the same nature; a dramatic or dramatico-musical work; a choreographic work or entertainment in dumb show; a musical composition with or without words; a cinematographic work to which are assimilated works expressed by a process analogous to cinematography; a work of drawing, painting, architecture, sculpture, engraving or lithography; a photographic work to which are assimilated works expressed by a process analogous to photography; a work of applied art; an illustration, map, plan, sketch or three-dimensional work relative to geography, topography, architecture or science; a performance; a broadcast; a phonogram; a compilation of data to the extent it is protected as a copyrightable work; or a work performed by a variety or circus performer to the extent it is not otherwise considered a literary or artistic work.

"You" means an individual or entity exercising rights under this License who has not previously violated the terms of this License with respect to the Work, or who has received express permission from the Licensor to exercise rights under this License despite a previous violation.

"Publicly Perform" means to perform public recitations of the Work and to communicate to the public those public recitations, by any means or process, including by wire or wireless means or public digital performances; to make available to the public Works in such a way that members of the public may access these Works from a place and at a place individually chosen by them; to perform the Work to the public by any means or process and the communication to the public of the performances of the Work, including by public digital performance; to broadcast and rebroadcast the Work by any means including signs, sounds or images.

"Reproduce" means to make copies of the Work by any means including without limitation by sound or visual recordings and the right of fixation and reproducing fixations of the Work, including storage of a protected performance or phonogram in digital form or other electronic medium.

2. Fair Dealing Rights

Nothing in this License is intended to reduce, limit, or restrict any uses free from copyright or rights arising from limitations or exceptions that are provided for in connection with the copyright protection under copyright law or other applicable laws.

3. License Grant

Subject to the terms and conditions of this License, Licensor hereby grants You a worldwide, royalty-free, non-exclusive, perpetual (for the duration of the applicable copyright) license to exercise the rights in the Work as stated below:

a. to Reproduce the Work, to incorporate the Work into one or more Collections, and to Reproduce the Work as incorporated in the Collections;

b. to create and Reproduce Adaptations provided that any such Adaptation, including any translation in any medium, takes reasonable steps to clearly label, demarcate or otherwise identify that changes were made to the original Work. For example, a translation could be marked "The original work was translated from English to Spanish," or a modification could indicate "The original work has been modified.";

c. to Distribute and Publicly Perform the Work including as incorporated in Collections; and,

d. to Distribute and Publicly Perform Adaptations.

e. For the avoidance of doubt:

vi. **Non-waivable Compulsory License Schemes.** In those jurisdictions in which the right to collect royalties through any statutory or compulsory licensing scheme cannot be waived, the Licensor reserves the exclusive right to collect such royalties for any exercise by You of the rights granted under this License;

vii. **Waivable Compulsory License Schemes.** In those jurisdictions in which the right to collect royalties through any statutory or compulsory licensing scheme can be waived, the Licensor waives the exclusive right to collect such royalties for any exercise by You of the rights granted under this License; and,

viii. **Voluntary License Schemes.** The Licensor waives the right to collect royalties, whether individually or, in the event that the Licensor is a member of a collecting society that administers voluntary licensing schemes, via that society, from any exercise by You of the rights granted under this License.

The above rights may be exercised in all media and formats whether now known or hereafter devised. The above rights include the right to make such modifications as are technically necessary to exercise the rights in other media and formats. Subject to Section 8(f), all rights not expressly granted by Licensor are hereby reserved.

4. Restrictions

The license granted in Section 3 above is expressly made subject to and limited by the following restrictions:

a. You may Distribute or Publicly Perform the Work only under the terms of this License. You must include a copy of, or the Uniform Resource Identifier (URI) for, this License with every copy of the Work You Distribute or Publicly Perform. You may not offer or impose any terms on the Work that restrict the terms of this License or the ability of the recipient of the Work to exercise the rights granted to that recipient under the terms of the License. You may not sublicense the Work. You must keep intact all notices that refer to this License and to the disclaimer of warranties with every copy of the Work You Distribute or Publicly Perform. When You Distribute or Publicly Perform the Work, You may not impose any effective technological measures on the Work that restrict the ability of a recipient of the Work from You to exercise the rights granted to that recipient under the terms of the License. This Section 4(a) applies to the Work as incorporated in a Collection, but this does not require the Collection apart from the Work itself to be made subject to the terms of this License. If You create a Collection, upon notice from any Licensor You must, to the extent practicable, remove from the Collection any credit as required by Section 4(c), as requested. If You create an Adaptation, upon notice from any Licensor You must, to the extent practicable, remove from the Adaptation any credit as required by Section 4(c), as requested.

b. You may Distribute or Publicly Perform an Adaptation only under the terms of: (i) this License; (ii) a later version of this License with the same License Elements as this License; (iii) a Creative Commons jurisdiction license (either this or a later license version) that contains the same License Elements as this License (e.g., Attribution-ShareAlike 3.0 US)); (iv) a Creative Commons Compatible License. If you license the Adaptation under one of the licenses mentioned in (iv), you must comply with the terms of that license. If you license the Adaptation under the terms of any of the licenses mentioned in (i), (ii) or (iii) (the "Applicable License"), you must comply with the terms of the Applicable License generally and the following provisions: (I) You must include a copy of, or the URI for, the Applicable License with every copy of each Adaptation You Distribute or Publicly Perform; (II) You may not offer or impose any terms on the Adaptation that restrict the terms of the Applicable License or the ability of the recipient of the Adaptation to exercise the rights granted to that recipient under the terms of the Applicable License; (III) You must keep intact all notices that refer to the Applicable License and to the disclaimer of warranties with every copy of the Work as included in the Adaptation You Distribute or Publicly Perform; (IV) when You Distribute or Publicly Perform the Adaptation, You may not impose any effective technological measures on the Adaptation that restrict the ability of a recipient of the Adaptation from You to exercise the rights granted to that recipient under the terms of the Applicable License. This Section 4(b) applies to the Adaptation as incorporated in a Collection, but this does not require the Collection apart from the Adaptation itself to be made subject to the terms of the Applicable License.

c. If You Distribute, or Publicly Perform the Work or any Adaptations or Collections, You must, unless a request has been made pursuant to Section 4(a), keep intact all copyright notices for the Work and provide, reasonable to the medium or means You are utilizing: (i) the name of the Original Author (or pseudonym, if applicable) if supplied, and/or if the Original Author and/or Licensor designate another party or parties (e.g., a sponsor institute, publishing entity, journal) for attribution ("Attribution Parties") in Licensor's copyright notice, terms of service or by other reasonable means, the name of such party or parties; (ii) the title of the Work if supplied; (iii) to the extent reasonably practicable, the URI, if any, that Licensor specifies to be associated with the Work, unless such URI does not refer to the copyright notice or licensing information for the Work; and (iv) , consistent with Section 3(b), in the case of an Adaptation, a credit identifying the use of the Work in the Adaptation (e.g., "French translation of the Work by Original Author," or "Screenplay based on original Work by Original Author"). The credit required by this Section 4(c) may be implemented in any reasonable manner; provided, however, that in the case of a Adaptation or Collection, at a minimum such credit will appear, if a credit for all contributing authors of the Adaptation or Collection appears, then as part of these credits and in a manner at least as prominent as the credits for the other contributing authors. For the avoidance of doubt, You may only use the credit required by this Section for the purpose of attribution in the manner set out above and, by exercising Your rights under this License, You may not implicitly or explicitly assert or imply any connection with, sponsorship or endorsement by the Original Author, Licensor and/or Attribution Parties, as appropriate, of You or Your use of the Work, without the separate, express prior written permission of the Original Author, Licensor and/or Attribution Parties.

d. Except as otherwise agreed in writing by the Licensor or as may be otherwise permitted by applicable law, if You Reproduce, Distribute or Publicly Perform the Work either by itself or as part of any Adaptations or Collections, You must not distort, mutilate, modify or take other derogatory action in relation to the Work which would be prejudicial to the Original Author's honor or reputation. Licensor agrees that in those jurisdictions (e.g. Japan), in which any exercise of the right granted in Section 3(b) of this License (the right to make Adaptations) would be deemed to be a distortion, mutilation, modification or other derogatory action prejudicial to the Original Author's honor and reputation, the Licensor will waive or not assert, as appropriate, this Section, to the fullest extent permitted by the applicable national law, to enable You to reasonably exercise Your right under Section 3(b) of this License (right to make Adaptations) but not otherwise.

5. Representations, Warranties and Disclaimer

UNLESS OTHERWISE MUTUALLY AGREED TO BY THE PARTIES IN WRITING, LICENSOR OFFERS THE WORK AS-IS AND MAKES NO REPRESENTATIONS OR WARRANTIES OF ANY KIND CONCERNING THE WORK, EXPRESS, IMPLIED, STATUTORY OR OTHERWISE, INCLUDING, WITHOUT LIMITATION, WARRANTIES OF TITLE, MERCHANTIBILITY, FITNESS FOR A PARTICULAR PURPOSE, NONINFRINGEMENT, OR THE ABSENCE OF LATENT OR OTHER DEFECTS, ACCURACY, OR THE PRESENCE OF ABSENCE OF ERRORS, WHETHER OR NOT DISCOVERABLE. SOME JURISDICTIONS DO NOT ALLOW THE EXCLUSION OF IMPLIED WARRANTIES, SO SUCH EXCLUSION MAY NOT APPLY TO YOU.

6. Limitation on Liability

EXCEPT TO THE EXTENT REQUIRED BY APPLICABLE LAW, IN NO EVENT WILL LICENSOR BE LIABLE TO YOU ON ANY LEGAL THEORY FOR ANY SPECIAL, INCIDENTAL, CONSEQUENTIAL, PUNITIVE OR EXEMPLARY DAMAGES ARISING OUT OF THIS LICENSE OR THE USE OF THE WORK, EVEN IF LICENSOR HAS BEEN ADVISED OF THE POSSIBILITY OF SUCH DAMAGES.

7. Termination

a. This License and the rights granted hereunder will terminate automatically upon any breach by You of the terms of this License. Individuals or entities who have received Adaptations or Collections from You under this License, however, will not have their licenses terminated provided such individuals or entities remain in full compliance with those licenses. Sections 1, 2, 5, 6, 7, and 8 will survive any termination of this License.

b. Subject to the above terms and conditions, the license granted here is perpetual (for the duration of the applicable copyright in the Work). Notwithstanding the above, Licensor reserves the right to release the Work under different license terms or to stop distributing the Work at any time; provided, however that any such election will not serve to withdraw this License (or any other license that has been, or is required to be, granted under the terms of this License), and this License will continue in full force and effect unless terminated as stated above.

8. Miscellaneous

a. Each time You Distribute or Publicly Perform the Work or a Collection, the Licensor offers to the recipient a license to the Work on the same terms and conditions as the license granted to You under this License.

b. Each time You Distribute or Publicly Perform an Adaptation, Licensor offers to the recipient a license to the original Work on the same terms and conditions as the license granted to You under this License.

c. If any provision of this License is invalid or unenforceable under applicable law, it shall not affect the validity or enforceability of the remainder of the terms of this License, and without further action by the parties to this agreement, such provision shall be reformed to the minimum extent necessary to make such provision valid and enforceable.

d. No term or provision of this License shall be deemed waived and no breach consented to unless such waiver or consent shall be in writing and signed by the party to be charged with such waiver or consent.

e. This License constitutes the entire agreement between the parties with respect to the Work licensed here. There are no understandings, agreements or representations with respect to the Work not specified here. Licensor shall not be bound by any additional provisions that may appear in any communication from You. This License may not be modified without the mutual written agreement of the Licensor and You.

f. The rights granted under, and the subject matter referenced, in this License were drafted utilizing the terminology of the Berne Convention for the Protection of Literary and Artistic Works (as amended on September 28, 1979), the Rome Convention of 1961, the WIPO Copyright Treaty of 1996, the WIPO Performances and Phonograms Treaty of 1996 and the Universal Copyright Convention (as revised on July 24, 1971). These rights and subject matter take effect in the relevant jurisdiction in which the License terms are sought to be enforced according to the corresponding provisions of the implementation of those treaty provisions in the applicable national law. If the standard suite of rights granted under applicable copyright law includes additional rights not granted under this License, such additional rights are deemed to be included in the License; this License is not intended to restrict the license of any rights under applicable law.

565666